John Pearce and the Rise of the Mass Food Market in London, 1870–1930

David W. Gutzke

John Pearce and the Rise of the Mass Food Market in London, 1870–1930

palgrave
macmillan

David W. Gutzke
Missouri State University
Springfield, MO, USA

ISBN 978-3-030-27094-0 ISBN 978-3-030-27095-7 (eBook)
https://doi.org/10.1007/978-3-030-27095-7

Cover illustration: Living London, ed. George R. Sims, 1903.

This Palgrave Macmillan imprint is published by the registered company Springer Nature Switzerland AG.
The registered company address is: Gewerbestrasse 11, 6330 Cham, Switzerland

For Trevor
and
Caitlin

Acknowledgements

In the years devoted to researching and writing this book, I have incurred many debts, which I now gladly acknowledge. I am thankful to the Missouri State University for its generous financial support with a faculty research grant, enabling my spending most of a summer researching this book in London. At an early stage in the manuscript's development, Matthew Hilton made valuable suggestions about the book's focus and content, and its possible publishers. Specialist in alcohol studies, David Fahey pointed to pertinent scholarly books and articles, and read as well as commented on parts of the manuscript. Another close friend, Malcolm Holmes, drawing on his extensive knowledge of London, read the entire book and ensured its accurate historical perspective. No one, however, gave more time, shared more insights or contributed more overall, with his invaluable proof reading skills, to the final book than my close friend and mentor Trevor Lloyd, who scrutinised this work with a dedication equal only to my own. With incredible patience, diligence and interest, he also brought to these diverse tasks an unrivalled knowledge of economics, business history, the changing nature of working-class life, social mobility and the City of London's evolution. Without his guidance, I would not have successfully grasped the spatial, social and business context in which the chief caterers worked. Let me loosely plagiarise myself in repeating what I said in my last monograph: in making shrewd comments about style, substance and interpretation, Trevor elevated my book's contributions to a much higher scholarly level. I am forever grateful for not just his selfless commitment to historical scholarship but his enduring friendship. Often it is said that we as scholars stand on the shoulders of those who preceded us: never was this truer than in my relationship with Trevor, to whom I am forever indebted. He has been a steadfast friend who constantly inspires me.

Thanks too go to Shannon Conlon (Missouri State University's Interlibrary Loan wizard), who repeatedly impressed me with her skills in locating obscure sources, finding creative ways to obtain materials for my research and renewing overdue items. She is indispensable and a cherished friend.

I am enormously grateful to Jacob Crusinberry, my graduate assistant. In administering my undergraduate courses and undertaking other duties going well beyond any reasonable expectation, he proved indispensable in giving me the necessary time to transform the manuscript into a monograph. At the same time, I tried to ensure he did not in any way neglect his roles as a new father and husband. He carried off this balancing of pedagogical, scholarly and parental obligations with aplomb, which did him credit and for which I want to acknowledge how deeply I appreciate support from his wife and daughter.

Finally, I am forever indebted to my older daughter, Caitlin, who utilised her outstanding computer skills in locating the historical images that did so much to convey visually the catering world of John Pearce. Her help was also indispensable in the final stages of copy editing, proof reading and indexing.

David W. Gutzke

Contents

List of Figures

List of Charts

List of Tables

CHAPTER 1

Introduction

This book is about a specialised and interesting part of the food trade and also a study (unavoidably incomplete) of a striking personality who lived his whole life in catering, changing London for the better in the process. Such an undertaking would have been impossible a decade ago, since all his company records were destroyed after his death. Complicating my investigations of John Pearce, all his competitors likewise preserved no records, except for several minute books. Joseph Lyons & Co. was quite unusual in having a company archivist, who had access to the firm's records and wrote an official history, though soon thereafter all the evidence vanished. Indispensable to my research was the recent digitising of major British newspapers, together with the then prevailing journalistic practices of publishing verbatim accounts of company meetings and annual reports.

Pearce looms so large as a historical figure because he became the quintessential rags-to-riches late Victorian, an astonishing figure whose social mobility many recognised, but whom few could rival. He benefited from having several intimate friends—two became his biographers, while the third served as editor of a leading catering journal—providing insights into not just London's changing catering world but Pearce himself. As a result of spearheading the emergence in the capital of the mass food market, he would become a familiar figure interviewed often in the press, where he disclosed some facets of his life as caterer. Finally, he also fully deserves to be the focus of this study owing to his longevity, remarkable

D. W. Gutzke, *John Pearce and the Rise of the Mass Food Market in London, 1870–1930*, https://doi.org/10.1007/978-3-030-27095-7_1

Table 1.1 Estimated customers served annually in the city, 1908

Company	*City shops*	*Estimated customers*
Aerated Bread Co. (ABC)	65	24 million
J. Lyons & Co.	57	23 million
British Tea Table Co.	37	10 million[a]
Express Dairy Co.	21	8 million

Source: *Temperance Caterer*, 15 Sept. 1908

[a]The figures for 1908 are the best comparison of all four companies at one time, but by then, Pearce had been forced out of the BTT by a few large shareholders, soon with disastrous consequences—the company heading towards bankruptcy. The number here was considerably bigger in the years 1900–1904, when Pearce served as managing director and the company flourished. One informed estimate in 1905 put the number of its annual customers at 32 million (*South London Chronicle*, 26 May 1905)

commercial success and commanding presence in the lives of lower- and middle-class workers in the City.

In 1908, the *Temperance Caterer* published statistics on the consumption of meals in the City of London that are reproduced here because they come from one of the few direct comparisons among the four big firms in London catering (Table 1.1). The proportion of teashops based in the City for the four largest firms—Aerated Bread Co. (ABC), J. Lyons, British Tea Table Co. (BTT; formerly Pearce & Plenty) and the Express Dairy Co.—is quite suggestive. Two-thirds of the British Tea Table Company's outlets were so located in 1908, far greater than those of the Express Dairy, which had around 50% based in the City. By far the biggest company, J. Lyons, catering more to middle- rather than working-class patrons, had nearly half of its outlets there. Altogether, these four companies ran 180 shops in the square mile, selling 65 million meals annually! Lyons had fewer overall depots[1] than the ABC, but still outsold its main rival: Lyons' 120 depots sold roughly 250,000 meals daily, whereas ABC's 130 depots counted just 100,000 meals daily.[2] The two largest companies, moreover, also catered to many patrons outside the City, giving them a wider customer base than their competitors.

[1] The precursor of the term "restaurant," depot described originally less exalted premises in the mid-Victorian era. Restaurant gradually replaced it, though the two terms were interchangeable until World War I.

[2] *Temperance Caterer*, 15 Sept. 1908; Peter Bird, *The First Food Empire: A History of J. Lyons & Co.* (Chichester: Phillimore & Co., 2000), p. 38; Express Dairy Company, Museum of English Rural Life, 1909 Annual Report, TR EXP/5/3. Slaters and Lockharts were excluded, presumably because reliable estimates were unavailable.

The City's dominance could also be measured numerically. In 1840, the EC postal code—embracing the City—had ranked first, with the most dining/coffee rooms and restaurants, accounting for nearly half of the capital's total. While this preponderance gradually declined during the next seven decades, the City still held over one-fourth of the total before World War I. In second place stood the Western postal code, where almost one-fifth of these establishments conducted business.[3]

John Pearce—involved in the revolution in retailing food in late Victorian London—has never received any detailed historical treatment. By writing about his business career, it is possible to set it against the development of the whole industry without going into considerable biographical details of his life, which remain sketchy and often unknowable, given limited available evidence. Pearce's career thus must be placed in a wider historical context to understand his role in pioneering the mass food market in London.

This approach also enables me to contribute to the growing literature on the concept of consumption. To broaden our understanding, historian James Obelkevich recommends that scholars engage in "detailed empirical research on … a particular group of consumers." In studying Pearce's companies as well as those of his competitors, this book illuminates changing consumption patterns for workers in the City of London, the birthplace of the mass market, over a half century.[4]

Scholars point to the years after 1850 as critical in the "revolution in retail distribution," and three factors indicate its catalysts: "new products and innovations in product manufacturing with changes in distribution channels," improved transportation and storage facilities, and emergence of the mass market in large urban areas fostering the development of multiple branches.[5]

While scholarship on the retail revolution is extensive, little serious investigation exists on the narrower concept of the mass market. In an early study (1966) on the social history of diet, John Burnett said nothing either about John Pearce or about the mass market, instead stressing

[3] Brenda Assael, *The London Restaurant, 1840–1914* (Oxford: Oxford University Press, 2018), pp. 19–20.

[4] James Obelkevich, "Consumption," in James Obelkevich and Peter Catterall (eds.), *Understanding Post-War British Society* (London: Routledge, 1994), p. 142.

[5] G. Shaw, "The Evolution and Impact of Large-Scale Retailing in Britain," in John Benson and Gareth Shaw (eds.), *The Retailing Industry*, vol. 2: *The Coming of the Mass Market, 1800–1945* (London: I.B. Tauris, 1999), p. 251.

Lyons' establishment of teashops in the 1890s.[6] Several subsequent historical studies, however, would break new ground in suggesting the pivotal role of a new concept—the mass market—in transforming retailing.

W. Hamish Fraser, in his *The Coming of the Mass Market, 1850–1914*, identified three developmental stages of the mass market.[7] Hawkers, fairs and street markets had flourished in the first half of the nineteenth century. "The street," Fraser wrote, "was the last refuge of the unemployed and the unemployable, the artisan who had hit hard times, the drunkard, the blind, the limbless." Little capital required and credit easily available with a loan from a pawn broker, penny capitalists burgeoned in numbers, particularly in London. Mobility, moving from place to place to what they called "stands," was one of their chief features. Mid-Victorian London social investigator Henry Mayhew estimated some 30,000 costermongers sold a wide array of goods—fish, fruit, vegetable, game, poultry and flowers.

Distinctly second, London street traders (4000) catered to those working-class denizens whose homes had no cooking facilities and so purchased food cooked on the spot, together with a beverage of astonishing choice—ranging from tea, coffee, cocoa and ginger beer to lemonade, elder cordial, peppermint water, rice milk and even fresh milk. "The poorest section of the working class" consumed the poorest quality of food, only escaping detection as often inedible or noxious owing to lax government oversight in an era of laissez-faire. Seen in a broader context, these Londoners, one step above the residuum, engaged in what contemporaries regarded as the "luxury trade" in which workers proved capable of buying "take out" meals. John Pearce became part of this broad group when he opened a mobile coffee stall, dubbed "the Gutter Hotel," in and around East and City Roads in 1866. Reflecting changes in the nature of catering, coffee stalls would be renamed coffee bars, which went well beyond offering a standard fare of coffee and "snacks." Plaice, haddock, sole and whiting, especially popular with the working class, sustained some 300 street fishmongers. Cheap and readily accessible, herring sales topped 875 million annually. These astonishing sales, too, preceded founding in

[6] John Burnett, *Plenty and Want: A Social History of Diet in England from 1815 to the Present Day* (London: Thomas Nelson, 1966). A later book likewise ignores the mass market as a concept, though the author employs the term itself (John Burnett, *England Eats Out: A Social History of Eating Out in England from 1830 to the Present* (London: Pearson Longman, 2004)).

[7] W. Hamish Fraser, *The Coming of the Mass Market, 1850–1914* (London: Macmillan Press, 1981), pp. 94–109.

the 1860s of what became a central institution for slum dwellers—fish-and-chip shops. Another group, comparable in numbers to street traders, sold diverse manufactured products—metal, glass, china and cloth. Unlike food retailers, this group preferred barter, not cash. Two final groups were numerically less critical but still important: sellers of street literature and a diverse, miscellaneous group of thousands defying easy generalisation.[8]

Bigger shops with more diverse stock and larger premises constituted the second stage of the mass market. To achieve this more enviable level, stationary shopkeepers required more capital than their peripatetic predecessors—the greater sums still remained quite small. At one extreme stood the Roberts' family in Edwardian Salford, the semi-skilled, working-class father investing £40 of his savings in a corner shop, stocked from nearby larger shops for £2. In what became a familiar pattern for such shopkeepers, the father continued working for wages, while his wife ran the shop and presumably benefited if the family became more prosperous as a result. For Londoner John Pearce, an unskilled labourer with more meagre savings (Fig. 1.1)—a week's salary of £1 earned from an herbalist shop—rental of a barrow cost 1s. weekly, his largest outlay. Given a slow start in which his morning's earnings for six months averaged just 30d., he took a part-time job as a packer earning 10s. for a 36-hour work-week to tide him over until business picked up. Social investigator Charles Booth learned that a London shopkeeper netted on average £2 15s., whereas John Pearce earned initially about one-fifth this amount. Steps upward in social mobility could involve small increments, requiring improvised strategies of survival.[9] By the 1870s, Pearce had the insight and saw the

[8] Ibid., p. 95; Burnett, *England Eats Out*, pp. 39, 44; John K. Walton, *Fish and Chips and the Working Class, 1870–1940* (Leicester: Leicester University Press, 1992), p. 23; Henry Mayhew, *London Labour and the London Poor* (Griffin, Bohn & Co., 1861): vol. 1: *The London Street-Folk*, pp. 160–207; S. J. Adair Fitz-Gerald, "Chats with Caterers: John Pearce," *Caterer and Hotel-Keepers' Gazette*, 16 Jan. 1905, p. 14; Marguerite Williams, *John Pearce: The Man Who Played the Game* (London: Religious Tract Society, 1928), pp. 92–3.

[9] John Benson, *The Penny Capitalists: A Study of Nineteenth-Century Working-Class Entrepreneurs* (New Brunswick, New Jersey: Rutgers University Press, 1983), pp. 115–16; Rev. James J. Ellis, *Pluck, Patience and Power: The Life Story of John Pearce of "Pearce and Plenty"* (London: H.R. Allenson, [1910]), pp. 62–3, 65, 70, 75, 77; Charles Booth, *Life and Labour of the People of London* (London: Macmillan & Co., 1903), 2nd series, vol. 3: *Industry*, p. 254; Robert Roberts, *The Classic Slum: Salford Life in the First Quarter of the Century* (Manchester: University of Manchester Press, 1971), p. 15.

Fig. 1.1 Gustave Doré wood engraving, "Coffee Stall—Early Morning" (1872)

potential of expanding through satellite stalls, with trained managers hired to oversee other stalls, not surprisingly called "Gutter Hotels" (Fig. 1.2).[10] Such branches were an echo of the general development of multiples—retail chains owned by the same company.

Expanding numbers of "multiples" marked the third stage of the mass market. Nothing was new about companies forming branches—called "multiples"—since the grocery and provisions trade had first pioneered

[10] *Daily Telegraph*, 27 March 1905.

MR. JOHN PEARCE AT HIS COFFEE STALL.

This is from a photo taken when Mr. Pearce had a stall in City Road. He saved £1,200 of his earnings by it.

Fig. 1.2 John Pearce at his "Gutter Hotel" coffee stall (City Road) in 1866 (Reproduced by permission of the Mary Evans Picture Library)

the concept. One of the first, Walton, Hassell & Port in London, counted thirty branches in 1870. What made the 1870s–1880s a distinct departure was that multiples exploded in numbers in these trades as the level of unemployment dropped. "The multiples were the shops of the mass market," observed W. Hamish Fraser. By 1885, thirty-one firms owned ten or more branches, with eight running at least twenty-five.[11]

Multiples embraced standardisation in design, products, value, service quality, and above all, branding as methods for differentiating themselves from competitors. "Multiple retailing developed where consumer convenience was significant," commented Michael Ball and David Sunderland in their economic survey of nineteenth-century London. The commercial imperative for establishing branches as a tactic for expanding business reflected the assumption that, regardless of how retailers packaged their products at one central site, growth would inevitably reach a maximum, even if premises became larger, more diverse and more attractive.[12] Establishing department stores, in contrast, assumed that people would travel a long way if they had a wide enough choice when they reached the store.

Scholars cite several factors as vital to promoting the rise of multiples from the late Victorian era: increasing imported foodstuffs, factory production and a new business philosophy. Central to multiples' marketing strategy was limiting the range of goods sold to enable purchasing in bulk, providing profits derived from minuscule transactions based on high turnover. In meat retailing, a profit margin of 0.5% seemed satisfactory; in John Pearce's mass catering to London's working class in the 1880s–1890s the figure was vastly higher—2.4%, five times the meat retailing's margin of profit per unit. To the Royal Commission in 1897, John Pearce explained what mass catering meant in practice: "We serve six customers in Pearce's houses before the person that has the capital in the business receives a farthing in dividend." None of his other houses rivalled the original Pearce and Plenty on Farringdon Street, where a huge staff of 50 preparing food and dispensing it almost with lightning speed fed some 6000 patrons daily, who ravenously devoured steak pudding, potatoes and mug of cocoa for 6d.[13]

Multiples emerged in specialist retailing, initially with W.H. Smith and the Singer Manufacturing Co. before spreading to other trades—footwear, grocery and meat. By the 1880s–1890s, the concept appeared in

[11] Fraser, *Mass Market*, pp. 111–18; *Daily Telegraph*, 27 March 1905; *Pearson's Weekly*, 5 Sept. 1914.

[12] Michael Ball and David Sunderland, *An Economic History of London, 1800–1914* (London: Routledge, 2001), pp. 134–35.

[13] Ibid., p. 136; *Evidence of the Royal Commission on Liquor Licensing Laws*, 1898, 36 (Cmnd. 8694), pp. 242, 244.

tailoring and patent medicines.[14] According to D.J. Richardson, "the dramatic rise of the multiples in the retail food trade established a pattern which was followed in many respects by catering." J. Lyons, for instance, distinguished itself in the 1890s in emulating the business strategy of earlier multiple caterers in the 1850s.[15]

In embracing uncomplicated shop fittings and introducing "standardised branch stock control systems," multiples achieved superior standards in quality as well as in service. In generating custom, premises "were attractively laid out and kept immaculately clean."[16]

Advent of the mass market in London from the mid-1870s drew meagre scholarly interest until A.E. Dingle's 1972 ground-breaking but largely ignored article. He advanced a compelling thesis in which he identified rising purchasing power, accessibility of consumer goods and stable beer retail prices as three essential causes. Consumer choice widened with imported foodstuffs, such as grain, meat, bacon, dairy products and fruit. Many consumer goods industries now industrialised, enabling inexpensive mass-produced boots, shoes, clothing and food processing to enter the market. Another development—the revolutionising of retailing and distributing practices—fostered falling prices, on the one hand, and rises in both real wages and demand, on the other. As the range of consumer goods broadened still further, consumer choice burgeoned in the 1880s. In the years 1860–1875, as prices fell while employment levels continued, real wages soared by 92%. Retail prices of beer, however, remained unchanged at 3d. per pint, inducing its consumers to see that their standard tipple had become relatively more expensive compared to an increasingly diverse array of consumer goods. The economic imbalance between 1875 and 1890 in which employment and money wages tended downwards while prices fell faster and real wages continued to rise prompted drinkers to switch purchases from beer to new consumables, explaining why beer consumption stagnated from 1876 rather than continuing its rise. Summarising the impact of these changes, John Burnett, in his *England Eats Out: A Social History of Eating Out in England from 1830 to the Present* (2004), argues that "there had been a substantial filtering-up

[14] Ball and Sunderland, *History of London*, pp. 134–35.

[15] D.J. Richardson, "J. Lyons and Co. Ltd.: Caterers and Food Manufacturers, 1894 to 1939," in Derek J. Oddy and Derek S. Miller (eds.), *The Making of the Modern British Diet* (London: Croom Helm, 1976), p. 161.

[16] Ball and Sunderland, *History of London*, p. 136.

from the lower ranks of labourers towards steadier, better-paid employment, and … more working-class families were beginning to enjoy an improved more varied and nutritious diet." Increasingly customers purchased consumer goods as prices fell faster than money wages. Stable beer and coffee prices now seemed relatively more expensive compared to new consumer goods, so the working class, formerly purchasers of alcohol and coffee, switched to buying consumer durables. Dingle's article was thus seminal, the first scholarly study to recognise the mass market as a concept and offer a persuasive thesis explaining its emergence.[17]

New types of coffee public houses in the 1860s–1880s, mimicking pubs in every way save in selling alcohol, suggested to some scholars that late Victorian temperance reformers had discovered a novel method of retailing—mass catering. Two broad reform groups emerged: those drawing on strong temperance convictions, whose lack of business acumen doomed such ventures, and a smaller but more commercially minded group, which elevated profits over philanthropy. None achieved true mass catering in London.[18]

Recently, Andrea Broomfield, in her *Food and Cooking in Victorian England*, maintains that from coffee public houses begun in the 1870s came "a corporate business model that worked," serving as the basis for commercialised catering.[19] In fact, at most qualified success characterised their efforts, as Chap. 2 on coffee public houses demonstrates. Those entrepreneurs with temperance roots who survived broke with prevailing policy, introducing ideas based on the innovative approach of massive volume sales with miniscule profits on each transaction—the dominant philosophy of multiple shops.

An entirely different case for coffee public houses' impact comes from the career of Ronald McDougall. A transplanted caterer to London in the

[17] A.E. Dingle, "Drink and Working-Class Living Standards in Britain," *Economic History Review* 25 (1972): 608–22; A.L. Bowley, "Changes in Average Wages (Nominal and Real) in the United Kingdom between 1860 and 1891," *Journal of the Statistical Society* 58 (1895): 225, 251–52; Burnett, *England Eats Out*, p. 40.

[18] The concept of mass food catering first appeared in Dublin, where chef Alexis Soyer established a vast soup kitchen capable of feeding 1000 people per hour in 1847 (Andrew Langley, *The Selected Soyer: The Writings of the Legendary Victorian Chef, Alexis Soyer* (Bath: Absolute Press, 1987), pp. 31–4). Just the Liverpool British Workman Public House Company achieved mass catering. See Chap. 5, note 2.

[19] Andrea Broomfield, *Food and Cooking in Victorian England: A History* (Westport, CT: Praeger, 2007), p. 56.

late 1870s and early 1880s, he assumed management of a coffee public-house company, the People's Café Co., which achieved remarkable—indeed astonishing—success. Interviewed in 1912, some three decades after massive market changes, he claimed he alone had initiated London teashops, one vital source of mass catering. Half a century later, historian Kathleen Heasman independently reached the same conclusion.[20] McDougall's case for achieving mass catering is debunked in Chap. 3.

Who then deserves credit as having achieved status as the first mass food caterer in Victorian London? Four traits were necessary to reach the level of being a mass food marketer: number of multiple branches; volume of daily meal sales; class of the clientele; and whether the company served hot meals (which entailed several courses), not just light refreshment.

Smaller catering companies doing business in the City are easily discounted from consideration. Numbers of multiples as well as volume of substantial hot meal sales disqualified both Slaters and Lockharts. Slaters had opened just one London depot in 1889, soon after the advent of the mass market, so sales it achieved at this one site could not—by whatever criteria—qualify as catering to the "masses." Lockharts, in contrast, having appeared in London in 1883 with its first shop, established multiples on a vast scale thereafter, opening another fifty-three houses in London alone by 1888. To earn recognition as a mass caterer, however, Lockharts needed to specialise in selling hot meals with joints of meat and vegetables, not just light fare—sandwiches, sausages, pies and pastry—on its menus throughout the 1890s.[21]

Was a more persuasive case possible for the largest catering companies? In a 2006 essay, three scholars contend that both the Aerated Bread Co. (ABC) and Lyons were responsible for having "revolutionised eating out." "By achieving large-scale production techniques, and standardising conditions, products, service and prices," the ABC and Lyons "dramatically transformed … the nature of catering." Compelling evidence for this thesis, however, is lacking. Bereft of data of total meal sales, the authors rely instead on Kelly's *Directories* of London, which enumerated total numbers of ABC depots but which offered no insight whatsoever into

[20] Kathleen Joan Heasman, "The Influence of the Evangelicals upon the Origin and Development of Voluntary Charitable Institutions in the Second Half of the Nineteenth Century" (University of London, Ph.D., 1959), p. 300. Though this thesis was the basis for her subsequent book, only the dissertation cited sources.

[21] See pp. 52–3.

what the company sold on such premises. Had the authors looked further, they would have discovered other evidence supporting an entirely different conclusion. The ABC, which had established depots from the 1870s, had enough multiples with seventy shops (1889) to stake a claim as initiating mass catering, but several defects disqualified it as having in fact "revolutionised" dining: it concentrated on attracting not masses of workers in the square mile, but lower-middle-class white-collar workers, together with those securely in the middle class; and it offered them its own version of "light refreshment"—bread, cakes and pastry. "Cakes and pastries," not sizable hot meals with meat and vegetables, Pearce knew, still characterised the ABC menu in 1897, when he testified before the Royal Commission on Liquor Licensing.[22] That same year in an interview in the *Caterer*, a reporter described the ABC's menu as consisting of little more than "tea and buns." Baroness Orczy's mystery stories, collected, published and entitled *The Old Man in the Corner* and set in an ABC shop (Norfolk Street, off the Strand), capture the Edwardian atmosphere of respectability, with her unescorted female journalist, Miss Mary J. Burton (*Evening Observer*), drinking tea and conversing with a nearby armchair detective, who sips milk with a bun or cheesecake while solving crimes (Fig. 1.3).[23] Lyons comprised an altogether different case from the ABC. "Through our teashops we were largely responsible for revolutionizing catering in London by introducing good and inexpensive food in clean and cheerful surroundings," argued its in-house magazine long after the transformation.[24] Indeed, Bird, as his conclusions and preconceptions stated clearly, entitles his chapter "The Restaurant Revolution."

Yet, he offers no information whatsoever about total meal sales at Lyons teashops. Nothing else could have more conclusively addressed whether Lyons did in fact revolutionise catering in the 1890s and early 1900s.

[22] Gareth Shaw, Louise Hill Curth and Andrew Alexander, "Creating New Spaces of Food Consumption: The Rise of Mass Catering and the Activities of the Aerated Bread Company," in John Benson and Laura Ugolini (eds.), *Cultures of Selling: Perspectives on Consumption and Society Since 1700* (Aldershot: Ashgate, 2006), pp. 86–8; Dora Greenwell McChesney, "The World of the ABC," *Daily Mail*, 15 Apr. 1903; *Evidence on Liquor Licensing Laws*, 1898, p. 240; A. Jepson, "The Coffee Tavern Movement in London," *Supplement to the Temperance Caterer*, 10 Sept. 1887; *Temperance Chronicle*, 15 Aug. 1906.

[23] "A People's Caterer," *Caterer*, 15 Jan. 1897; Baroness [Emmuska] Orczy, "The Fenchurch Street Mystery," *Royal Magazine* 6 (May, 1901). The ABC's appeal to higher social strata first came in 1906 (*Financial Times*, 6 Nov. 1906).

[24] J. Lyons & Co., *Lyons Mail*, Oct. 1934, Acc. 3527/230, London Metropolitan Archives.

Fig. 1.3 Solving Crime at an ABC, 1901 (Baroness [Emmuska] Orczy, "The Fenchurch Street Mystery," *Royal Magazine* 6 [May, 1901])

Surely such data would have survived when Bird came to write his company history, though as an unofficial archivist, not a trained historian, he perhaps lacked appreciation of this topic's overall importance. Within the City through its teashops, Lyons catered chiefly to London's middle class, a prosperous clientele which could afford costlier meals than those socially below them. Such meals fell far short of what workers wanted—hot, generous portions of meat and vegetables. "There was almost no cooking except for toasting … and [it was] warmed on hot plates," commented John Burnett. At its teashops, Lyons thus catered to those seeking light refreshments. Between 1894 and 1900, Lyons multiples expanded from three to thirty-seven. In targeting primarily bourgeois male patrons in the City, Lyons sacrificed mass food sales—dependent on service as quick and as rapid as consumption—for greater profits.[25] We are left therefore with aggregate numbers of teashop openings and company profits and dividends as sole indicators of Lyons' claim as a mass caterer. Evidence of Lyons' pioneering mass caterer is simply non-existent: its universal appeal spanning the propertied classes really pre-empted its role as a mass caterer to the masses. Pearce earned his inevitable reputation as a mass caterer with his 3d. meat pies, whereas Lyons a decade later offered patrons mutton pies at 7d.[26]

No one but John Pearce thus fulfils the four traits requisite for establishing the leading part in spearheading London's mass food catering. In gradually transiting from coffee stall vendor to coffee house proprietor, he spent thirteen years (1866–1879) acquiring experience, capital and novel ideas for competing in an intensely competitive market. Accumulating investment funds proved daunting but not insuperable: first, he began humbly at his "Gutter Hotel" coffee stall, where eventually he generated £6 pounds of business daily, working between 4 a.m. and 8 a.m.; then he bolstered business and profits with other satellite "Gutter Hotel" coffee stalls in which he installed managers; and finally on selling this business he received £200 for the stall and its custom, which, together with his savings of £1000, provided the financial nucleus for opening his first depot at 58 Aldersgate Street in 1878, commencing his career's second stage. Here, we know, Pearce–displaying immense self-confidence—gambled it all, investing his entire life savings, £1400!

To supplement his depleted funds, he entered the hotelier business at 84 Farringdon Street, building the first "poor man's" temperance hotel atop a new depot in 1882. Strategically, this constituted a shrewd decision: his sixty beds produced enough revenue covering the entire building's rent; and his profits from daily sales of 6000 meals generated £1000 annually (1882–1886).[27]

Just one depot (together with a hotel) sustained him until 1886 when, with Sir Edward Sullivan and others as investors, he formed a limited liability company in what became Pearce & Plenty. Inevitably the result of

[25] Bird, *First Food Empire*, p. 43, and Appendix 4; Evidence of the Royal Commission on Licensing (England and Wales), 11 Apr. 1930. The Commission's evidence was printed but never published.

[26] Burnett, *England Eats Out*, p. 124.

[27] "Coffee-Stall Crisis," *Daily Telegraph*, 3 Apr. 1901; John Pearce, "'I Started Gutter Hotels': Founder of the Famous Poor Man's Restaurants," *Pearson's Weekly*, 5 Sept. 1914; *Coffee Public-House News*, 1 Feb. 1883.

overstretched investment funds delayed his expansion and was crucial to his endurance: it enabled Pearce to withstand the mass market's turbulent arrival early in the 1880s; and it avoided a financial crisis owing to plummeting sales (as in McDougall's case).[28] When Pearce & Plenty became established with a capital of £20,000, three more depots duly appeared in the City the following year. Slow entry into the City's market constituted one vital reason for Pearce's persistence. Thereafter, expansion came quickly, as multiples became an integral part of Pearce & Plenty: they counted twelve (1889), and then, twenty-two (1896). In achieving this level, Pearce met one criterion for qualifying as a mass food caterer—formation of satellite branches called multiples. Now he entered the third stage of his career.

Total meal sales tell their own story about John Pearce as a mass caterer. Whether insisting on freshly brewed coffee or meat pies, steamed rather than boiled, witty advertising or going upmarket in search of a new clientele, Pearce was committed to innovative practices throughout his career. None of these matched in either imagination or conceptualisation, however, his role in instituting mass catering on an unprecedented scale. Long before Lyons' so-called teashop revolution began in 1894, as Bird would have it, Pearce was selling more than 30,000 hot meals daily in the City, soon rising to 65,000 (Table 1.2). By 1905, his two companies were serving 120,000 patrons, not just light refreshments offered by his competitors, but hot substantial meals daily, at 84 depots largely in the City and its surroundings to Londoners (Table 8.3). By whatever rubric, this ranked

Table 1.2 John Pearce and the mass market's arrival in the City of London, 1887–1905

Year	*Daily meal sales*	*City depots*
1887	14,000	4
1889	30,000	11
1896	65,000	46
1898	70,000	52
1905	120,000	84

Sources: See Tables 5.1 and 5.2

[28] Cost of outfitting a new depot, even in a rudimentary style, was far beyond the savings of the former Gutter Hotel proprietor. As the depot opened on Farringdon Street in 1882, Pearce had to find between £700 and £800, a sum which almost equalled what he had saved in thirteen years as a coffee stall entrepreneur ("Pearce's Coffee Bar, Farringdon Street, London," *Coffee Public-House News*, 1 Feb. 1883).

clearly as pre-eminent in London's catering world. In concentrating from his beginning on the City, drawing almost exclusively a working-class clientele seeking ample, inexpensive hot meals with meat as an essential ingredient, dispensed with almost lighting speed, and opening new "depots" as quickly as his burgeoning working-class clientele demanded, he alone achieved distinction as indisputable caterer to the masses.[29]

In exploring the advent of mass catering in the City of London's working class, John Pearce, founder of Pearce & Plenty, stands out as the central figure from the late 1870s well into the 1920s. In part this was because he began life early as a caterer, gradually moving socially upwards to graft a loyal middle-class clientele onto his broader working-class base; and in part, because his career spanned six decades of dramatic changes in feeding Londoners, making him pivotal to understanding the wider catering context.

Pearce, though premier caterer of the City of London's working class, received little scholarly attention—not even a popular, undocumented history comparable to Peter Bird's book on Lyons.[30] Certainly, this was not the result of lack of historical interest. Utter destruction of Pearce's personal and business archives, the same fate befalling all other major London catering companies except for Lyons (granted only a brief reprieve), had seemingly precluded serious historical study of him. Bereft of essential business documents—detailed minute books covering the Board of Directors, depot superintendents, employee information, estate properties and vital statistics, together with the plethora of other matters (notably advertising, newspaper clippings and critically correspondence) that any company typically generates—little wonder then that John Pearce languished in obscurity. Even the new *Oxford DNB* thought Pearce's credentials unworthy of scholarly recognition, a damning verdict historian John Benson had already endorsed in his study of penny capitalists in

[29] Outside London, philanthropic employers—the cocoa and chocolate firms of Cadbury, Rowntree and Fry; the soap manufacturer Lever Brothers; and the mustard producer Colmans—all established huge canteens in which workers received meals speedily delivered at cost prices. At Cadbury's Bournville, women workers numbering 3600 got just 15 minutes for mid-morning lunch. Burnett points to these firms as early examples of mass catering "unique in scale outside military establishments." However impressive in terms of their working-class clientele, daily meal sales and hot meals, such firms lacked the fourth trait of the mass caterer, the establishments of multiples (Burnett, *England Eats Out*, pp. 110–12).

[30] Burnett offers a brief overview of Pearce's business career (Burnett, *England Eats Out*, pp. 117–18).

which he overlooked Pearce entirely.[31] A still more recent scholarly assessment of Pearce's career dismissed it as worth no more than a brief encyclopaedic entry, too insignificant surely for even an article, much less a book.[32] Does this perhaps reflect what E.P. Thompson expressed so many years ago about historical figures at the base of the social system receiving little more than "the enormous condescension of posterity"?[33] How is one, then, to reconcile Pearce's unexamined scholarly dismissal, on the one hand, with his striking public persona, on the other? "He was probably better known personally to his thousands of customers than any other caterer," thought biographer Marguerite Williams, who knew him better than most, possibly anybody, certainly in his later years.[34]

His two biographers, both contemporaries and friends, wrote disappointing studies, apparently dissuading scholars from exploring Pearce and his catering world. Familiar with Pearce's religious views, beliefs and convictions, the Rev. James J. Ellis published the first biography in 1910, naturally assuming that Pearce's business career at age 63 was virtually over (as so many of his critics with shares in the company believed). Pearce, himself, in his more pessimistic mood, might well have agreed. As he once reflected about his early life and prospects for success: "I never had a chance." In elaborating on this statement, Pearce stressed, "I had no education, no money, and no proper start in life."[35] Second biographer Marguerite Williams, whose study appeared in 1928 after his active second career had finally ended, might have examined the intervening years since Ellis had published his study, but her overriding religious concerns—the Religious Tract Society published her book—and view of Pearce's business career as a subordinate subject, meant she too devoted little space to this neglected but vital period in which he re-invented himself as an evolving, creative and imaginative London caterer with few peers. So important was religion as a factor in his life and work as well as relationship with his mother that it seemed perfectly natural to both biographers that Pearce as

[31] Benson, *Penny Capitalists.* One of his subsequent surveys, *The Rise of Consumer Society in Britain, 1880–1980* (London: Longman, 1994), likewise ignored Pearce as well as other mass working-class caterers.

[32] Such sentiments were expressed in an anonymous referee's assessment of this manuscript at an earlier stage.

[33] E.P. Thompson, *The Making of the English Working Class* (London: Victor Gollancz, 1963), p. 12.

[34] Williams, *Pearce*, p. 226.

[35] Ellis, *Pluck*, p. 208.

the City's foremost caterer be treated as ancillary. His biographers, moreover, set their studies in a narrow historical context, their primary focus illuminating less about Pearce as businessman and caterer than about Pearce the Baptist, temperance adherent and upright Christian. In short, they afford little insight into what made Pearce a progressively adept entrepreneur, one of London's pre-eminent caterers for over half a century. Nor was this shortcoming remedied in their other published work: nothing else in fact from them ever appeared in print about Pearce.[36] These sources, while providing an indispensable overview of his salient character traits, said little about marketing strategies, boardroom conflicts, market assessments, prices and menu offerings as well as enumerable other vital topics. Without insight into such matters, no author could write a worthwhile, reliable business history.

What then justifies a book on catering that is neither a biography nor a business history? Brenda Assael's recent study, *The London Restaurant, 1840–1914* (2018), exploring the restaurant as an institution, suggests one possible approach. Hers is best suited for giving people of the present day a vivid, revealing glimpse of what constituted dining in the capital before World War I. In it she chooses to write about the specialised world of the expensive, more or less Frenchified, places too expensive and too formal for anyone outside the top 5% or 10% of the population to visit. Assael has decided to say little about the arrangements for eating out of the 90% or 95% who did not go to restaurants in her sense of the word. Yet, cultural and social developments for the preponderance of the population are important and deserve attention. She rightly says that "social historians of London's economy have shown negligible interest in the restaurant," but her own scope for study still leaves much unexplored, notably caterers with numerous branches based primarily in the City of London.[37] As a study of a milieu and John Pearce's role in it, my book inevitably is quite different from Assael's.

Recently, the British Library's digitising of newspapers, both national and regional, has offered entry into this previously closed world of catering. Two major London daily newspapers—the *Financial Times* and *The Times*—reproduced speeches at annual shareholders' meetings, interviews with chairmen, general managers, managing directors and disgruntled

[36] I failed to locate a copy of James Ward's brief biographical sketch, *The Life of John Pearce* (c. 1905).

[37] Assael, *London Restaurant*, p. 3.

shareholders, offering lengthy editorial comments and assessments of catering companies' economic performance as well as changes in the catering market and consumer habits. To some extent, these sources serve as substitute for lost company records. Basic information about net profits and losses, dividends, numbers of depots/restaurants, stock prices, reserves, goodwill, depreciation and capital can generally be extracted, though companies sometimes chose not to divulge data seen as potentially damaging or perhaps helpful to rivals. Unfortunately, because catering companies regarded meal sales as highly confidential, little is known save the figures provided earlier (Table 1.1). Pearce broke with this policy, enabling the charting of his expanding sales of meals, which provides solid evidence of his rightful claim as the pre-eminent mass food caterer of London's working classes (Table 1.2).

However indispensable digitalised databases are for historical research, more traditional but far more labour-intensive methods of gathering historical material must be adopted. Friend and admirer of Pearce, Joseph Bentley was a crucial source for understanding the catering world of late Victorian and Edwardian England. As general manager and Secretary of the Bradford Coffee Tavern Company as well as Secretary of the National Coffee Tavern Association, he possessed vast insight, unmatched among journalists writing about not merely the coffee public-house movement but more broadly catering. From becoming editor of the *Temperance Caterer* early in the 1890s until his retirement in 1917, Bentley's keen insight into catering enlivened, informed and disseminated a distinctive voice for almost thirty years. While he left no reminiscences, memoir or an autobiography, his monthly columns in the *Caterer* afford indispensable informed, impartial and knowledgeable commentary. Since this newspaper has not yet been digitised, I read the entire run of the *Caterer*. Several other non-digitised newspapers, notably, the *Coffee Public-House News*, *Refreshment News* and *Temperance Chronicle*, were likewise read comprehensively.

Unanticipated when I began exploring this catering world was the discovery of a dozen lengthy interviews with Pearce, published in newspapers often not yet digitised, together with his detailed testimony before a royal commission at a pivotal moment in his business career. These materials were indispensable in understanding Pearce and his business career.

My thesis is that John Pearce alone possessed the characteristics, personality and imagination for spearheading the catering revolution for London's working-class and petite bourgeoisie in the City, not much outside the underground's line encompassing what might be called the inner circle. Intuitively, Pearce drew on his own background—slum-born, raised by a single parent, little formal education, exposed to diverse trades as well as some disquieting personalities, and driven by a powerful, abiding work ethic, together with an uncompromising moral code—to earn money sufficient to make the transition from penny capitalist to fixed shopkeeper and finally to owner of numerous multiples. Pearce's experiences and personal insights, together with the training of his sons in the catering business, created an amalgam, a dynamic business culture which appreciated experience as much as education, but which still remained receptive to new ideas with a penchant for experimentation. What emerges ultimately is the portrait of a significant figure in London and a leader of the "the temperance catering movement."[38]

From whatever perspective, John Pearce appears as the quintessential penny capitalist, a progenitor of the mass food market and an innovative, imaginative businessman who grasped intuitively how working- and middle-class catering was evolving from the late Victorian era into the 1920s. To diverse influences—family (pre-eminently his mother, wife and sons), class consciousness (born near the residuum), temperance, fundamentalist religion (especially the Rev. William Carter's unadorned beliefs in God's love), John's philanthropy, a deeply engrained, uncompromisingly moral code, and distinctive temperament—John Pearce owed his success as a mass caterer. How these influences in turn shaped him and more generally the milieu of late Victorian and Edwardian England constitute themes of the following chapters.

[38] *Financial Times*, 10 Aug. 1906 and 13 Feb. 1913.

CHAPTER 2

Pubs without Beer

Promoting coffee public houses—pubs without alcohol—began in earnest early in the 1870s, spearheaded by temperance reformers and philanthropists. Several temperance organisations—the Church of England Temperance Society, the National Temperance League and the Dublin Total Abstinence Society—individually, less often jointly, became the most receptive because they saw establishing coffee public houses as a viable strategy for promoting temperance. According to one informed observer, "one way of getting an idea of our fellow-countrymen's miseries is to go and look at their pleasures."[1] Not much more than a decade later, coffee public houses had allegedly peaked, with contemporaries and subsequent scholars convinced of unmistakable signs of decline quite evident.

Myths, confusions and obfuscations dominate the movement's history. Indeed, even its name remained controversial: some early proponents called it the Temperance Refreshment House movement; others dubbed it the British Workman's Public House movement; while still others referred to it as the reformed public-house movement; and finally and most commonly, numerous supporters designated it the coffee public-house

[1] Brian Harrison, *Drink and the Victorians: The Temperance Question in England, 1815–72*, 2nd ed. (Keele University: Keele University Press, 1994), p. 296; [J.J. Manley], "The Temperance Refreshment House Movement," *British Almanac Companion* 53 (1880): 47; "The Coffee Public-House Movement," *Chambers's Journal* 56 (1879): 144; Eve Lockington and Win Trickey, "The Coffee House Movement," *Loughton & District Historical Society* 154 (Oct. 2002): 3.

D. W. Gutzke, *John Pearce and the Rise of the Mass Food Market in London, 1870–1930*, https://doi.org/10.1007/978-3-030-27095-7_2

movement. Contemporaries repeatedly asserted that the movement was non-sectarian, that private philanthropists considerably funded the enterprises, that temperance pledges were not solicited, and that well-run coffee public houses contained separate areas for women. None of these were entirely true. Joseph Bentley (secretary of the National Coffee Tavern Association) asserted that "in the ideal Coffee Tavern all that is good in the best public-house is retained; it is simply minus the pernicious drink and its evil associations." Had this been in fact the case, coffee public houses would have stood a much better chance of wider popularity.

Lower taxes on tea and coffee in the early nineteenth century enabled consumption of these beverages, priced at 1–3 d. per cup, to compete with beer, sold at 3d. per pint, and move socially downwards into the middle and lower classes. Coffee houses soared in numbers, reaching between 1600 and 1800 in the early 1840s, but not with temperance support. Family-centred leisure dominated this era, so men consuming even non-alcoholic drinks in coffee houses drew criticism. In opening a coffee house in Dundee in 1853, Lord Kinnaird inaugurated a movement dedicated to catering to working-class patrons on a philanthropic basis. Ironically, it owed its survival to attracting socially upward bourgeois customers who could afford to pay more for coffee.[2]

Much of the impetus for creating coffee public houses came from growing distances working- and middle-class men had to travel to work, making impossible earlier habits of returning home for a mid-day meal. Even when workers had carried lunch with them to consume in a pub, they now expressed a desire for hot food. Greater demand for restaurants and cafes created opportunities for enterprising entrepreneurs and temperance advocates. Inexpensive tram and railway fares enabled workers in suburban London to emulate in a modest way the behaviour of their social betters.[3]

Parliamentary legislation enacted in 1855–1856 and 1862 permitted a new form of enterprise—limited liability companies—facilitating rapid emergence of commercialised catering. Between May 1876 and June

[2] Harrison, *Drink and the Victorians*, pp. 302–04.

[3] Robert Thorne, "Places of Refreshment in the Nineteenth-Century City," in Anthony D. King (ed.) *Buildings and Society: Essays on the Social Development of the Built Environment* (London: Routledge & Kegan Paul, 1980), p. 244; Malcolm Elliott, "The Leicester Coffee-House and Cocoa-House Movement," *Transactions of the Leicestershire Archaeological and Historical Society* 47 (1971–1972): 56; H.J. Dyos, "Workmen's Fares in South London, 1860–1914," *Journal of Transport History* 1 (1953): 3–19.

1879, 156 coffee and cocoa companies became incorporated.[4] Census returns record the explosion of eating facilities, with coffee and eating houses nearly tripling in the three decades after 1861.[5]

Two rival northern cities claimed to have originated the coffee public-house movement. In honour of Thomas Bywater Smithies, a prominent teetotal who had founded the *British Workman* newspaper in 1855, Mrs R.S. Hind Smith named the first coffee house the British Workman Public House, opened in Leeds in 1867.[6] On its façade ran the following verse:

A public-house without the drink,
Where men can, talk, read and think,
They safely home return,
A stepping-stone this house you'll find,
Consent to leave your beer behind,
All truer pleasure learn[7]

Coffee and tea, the mainstay of the beverages, cost 1½d. per cup. This city remained the stronghold of the embryonic movement, with Leeds accounting for nearly half of other such ventures in the next five years. Of the thirty-seven coffee public houses established, all but seven were located in the North.[8]

In appearance such establishments rejected traditional concepts of coffee houses and instead copied public houses in outward appearance and inner decorations. Further emulating pubs, such Workman Public House establishments afforded diverse amenities, ranging from newspapers and entertainments to overnight lodging and employment information. New beverages were likewise marketed, notably Winterine, Anti-Burton and aerated milk. Admirers pointed to widespread changes in social habits:

[4] H.A. Shannon, "The Limited Companies of 1866–83," *Economic History Review* 4 (1933): 308; Thorne, "Places of Refreshment," p. 239; E.T. Bellhouse, "The Coffee-House Movement," *Transactions of the Manchester Statistical Society* (1880): 122–23.

[5] Harrison, *Drink and the Victorians*, p. 303.

[6] Mrs Hind Smith, "British Workman Public-Houses; or, Public-houses without the Drink," *Transactions of the National Association for the Promotion of Social Science* (London: Longmans, Green, Reader & Dyer, 1872), p. 591; see also Peter Roger Mountjoy, "Thomas Bywater Smithies, Editor of the *British Workman*," *Victorian Periodicals Review* 18 (1985): 46–56.

[7] E. Hepple Hall, *Coffee Taverns, Cocoa Houses and Coffee Places: Their Rise, Progress, and Prospects* (London: S.W. Partridge, [1878]), pp. 15–16.

[8] Ibid., pp. 34–5, 38; National Temperance League 1881 Annual Report; Smith, "British Workman Public-Houses," p. 591.

> Drinking habits were broken; desires for self-improvement were awakened; … desolated homes were refurbished, and neglected families reclothed; Sabbaths were better spent; … public-houses … were losing custom and shopkeepers were gaining it; the general character of the neighbourhood was improved; [and] bad language was given up….[9]

Liverpool was the second home of coffee public houses. Total abstainers affiliated with the National Temperance League claimed it had commenced the Temperance Refreshment House movement.[10] In 1875 philanthropists established the Liverpool British Workman Public-House Company, a limited liability company with £20,000 of capital that aimed at providing cheap, plain food for workmen. Huge northern provincial cities such as Liverpool provided fertile ground for the National Temperance League's expansion with such a venture (Table 2.1). Within several years, the company was running thirty-nine houses, one-third of them sited on the docks, and doubling its capital to £40,000.[11] By 1884, the total number stood at sixty. Statistics indicate this venture filled a huge need. Opening its first house in 1875 equipped to accommodate some 500 customers, dockers thronged to it and easily overfilled the available seating. Opposite the Huskisson Dock, an even larger structure soon appeared, seating 1090 patrons. Mass catering had arrived here: altogether the houses catered to 25,000 patrons daily generating £85,000 in annual revenue (Table 2.1). Nothing like this then existed in London.[12] Instead of

Table 2.1 Spread of coffee public houses, 1884

	Affiliated public companies	*Coffee public houses*
National Temperance League	232	667
Independently run coffee public houses	646	646
Total		1313

Source: *Coffee Tavern Guide*, 1884

[9] The Northerner Blog, "Newcastle Latest City to Open 'Dry Bar'"; Hind Smith, "British Workman Public-Houses," p. 591; Hall, *Coffee Houses and Coffee Palaces*, p. 15.

[10] C.C. Smith's untitled paper, National Temperance League Congress, Liverpool, June, 1884 (Liverpool: National Temperance Publication Depot, 1884).

[11] Hall, *Coffee Taverns and Coffee Palaces,* pp. 21–4, 39–40.

[12] See Chap. 1, n. 18, Table 1.2, and Chap. 5.

Fig. 2.1 British Workman's Coffee Tavern at Liverpool, 1878 (*The Graphic*, 12 Jan. 1878)

rum and milk for breakfast, workers could enjoy a hot breakfast costing 1d.–2d.[13] In the ensuing years, the menu expanded to pea soup, hot pot and sausages, and patrons in central cafes could order hot meats and

[13]W. Peskett, "Work in Liverpool," *Coffee Public-House News*, 1 Aug. 1884.

puddings. Not until 1888, however, could diners at larger houses order dinners.[14]

Total abstinence dominated the entire enterprise, its 400 employees all taking the pledge to teetotalism and to joining the company's total abstinence society. Each bar carried a notice advertising a pledge book for patrons to sign, committing themselves to disavowing alcohol; some 30,000 had done so by 1884.[15]

The National Temperance League's British Workman Public House Company represented a radical departure in philosophy: instead of relying on philanthropists, the focus shifted to enticing humanitarian contributors who wanted to dispense, not charity but philanthropy with a reasonable financial return, at least 5% annually and preferably higher. Working-class denizens, so the argument ran, would resent outright charity but not philanthropy grounded on respectable financial return. Liverpool became the first to float a public company with the coffee public-house philosophy as its basis.

For the first time, the League acknowledged that pubs as social agencies promoting socialisation had a legitimate right to exist, provided they were stripped of their role as dispensers of alcohol. Such reformed pubs could provide customers with refreshments, while simultaneously earning investors adequate profits. Though total abstainers spearheaded the movement, non-abstainers played an important but subordinate function. In an article recounting the origins of coffee public houses in 1881, Thomas Hogben disclosed his own commitment to abstainers' superior beliefs that would bedevil the movement's subsequent development. Both groups, he noted, had "amicably worked" together, and over time, he fully expected the non-abstainers, discovering their flawed beliefs, would ultimately embrace the total abstinence position.[16]

Initially, coffee public-house promoters began as philanthropists who discovered rather surprisingly that charity and profit could co-exist successfully, much like philanthropic housing projects. Efforts in the country's twenty-three largest towns yielded dividends of 10%, save in the

[14] P.T. Winskill and Joseph Thomas, *History of the Temperance Movement in Liverpool and District, from its Introduction in 1829 Down to the Year 1887* (Liverpool: Joseph Thomas, 1887), p. 214.

[15] Peskett, "Work in Liverpool"; "Representative Temperance Caterer, No. 2: Mr. W.H. Preskett," *Temperance Caterer*, 3 Sept. 1887.

[16] Thomas Hogben, "The Coffee Public-House Movement," *A Hand-Book of Temperance History* (London: National Temperance Publications Depot, 1882), pp. 119–20.

metropolis, where as one observer noted, "London has been a source of anxiety."[17] Public-house companies established varying yardsticks, usually 5% but sometimes as much as 12–15%, of what investors could reasonably expect in return for their philanthropy.[18] While not members of temperance societies, these philanthropists regarded coffee public houses as a valid way of discouraging intemperance with counter-attractions. Cash, however, ultimately trumped the disapproval of insobriety. Dominating the movement, these temperance-minded philanthropists espoused the philosophy that "coffee Public-houses must be made to pay their way like any other business."[19] The movement's chief newspaper, the *Coffee Public-House News*, aligned with these philanthropists, but argued less from hard-headed investments than from a more pragmatic perspective—the clientele most inclined to frequent such establishments. As responsible family men with duties and obligations, abstainers would spend evenings at home with wives and children after signing pledges, whereas moderate drinkers would resort to coffee public houses as an alternative to consuming alcoholic beverages regularly. "Few persons," remarked the *News* in 1885, "fully realize the advance which has taken place in the direction of moderate drinking among business men, clerks, and many other sections of the community."[20] Similar sentiments had appeared three years earlier in an article in *Punch*, which portrayed the clientele of the metropolis' coffee houses as constituting "poor respectability," defined as "labourers, cabmen, and the poorer grades of shop men and clerks."[21] Women went unmentioned.

Nearby Manchester launched the Manchester Coffee Tavern Company in 1877 with £20,000 capital and soon was overseeing twelve coffee taverns. As in other companies, prominent figures—here, Dr Fraser, Bishop of the diocese—had become major contributors. Two years after opening, the coffee-house taverns had generated impressive earnings of over

[17] John N. Tarn, *Five Per Cent Philanthropy: An Account of Housing in Urban Areas between 1840 and 1914* (Cambridge: Cambridge University Press, 1973); National Temperance Congress: Liverpool, June, 1884 (Liverpool: National Temperance Publication Depot, 1884), p. 195.

[18] Bellhouse, "Coffee-House Movement," p. 123.

[19] *Coffee Public-House News*, 1 Apr. 1884; W.R. Lambert, *Drink and Sobriety in Victorian Wales, c. 1820–c.1895* (Cardiff: University of Wales Press, 1983), p. 105.

[20] *Coffee Public-House News*, 1 Jan. 1885.

[21] "The Coffee-Shop," *Punch* 82 (1882): 84.

£16,000.[22] Likewise, Hull, in the northeast, expanded quickly, having established eight coffee taverns in the second year after its opening in 1877. Almost exactly the same figures applied to the Birmingham Coffee House Company.[23]

Sharing this philosophy of competing with gin palaces but displeased with the British Workman Public House Company's plebeian houses in the North, noted philanthropist Dr Thomas Barnardo financed several East End coffee public houses, and positioning a tent outside the Edinburgh Castle, an infamous East End gin palace in Limehouse, he and several friends collected 4000 teetotal pledges in the summer of 1872. So effective was this tactic that the Castle, deprived of much business, had to shut, and Bernardo then bought what he called the "Citadel of the Enemy" before radically renovating the premises. To differentiate it from the more modest northern efforts, Bernardo rechristened the Castle as the Edinburgh Castle Coffee Palace, its name reflecting the palatial interior with a seating capacity of 3000. Still more ambitiously, he had the Dublin Castle, Mile End Road, reconstructed at a cost of £5000 in 1876. One impressed writer on coffee public houses described the Dublin Castle Coffee Palace as "the best adapted coffee-house in the metropolis."[24] Not so easily impressed, however, was Mr Jepson, who visited Barnardo's East End houses in 1884. He disliked that limited menus, confined to non-intoxicants and light food, fell far short of dinner meals.[25]

Coffee became the featured beverage because of its low cost, primarily the result of adulteration. Chicory, a cheap ingredient, was the standard adulterant, giving minimal coffee beans the black colour and bitterness drinkers had come to expect. Throughout the Victorian era, various investigators exposed the pervasive practices of adulterators, discrediting coffee as a suitable beverage for middle-class patrons who could afford to pay more for cocoa or tea. Adulteration nevertheless survived not just exposure of most samples being laced with chicory published in the press, but

[22] Bellhouse, "Coffee-House Movement," p. 121.

[23] Ibid., pp. 121–2; *Coffee Public-House News*, 2 Dec. 1878.

[24] Hall, *Coffee Taverns and Coffee Palaces*, pp. 54, 58; James Freeman Clarke, *Coffee Houses and Coffee Palaces in England* (Boston: George H. Ellis, 1882), pp. 17–20; P.T. Winskill (ed.), *The Temperance Movement and its Workers: A Record of Social, Moral, Religious, Political Progress* (London: Blackie & Son, 1891), 3: 175; "Dr. Barnardo Turned a Gin Palace into a Coffee House," *Look & Learn* 666 (9 Nov. 1974).

[25] J. Jepson, "The Coffee House Movement in London," *Coffee Public-House News*, 1 May 1884.

government legislation (Sale of Food and Drug Act (1875)). "We have Adulteration Acts," complained one critic after enactment of the key bill, "but nobody to enforce them." Having invested £100,000 in Birmingham coffee public houses, shareholders confronted the harsh truth that "there was not a drop of tea or coffee in the town fit to drink." As rivals to coffee, tea and cocoa benefited from technological changes that enabled the sale of superior beverages largely free of adulteration. By the 1870s, tea cost more but cocoa less than coffee. To differentiate it from coffee, cocoa was marketed as a wholesome beverage necessary for a healthy diet. Per capita consumption of coffee had been declining steadily from mid-century, while that of tea—and later cocoa—had risen sharply. Inexpensive, vile-tasting coffee with a dubious reputation became the beverage with which coffee public houses sought to attract patrons. In showcasing coffee, however, coffee houses prolonged outdated wholesale techniques and sale of an adulterated product. "Aiming at the poorest stratum of society, and being essentially local-based organisations, the coffee public-houses tended to provide an outlet for the cheap product of the small, local manufacturer," maintains John Othick.[26]

Promoters of the coffee public house advised that enthusiasts not just copy but replicate "gin palaces" (Fig. 2.2). Coffee public houses should be virtually indistinguishable from pubs, from the "massive plate glass window, with the lower part frosted and lettered" to the bar dominating the interior with seats and tables.[27] This was especially true of poor districts, maintained the secretary of the Blackburn Coffee House Company, because "men are shy of going into places where the arrangements are all different to what they have been accustomed to." Meticulously replicating pubs sometimes seriously confused the intoxicated: "It is no rare circumstance for a toper to find his way into a coffee tavern in the sweet delusion

[26] John Burnett, *Liquid Pleasures: A Social History of Drinks in Modern Britain* (London: Routledge, 1999), pp. 84–6; John Burnett, *Plenty and Want: A Social History of Diet in England from 1815 to the Present Day* (1966; rev. ed.: London: Methuen & Co., 1983), p. 263; J. Othick, "The Cocoa and Chocolate Industry in the Nineteenth Century," in Derek Oddy and Derek Miller (eds.), *The Making of the Modern British Diet* (London: Croom Helm, 1976), pp. 77–8, 86–7; *Coffee Public-House News*, 1 Nov. 1886; Anon. to Editor, 16 Oct. 1886, *Coffee Public-House News*, 16 Oct. 1886.

[27] *Practical Hints for the Management of Coffee Taverns* (London: Coffee Tavern Company [1878]), p. 8.

Fig. 2.2 Queen Coffee and Cocoa Tavern, Ashton-under-Lyne, 1882 (*Coffee Public-House News*, 1 Nov. 1882)

that it is a gin-palace and call loudly for a pint of 'half and half.'"[28] To counter appeals of pubs and beerhouses, coffee-house promoters shrewdly opened their doors and private rooms to meetings of friendly societies and clubs.[29]

[28] Norman Longmate, *The Waterdrinkers: A History of Temperance* (London: Hamish Hamilton, 1968), p. 209.

[29] Joseph Bentley, "Temperance Restaurants and Coffee Houses in Britain," in John Newton Stearns (ed.), *Temperance in All Nations: History of the Cause in All Countries of the Globe* (New York: National Temperance Society & Publication House, 1893), 2: 382; H. Birch, "About Coffee Houses—How to Manage Them," *Coffee Public-House News*, 2 Jan. 1882.

Coffee public houses, three small floors high, could be built for a modest £300, and some companies such as Leicester Coffee and Cocoa House Company preferred these purpose-built houses.[30] But other companies, eager to draw workers from nearby gin palaces, had more grandiose aspirations: the Bedfordshire Tavern Company outfitted what came to be called the Cowper Arms for £2815, while companies in Bradford and Bootle constructed purpose-built structures costing £3500 and £10,000, respectively.[31] With huge weekly sales of 800 gallons of soup driving sales averaging over £500 weekly, the Bradford Coffee Tavern Company found such heady success so overwhelming that it purchased the premises of its first coffee house for £6750, and still paid investors a dividend of 10%. This feat especially impressed the National Temperance League: "Legally secure your investment, so that it cannot be prostituted for the sale of alcoholic drinks."[32] The quintessential coffee public house, the Ossington Coffee Palace, appeared in Newark-on-Trent in 1882, for which its owner, Viscountess Ossington, laid out a staggering £20,000.[33]

Unlike the provinces, private temperance proponents initially pioneered London's coffee public houses. Of the first three efforts, two succeeded, with the establishment opened on Bell Street, Edgware Road, impressively earning 30% profits. Whatever the profits, proselyting was central to the "mission" work. Dr Barnardo's Edinburgh Castle Coffee Palace was less a place for drinking coffee or cocoa than an outreach agency, replete with mission church and education, recreation and training institute.[34]

In these same years, five public companies primarily promoted London coffee public houses. The first to incorporate on a large scale, the People's

[30] "Coffee Public-House Movement," p. 144; Elliott, "Leicester Coffee-House Movement," p. 57.

[31] "British Workman Public-Houses and Other Aids to Temperance," in P.T. Winskill (ed.), *Temperance Movement,* 3: 213; *Coffee Public-House News,* 1 July 1881 and 1 Nov. 1882.

[32] Bellhouse, "Coffee-House Movement," p. 122; National Temperance League, 1881 Annual Report.

[33] Andrew Davison, "'Try the Alternative': The Built Heritage of the Temperance Movement," *Journal of the Brewery History Society* 123 (summer, 2006): 103–04.

[34] Hogben, "Coffee Public-House Movement," p. 123; J. Jepson, "Coffee House Movement in London"; P.T. Winskill and Joseph Thomas, *History of the Temperance Movement in Liverpool and District, from its Introduction in 1829 Down to the Year 1887* (Liverpool: Joseph Thomas, 1887), 3: 175.

Café Co. was established in 1875, with £10,000 of capital and the Earl of Shaftesbury as president and Samuel Morley, MP, as a director.[35]

London coffee public houses were also the base of the Coffee Tavern Company. Founded in 1876 with £10,000 of capital (soon raised to £50,000), the company established twenty-seven coffee public houses in "the poorest parts of the metropolis." Like the Café Co. the vice presidents were a list of some seventy luminaries, with peers (such as the Duke of Westminster and Viscount Portman) and politicians (W.E. Gladstone, W.F. Cowper Temple and Sir Harcourt Johnstone). It quickly earned one observer's admiration: "The Company has not shrunk from pushing its experiments into the poorest parts of the metropolis." Perhaps this approach explained its qualified success as it "paid a moderate dividend."[36]

Throughout the early 1880s, British coffee public-house companies expanded, with about eighty owning between 2500 and 3000 coffee houses.[37] Spread across the country, especially in northern industrial cities, coffee houses drew considerable support in Liverpool, the leading provincial city where fifty-eight had been established. Next in size came the Bradford Coffee Tavern Company, which counted twenty-five houses (Fig. 2.3). Manchester and Birmingham ranked fourth and fifth, with twenty-one and nineteen, respectively. Outside the industrial north, Oxford and Nottingham represented other towns with flourishing coffee public houses. London took pre-eminence with 121 coffee houses in 1884.[38]

Of twenty-four coffee public-house companies in 1879, half paid 10% dividends, while the other half paid 5–6%. Moreover, these statistics would have been higher save for the fact that many companies added to their reserve funds instead of earmarking them for profits. Such buoyant developments led one observer to anticipate that coffee public houses would "revolutionise the drinking habits of our country." He went further in asserting that, when measured against other enterprises, coffee public houses would "compare [favourably] with any other retail business."[39]

[35] Bellhouse, "Coffee-House Movement," pp. 119–20.

[36] Hall, *Coffee Taverns*, p. 39; [Manley], "Temperance Refreshment House Movement," p. 49; Hogben, "Coffee Public-House Movement," p. 123.

[37] Clarke, *Coffee Houses*, p. 22.

[38] *Coffee Public-House News*, 1 May 1884; Bellhouse, "Coffee-House Movement," p. 123; Thorne, "Places of Refreshment," p. 245.

[39] Bellhouse, "Coffee-House Movement," p. 123; Hogben, "Coffee Public-House Movement," pp. 119, 125.

Fig. 2.3 College Road Branch, Bradford Coffee Tavern Co., 1881 (*Coffee Public-House News,* 1 July 1881)

The movement's subsequent history was far less successful. In an early but brief appraisal in *Country Life*, architectural historian Mark Girouard ridiculed the movement as run by well-meaning but incompetent members of the landed classes. Though he provided minimal evidence, there was some truth in what he argued.[40]

What Liverpool and Birmingham had achieved mesmerised early proponents of coffee public houses, recalled Joseph Bentley. Rushing forward in emulation, they committed many mistakes:

[40] Mark Girouard, "Pubs with No Beer: The Victorian Coffee Public House," *Country Life*, 9 Oct. 1975, pp. 926–28.

> Too much money was available in some places, causing reckless expenditure, too much condescending patronage and interference by wealthy and well-meaning, but inexperienced friends; too much display of good mottoes on the walls and bad teas in the urns.[41]

Again Girouard speculated that these problems were scarcely confined to amateurish upper-class philanthropists:

> The managers they installed tended to be incompetent or dishonest, the food inadequate, the coffee disgusting, and the rooms chilly and unwelcoming.[42]

There was no shortage of Victorian critics who agreed with him. "In the usual run of coffee-houses," complained the *Chambers's Journal*, "the coffee, tea and cocoa are of such poor quality as to contain scarcely any stimulating or nourishing properties."[43] The *News* cited high turnover of managers as an indicator of serious shortcomings in the business.[44] Part of the difficulty was that companies recruited individuals experienced in running public houses who often "have acquired habits of insobriety which they find it difficult to shake off."[45] Drunkenness contributing to "the slovenly and even dirty habits of the managers" also drew the paper's ire.[46] What Girouard might too have mentioned was that coffee public houses' shabby exteriors and interiors, dismal goods and discourteous staff all inspired their "evil reputation."[47]

Girouard's portrayal of the movement's irreversible decline, in which he stressed factors inherent in the quality of the goods, sales environment, deficient managers and staff, poor locations and hefty rents, saw failure as the product of the broadly conceived nature of the premises and employees. Subsequent commentaries have largely endorsed his interpretation without probing the roles of broad philosophy dictated by promoters. The

[41] Bentley, "Temperance Coffee Houses," 2: 378–79.

[42] Girouard, "Pubs with No Beer," p. 928; C.C.Smith's paper at the National Temperance Congress, June, 1884, p. 195.

[43] "Coffee Public-House Movement," p. 144; also see *Coffee Public-House News*, 2 Oct. 1882 and 1 May 1884; Hogben, "Coffee Public-House Movement," p. 125.

[44] *Coffee Public-House News*, 1 July 1882.

[45] Stephen Bourne, "The Social Influence of the Coffee-House Movement," *Coffee Public-House News*, 1 Sept. 1881.

[46] *Coffee Public-House News*, 1 March 1883.

[47] Ibid., 1 July 1882.

movement's shortcomings had greater complexity, deeper internal conflicts and sharper irreconcilable beliefs than Girouard and many others grasped.[48]

Christianity's role, conflicting goals (sobriety versus total abstinence), class prejudices, condescension to working-class culture, rational recreation, an almost exclusive male clientele, widespread misunderstanding of the residuum's income and tantalising cash—all contributed to the demise of a movement in which reformers had invested sizeable sums of money, estimated at £2,000,000.[49] But pre-eminently, coffee public houses as a group were far from being as homogeneous as Girouard assumed.

How the movement developed from the mid-1880s depended much on the companies' locations. Those in leading northern and midland industrial towns grew slowly or not at all in the decade after 1884: Liverpool added just six houses and Bradford seven, while Birmingham stagnated with nineteen. Coventry's houses were steadily contracting, and Sheffield's one British Workman Public House Company shut down. Smaller towns like Yeovil did establish a coffee public house in the early 1880s, but this soon disappeared altogether.[50] In the capital, it was not so much decline as disaster.

[48] Peter Haydon attributed the movement's failure to the withdrawal of financing by wealthy supporters, though he provided no evidence of this. This view was reiterated in a later study. Another study focused more on the defects of day-to-day business operations, citing poor locations, inept managers and high rents as the most important factors (Peter Haydon, *The English Pub: A History* (London: Robert Hale, 1994), p. 241; Michael Flynn, Caroline Ritchie and Andrew Roberts, *Public House and Beverage Management: Key Principles and Issues* (Oxford: Butterworth-Heinemann, 2000), unpaginated; D.J. Richardson, "J. Lyons & Co. Ltd.: Caterers & Food Manufacturers, 1894 to 1939," in Derek Oddy and Derek Miller (eds.), *The Making of the Modern British Diet* (London: Croom Helm, 1976), p.163).

[49] Bentley, "Temperance Coffee Houses," 2: 379.

[50] Bellhouse, "Coffee-House Movement," pp. 119–20; Bentley, "Temperance Coffee Houses," 2: 382; Bob Osborn, *The History of Yeovil's Pubs* (n.p., n.d.); Caroline Oldcorn Reid, "Middle Class Values and Working Class Culture in Nineteenth Century Sheffield" (Unpublished University of Sheffield, Ph.D., 1976), p. 477. The pace of decline varied considerably. Nottingham had five coffee houses in 1881, four of them still doing business in 1895. By 1900, however, only one appeared in *Kelly's Directory*. Leicester coffee public houses, in contrast, flourished until 1900. Beverley's two establishments endured until the turn of the century, with one shedding its temperance ethos and becoming a commercial proposition (Terry Fry, "The Pleasures of Tea and Coffee: An Account of Tea Gardens and Coffee Houses in and Around Nottingham in the 18th and 19th Centuries," *Nottinghamshire Historian* 57 (Autumn/Winter, 1996): 10; Davison, "Built Heritage of the Temperance

Whether in London or the provinces, tension between Christianity and temperance plagued the movement. Some large contributors wanted both emphasised equally: "Each Coffee-house should be a centre of temperance [and Christian] work, and should have in connection with it a Temperance Hall." Without Christianity, one proponent warned, "the main object in view would be defeated."[51] But practical experience convinced many others that working-class denizens reviled religiosity. "Our object," stressed the secretary of the Blackburn Coffee House Company, "is to draw men and woman away from one particular form of temptation, and I am certain that if they knew that religious meetings were carried on in the houses they would fight shy of them, think they were merely traps." Another critic of making Christianity central to philanthropy agreed. Working-class inhabitants, he urged, would not want "religion thrust down their throats." The stronghold of those for whom religion acted as the chief catalyst was London, where numerous private (often anonymous) persons sponsored individual houses with modest expectations about profits. Religious texts and pictures graced the bar, transforming such establishments into "centres of a religious propaganda." Inscribed on the plate glass at Bernardo's Edinburgh Castle Coffee Palace were evangelical verses, such as "The coming of the Lord draweth nigh."[52] Joseph Bentley as secretary of the National Coffee Tavern Association attacked the merging of temperance and Christianity from another perspective altogether. Given that numerous coffee public-house patrons were in fact already teetotallers, he argued that disseminating religious and temperance beliefs of coffee-house owners would simply alienate these individuals. Nevertheless, he admitted to his total abstinence stance. The coffee public house, he asserted, "is the Army Service and Ambulance Corps of the teetotal forces."[53]

Movement," p. 106; Brad Beven, *Leisure, Citizenship and Working-Class Men in Britain, 1850–1945* (Manchester: Manchester University Press, 2005), p. 68; Paul Gibson, *A Toast to the Town: A History of Beverley's Public Houses* (Kingston upon Hull: n.p., 2001)).

[51] *Coffee Public-House News*, 1 May 1884. See also Elizabeth R. Cotton [Lady Hope]: *Our Coffee-Room* (London: James Nisbet & Co., 1878); *More about Our Coffee-Room* (London: J. Nisbet & Co., 1878); *Lines on a Dark Ground* (n.p., 1879).

[52] Birch, "Coffee Houses"; [Mamley], "Temperance Refreshment House Movement," pp. 46, 51–2; Antony Clayton, *London's Coffee Houses: A Stimulating Story* (London: Historical Publications, 2003), p. 126.

[53] Bentley, "Temperance Coffee Houses," p. 381.

Coffee public houses' real problem stemmed not just from Christian temperance work but from tacit espousal of teetotalism, a conviction which permeated deeply into the movement and which reflected its origins in the National Temperance League (Table 2.1). Like many other coffee-house companies, the Liverpool British Workman Public-House Company, for example, prided itself on hiring a staff of some 400 total abstainers.[54] In a paper on the social influence of the coffee-house movement, Stephen Bourne discountenanced hiring anyone but teetotallers.[55] Publicly, the movement remained unaffiliated with temperance societies; privately, "a vast amount of unobtrusive temperance work is done in the [Coffee] Taverns." A teetotal manager, for instance, could exploit opportunities to press his case for abstinence quietly. Again, publicity about the house disclosed no fervent temperance stance, but patrons still knew they could obtain a total abstinence pledge form and "a word of sympathy." Greeting sailors on the docks in what the company called cocoa rooms, the Liverpool Company's employees collected some 11,000 voluntary total abstinence pledges in three years.[56] Some coffee pubs went further: Sheffield's Stag Home held temperance meetings on Sunday nights.[57]

Central to the movement's philosophy was the unshakable faith in total abstinence as a cure for poverty. Once workers renounced alcohol, the temperance critique went, their much improved homes would become the focus of leisure time. Coffee public house promoters expected not to grow at such a rate as to displace pubs and beerhouses, but to wean drinkers from alcohol and stimulate demand for temperance beverages, so that ultimately alcohol retailers would gradually be forced to embrace the sale of non-alcoholic drinks.[58]

Non-teetotallers rejected these covert tactics. First-hand experience of acting as secretary of the Blackburn Coffee House Company convinced H. Birch that promoters must "keep the Coffee Taverns free from all teetotalism." Above all else, he knew, "don't try to make teetotallers of your customers." E.T. Bellhouse likewise questioned the wisdom of

[54] *Coffee Public-House News*, 1 Aug. 1884; Clarke, *Coffee Houses*, pp. 15–16.

[55] Bourne, "Social Influence of the Coffee-House Movement"; also see Hogben, "Causes of Failure in London."

[56] Bentley, "Temperance Coffee Houses," 2: 381–82; Hogben, "Causes of Failure in London"; Hall, *Coffee Taverns*, p. 40.

[57] Oldcorn Reid, "Middle Class Values," p. 477.

[58] Bourne, "Social Influence of the Coffee-House Movement"; *Coffee Public-House News*, 1 Jan. 1885.

pledge-taking activities at coffee houses or cocoa rooms. "There can be as much bitterness and intolerance imported into the advocacy and discussion of the teetotal question as in any other direction." For Bellhouse, drunkenness resulted more from the desire for convivial companions rather than from "love of drink itself," a minority view in the movement.[59]

Class overlaid these divergent views towards drinking, resulting in condescending attitudes to the impoverished. The *Coffee Public-House News* recalled a then common phrase describing the movement's mission: "to cater for the gutter."[60] Entering coffee houses, workers were pointedly cautioned: "No bad language permitted." Elsewhere swearing, gambling and smoking were prohibited. Yet, H. Birch expected such posters would affront workers. "Don't invent rules and regulations for the houses," he advised. His logic about workers' reactions was straightforward: "Don't treat them as if they were 'reclaimed' individuals": "they will resent it."[61]

Viability of working-class culture especially aroused hostility. Music hall companies with a temperance orientation were assailed for "low music-hall songs of an almost indecent character" and "vulgar dancing by ballet girls." Overall, critics charged, the entertainment was degenerate and immoral. So contemptuous of these entertainment companies was the *Coffee Public-House News* that it argued temperance could be best advanced if they closed altogether.[62]

Based in London's poor districts, the Coffee Tavern Company published a pamphlet in 1878, offering advice on managing coffee taverns and urging that the movement should be dedicated to the "improvement and elevation of the national character." Rational recreation in practice meant at least newspapers and books; in some cases, amenities included a piano for concerts and games such as chess, draughts and billiards.[63]

But these sentiments conflicted sharply with class prejudice. According to the *Coffee Public-House News* in 1879, "the mistake has sometimes been made of measuring the intellectual capacity of frequenters of coffee

[59] Birch, "Coffee Houses"; Bellhouse, "Coffee-House Movement," p. 126.

[60] *Coffee Public-House News*, 1 Apr. 1884.

[61] Birch, "Coffee Houses"; also see Frederick Gore, "The Causes of Success and Failure in the Coffee House Movement," *Coffee Public-House News*, 16 July 1885.

[62] *Coffee Public-House News*, 1 Feb. and 1 Aug. 1881, 1 Apr. 1884, and 16 July 1885; Hall, *Coffee Taverns*, p. 36.

[63] *Coffee Public-House News*, 1 May 1884; Bentley, "Temperance Coffee Houses," 2: 379–80; *Practical Hints*, p. 1. See below n. 75 for sources on rational recreation.

public-houses by the degree of education they are supposed to possess." Yet, the paper's approval of uplifting leisure did not extend to music halls, even when stripped of their alcohol. "Notorious for their evil influences," music halls needed to provide "entertainment … of a more refined and elevating tendency," urged the *News*.[64]

Some proponents disagreed. Frederick Gore (secretary of the Coffee Public House Association) delivered a paper, "The Causes of Success and Failure in the Coffee House Movement," (1884) in which he argued that "if the Coffee-house is to take the place of the gin palace, there must be as much liberty in the one as in the other."[65] Not all coffee houses subscribed to perpetuating class differences. Sheffield's Stag Home appointed an artisan as manager, and elected representatives of the working class to the board of management. Likewise, Sheffield's British Workman Public House adopted such policies.[66]

Impoverished women, however, were frequently discriminated against in many coffee public houses, their presence clearly offensive. "They could hardly venture to sit down without being stared at and made to feel uncomfortable, and so they naturally stay away." The tacit prohibitions against women extended well into Knightsbridge's shopping district, where the Church of England's Rose and Crown proclaimed its status as a "Men's Coffee Palace." Frederick Gore strongly criticised these attitudes: "women of the working classes have surely a right to admission to the Coffee-houses on the same terms as men." His was a perceptive attitude. To charge hard-pressed women more money to sit in a segregated room, he observed, scarcely showed any insight into their poverty-stricken status.[67]

Keen temperance reformers, as Bellhouse's shrewd insight demonstrated, coffee public house advocates misunderstood poverty. "The movement," one candid supporter admitted, "has not got at the lower rank of the working-classes." Few houses charged ½d. for a cup of coffee, tea or cocoa, the threshold of what impoverished slum dwellers could afford with weekly salaries of 12s. to 20s.[68] Even wholly philanthropic efforts, such as the Anglican Beckenham Rooms, charged working-class

[64] *Coffee Public-House News*, 1 March 1879.

[65] Gore, "Causes of Success and Failure"; *Coffee Public-House News*, 2 Aug. 1880.

[66] Oldcorn Reid, "Middle Class Values," p. 471.

[67] Thorne, "Places of Refreshment," p. 245; Gore, "Causes of Success and Failure".

[68] *Coffee Public-House News*, 1 May 1884. Both the Hull People's Public-House Company and Liverpool's British Workman coffee public houses charged ½d. per cup of coffee (Ibid., 2 Dec. 1878; "British Workman Public Houses," p. 213).

men 1d. for a cup of coffee and 1½d. for a cup of tea or cocoa.[69] Philanthropy clashed with profits, preventing promoters' assistance to the impoverished that had served originally as one of the movement's chief motivations. Coffee at 1d. or more per cup enabled these companies to envision generating profits necessary for economic survival, but the cost drastically circumscribed the movement's philanthropic philosophy as well as impact.[70] One compromise tried at Leicester (and doubtless elsewhere) was to permit coffee public houses with central sites to cater to more refined customers, whose patronage generated profits for subsidising houses with working-class clienteles.[71] Assisting uneconomic houses, however, contributed to "indifferent and careless" management. As one anonymous writer stated to an editor of a periodical, "the comfort of the visitors is not studied in any way," with the end result of customers receiving inferior goods.[72]

In the movement's first phase (1874–1876), northern coffee houses focused on workmen, seamen and navvies as their chief customers, but a second phase soon broadened the clientele. Lure of middle-class patrons with their more profitable custom led some companies increasingly from the late 1870s to target them rather than those for whom the movement had been originally established. The National Temperance League endorsed a philosophy of class inclusiveness in 1881: "This movement must not cater exclusively for the poorer member of society; but invite the commercial and upper classes." Begun in northern cities, the practice of catering to two distinct classes with different menus and prices spread southward. Doctors, solicitors and other professionals, for example, frequented coffee pubs in Leicester's city centre, famed for enticing food and an attractive environment. First-floor refreshment rooms charged higher prices reflecting the better quality of products dispensed. Without such middle-class custom subsidising profits, many coffee houses catering exclusively to workers would not have produced enough revenue to earn requisite dividends.[73]

[69] Cotton, *Our Coffee-Room*, p. 70. Many coffee public houses charged 4d. per cup for cocoa (Antony Clayton, *London's Coffee Houses: A Stimulating Story* (London: Historical Publications, 2003), p. 130).

[70] "Coffee House Movement," p. 144; Anon. to Editor, *Coffee Public-House News*, 16 Oct. 1886.

[71] Elliott, "Leicester Coffee –House and Cocoa-House Movement," p. 59.

[72] Anon. to Editor, *Church of England Temperance Chronicle*, 1 Jan. 1882.

[73] Elliott, "Leicester Coffee-House Movement," p. 59; *Coffee Public-House News*, 1 Jan. 1880, 1 Sept. 1881, 1 May 1883 and 1 Apr. and 1 May 1884.

This caused a schism in the movement. James Freeman Clarke espoused the view of coffee public houses as being dedicated to catering to the "roughest and poorest of those [of the working-] classes." In an uncompromising assertion of purpose, he insisted that coffee public houses should not allocate space specifically for any class of customers. The serious result of moving towards commercialising the movement was that companies "incline to the business of the better kind and unconsciously and unintentionally … neglect … the working-class houses."[74]

Coffee public houses' profits and philanthropy, on the one hand, proved as incompatible as rational recreation and new leisure habits, on the other. Rational recreation implicitly endorsed two ideologies, the doctrine of separate spheres and the cult of domesticity, limiting not only women's leisure opportunities but its potential appeal. People historically had engaged in recreation as a method of meeting prospective spouses. Yet rational recreationists—males drawn primarily from the middle class—concentrated on attracting working-class men, and envisaged new forms of leisure which eliminated class, not gender, boundaries. Bereft of female participants, rational recreation stood little chance of achieving wide popularity. Even when new sports, most conspicuously tennis, hunting or golfing, transcended this drawback, men and women of the propertied classes interacted in controlled settings, where parents successfully replicated the small genteel world of times past from which class interlopers had been excluded.[75]

The wider economic context in which the movement competed for profits merits examination. No one has appreciated that coffee public houses were struggling with an unforeseen development, the mass market's arrival in the 1880s.[76] Between 1876 and 1882, money wages stagnated, and with prices falling, the purchasing power of money wages went up.

[74] *Coffee Public-House News*, 1 Jan. 1880 and 1 May 1883; Clarke, *Coffee Houses*, pp. 29–30; National Temperance League, 1881 Annual Report.

[75] Richard Holt, *Sport and the British: A Modern History* (Oxford: Oxford University Press, 1989), pp. 124–28. The standard source on rational recreation is Peter Bailey, *Leisure and Class in Victorian England: Rational Recreation and the Contest for Control, 1830–85* (1978, reprint ed.: New York: Methuen & Co., 1987). See also J.M. Golby and A.W. Purdue, *The Civilisation of the Crowd: Popular Culture in England, 1750–1900* (New York: Schocken Books, 1985), pp. 88–114; and Catriona M. Parratt, "Making Leisure Work: Women's Rational Recreation in Late Victorian and Edwardian England," *Journal of Sport History* 26 (1999): 471–87.

[76] *Liverpool Mercury*, 17 Nov. 1879.

This benefit to the working class had its disadvantages; jobs were harder to find than they had been in the early 1870s. Consumers had wider ranges of imported goods, such as foodstuffs, meat, bacon, grain, dairy products and fruit from which to choose. Attending horse races also became popular. Coffee prices, however, remained pegged at 1d. per cup, making them relatively more expensive compared to these other products. Beer prices likewise became relatively more expensive at the unvarying price of 3d. per pint. Faced with new attractive consumer choices, workers turned from buying coffee and beer, and substituted these other items. Per capita consumption of coffee and beer, reflecting new patterns of consumer purchasing, fell almost 20% in the decade from 1880. The story was the same with beer consumption. These were the years when coffee public houses strove for economic success in a most unfavourable market. Regardless of other contributing factors, this one alone affords insight into why the movement seemed to decline so quickly.[77] Other deficiencies previously mentioned merely exacerbated the waning support. "Nothing short of thoroughly good coffee or tea," warned *Chambers's Journal*, "will furnish a satisfactory substitute for beer." Without first-rate coffee, the flight from it intensified when the market offered widening competing consumer goods.[78]

That coffee public houses did not more rigorously exploit opportunities for attracting customers from a wider demographic base offers another explanation for the economic crisis. In cities, working-class bachelors had few alternatives to spending evenings in the pub or beerhouse. "I live in a miserable lodging," complained one unmarried lodger. "I have nowhere to go but to the public-house, nowhere to sit down, often nowhere to take my meals." Returning to his lodging at night, he and others like him "often sleep in one room with two or even more generations of the same family." This was hardly a closely guarded secret. *Chambers's Journal* published an article in which it noted that where coffee public-house proprietors accommodated these bachelors, "the profit is considerable." The

[77] Othick, "Cocoa and Chocolate Industry," p. 78; A.E. Dingle, "Drink and Working-Class Living Standards in Britain, 1870–1914," in Oddy and Miller (eds.), *Modern British Diet*, pp. 125, 127–29; Wray Vamplew, "The Sport of Kings and Commoners: The Commercialization of British Horse-Racing in the Nineteenth Century," in Richard Cashman and Michael McKernan (eds.), *Sport in History: The Making of Modern Sporting History* (St. Lucia, Australia: University of Queensland Press, 1979), pp. 314–15; Jepson, "Coffee House Movement in London," *Coffee Public-House News*.

[78] "Coffee-House Movement," p. 144.

National Temperance League likewise saw accommodation as vital to drawing patrons. Nevertheless, strikingly few bachelors found an opportunity to take lodgings in coffee public houses. One notable exception was Knightsbridge's Rose & Crown Coffee Palace, a privately run establishment with ardent Christians as the backers where bachelors could sleep in either first- or second-class accommodation for 9d.–1s. nightly. According to the manager, he "seldom has an empty bed," easily filling the thirty-seven separate beddings. This was possible in part because the proprietor offered coffee, tea or cocoa for 2d. per pint.[79]

Whatever the geographic location or type of managerial basis, studies of coffee public houses portray their success as transitory, with irreversible decline unmistakable early in the 1880s. A broader type of evidence contradicts this view. The movement's chief organ, the *Temperance Caterer*, published data about the status of coffee houses throughout the country. With 60% of coffee-house companies declaring dividends in 1889, they exhibited clear signs of recovery and capacity to continue expanding (Table 2.2). Though twenty companies went out of business, existing or new companies established forty-one new houses. These statistics were scarcely an anomaly. Joseph Bentley reported in 1893 that most coffee public house joint stock companies earned dividends of 10% annually, with the average for all of them 8%. "The financial position of most of the larger companies is regarded

Table 2.2 Dividends of coffee-house companies, 1889

Declared dividends	*Number*	*Proportion*
10–15%	13	13%
6–9%	15	14%
5%	28	27%
2–4%	8	8%
None	20	19%
Liquidated	20	19%
Totals	104	100%

Source: Compiled from "Dividends Paid by Coffee Tavern Companies in 1889," *Temperance Caterer*, 2 Aug. 1890

[79] Ibid; Clarke, *Coffee Houses*, pp. 24–5; Hogben, "Coffee Public-House Movement," p. 126; *Daily News*, 30 March 1878. One official thought "a fair proportion of those engaged in directing the movement now provide sleeping accommodation in connection with their taverns" (Bentley, "Temperance Coffee Houses," p. 381).

as solid as that of banks; their shares rank with railway stock, and often fetch abnormal premiums." By then, too, the industry was extensive with an impressive capital of £2 million funding huge numbers of establishments: some 7000 coffee houses, temperance restaurants and hotels employed 56,000 people.[80] A decade later coffee houses still flourished, with 100 companies responsible for 3000 of them. In London alone, some 1700 coffee houses conducted business and, together with over 400 refreshment rooms and nearly 800 dining rooms, served 600,000 meals daily. To suburban coffee houses came increasing numbers of men and women stopping for refreshment on cycling outings, the craze of the 1890s.[81]

The movement is best understood as divided into three phases: in the first (early 1870s), coffee public houses experienced explosive growth[82]; in the second (from the late 1870s onwards), when mass produced items appeared, profits stagnated, and in many cases, especially in London, some companies collapsed; and finally, in the third (from the late 1880s), the movement overall revived, though stability rather than growth now characterised it.

Liverpool, the movement's acknowledged home, exemplified the latter two stages. Not immune to the movement's temporary declining patronage, the Liverpool Company lost one-fourth of its houses in five years, while still retaining its pre-eminence over its nearest rival, Bradford (Table 2.3).[83] Thereafter it displayed remarkable recovery, with all but two of the houses being profitable and earning dividends of 18% in 1895. With gross takings of £18,000 annually and capital increasing to £50,000 (two and a half times greater than when founded in 1875), the company retained its position as the leading coffee public-house company. Thus, coffee public houses nationally should be viewed in the 1880s as undergoing economically difficult but hardly catastrophic problems.

[80] Bentley, "Temperance Coffee Houses," p. 379.

[81] "Coffee-Houses in Great Britain," in Charles E. Bolton (ed.), *A Model Village of Homes, and Other Papers* (Boston: L.C. Page & Co., 1901), pp. 63, 65–6; *London Directory for 1901*, quoted in *A Pictorial and Descriptive Guide to London: Its Public Buildings, Leading Thoroughfares, and Principal Objects of Interest* (London: Ward, Lock & Co., 1902), p. 21.

[82] One indication of the movement's recovery in the early 1880s was that advertisements in the *Coffee Public-House News* suggested more people wanted managers' jobs than were available for applicants (Lockington and Trickey, "Coffee House Movement," p. 4).

[83] Rev. Charles Garrett, "The History of the British Workmen Public-House Company in Liverpool," *National Temperance League Conference, Chester, 1895* (London: National Temperance League Publication Depot, [n.d.]), pp. 255–56.

Table 2.3 Evolution of coffee public houses in large cities, 1880–1901

City	*1880*	*1881*	*1884*	*1885–1886*	*1892*	*1895*	*1900–1901*
Bradford	13	15	25	27	32[a]		34
Birmingham	16	20	19	21	19	22	18
Hull	11	11	4	17	18	18	19
Liverpool	35	40	58	45	64	65	49
Manchester	15	33	21	18	16	11	15
Leicester	6	8	12	7	13		12

Sources: *Coffee Public-House News*, 1 June 1883, 1 May and 1 Oct., and 1 May 1884, 16 July 1885, 16 Feb. and 25 Dec. 1886, 22 Feb. 1887; *Coffee Tavern & Temperance Hotel Guide*, 1885; Calkins, *Substitutes for the Saloon*, pp. 246, 248–49; Garrett, "History of British Workman Company in Liverpool," p. 256; Freeman Clarke, *Coffee Houses*, p. 7; Elliott, "Leicester Coffee-House and Cocoa-House Movement," pp. 56–60; [S.H. Hilliard], "Coffee-Houses," *Cyclopaedia of Temperance and Prohibition* (n.p., 1891), pp. 83–4; Bentley, "Temperance Coffee Houses," p. 382; Bellhouse, "Coffee-House Movement," pp. 120–22; Bolton, "Coffee-Houses in Great Britain," pp. 65–6; Thomas Hogben, "The Coffee Public-House Movement," in Robert Rae (ed.), *The National Temperance League's Annual for 1881* (London: National Temperance Publications Depot, 1881), pp. 123–24; county directors: Birmingham, 1892; Manchester, 1881, 1895; Sheffield, 1881, 1884, 1895

[a]Bradford slumped to 20 houses in 1891 (Hilliard, "Coffee Houses," p. 251)

Contemporaries, however, view coffee public houses in retrospect, projecting the successes of mass catering companies and emergence of alternative reform strategies in the 1890s backwards as an explanation for the movement's death. Confusion here derived in part from coffee-house proponents themselves, as a survey noted in 1901: "the leaders of the movement have not chosen to summarize their operations or to issue statistics." A related problem was that temperance organisations deliberately adopted a quite distant relationship with coffee public houses, so disguised their role in their expansion and thereby muddled a clear understanding.[84] The movement regained stability, if not robust vitality, with some 1700 coffee houses in London alone recorded in a 1900 guide. Nationally, coffee-house companies numbered 100, which had opened some 3000 houses.[85]

[84] Raymond Calkins, *Substitutes for the Saloon: An Investigation Made for the Committee of Fifty Under the Direction of Francis G. Peabody, Elgin R.L. Gould and William M. Sloane* (Boston: Houghton Mifflin Company, 1901), p. 244; Rev. Charles Garrett, "The History of the British Workman Public-House Company in Liverpool," *National Temperance Conference, Chester, 1895* (London: National Temperance League Publication Depot, [1895]), p. 256.

[85] *Descriptive Guide to London,* p. 21; "Coffee-Houses in Great Britain," in Bolton (ed.), *A Model Village of Homes,* p. 63.

As the movement evolved, companies expanded their services, with meals a critical facet in their survival. No other department of coffee houses generated more revenue or provoked more criticism than food sales.[86] But this caused difficulties with the movement's dual philosophy—philanthropy and profit. Too much emphasis on food revenue thwarted sale of inexpensive meals as well as the strategy of giving workmen places to socialise.[87] One impediment to selling workmen cheap, well-cooked meat was that they sought it from the joint, a quite expensive requirement. So formidable did this prove in fact that not until 1878 did someone south of the Tweed advertise inexpensive, thoroughly cooked meat on a mass catering basis.[88] Slumping trade prompted new attitudes, and proprietors began introducing food as a marketing strategy for survival.[89]

According to contemporary accounts and later historians, few women—estimated at just 5% of all customers—used coffee public houses.[90] Ostensibly, coffee public houses encouraged women to join husbands but ironically perpetuated the doctrine of separate spheres in which men and women occupied different physical spaces. If men brought wives or other females, the couple typically sat in a segregated room for females, replicating informal practices in pubs.[91]

Previous studies of the role of gender in coffee public houses, however, depend entirely on E. Hepple Hall's survey, published in 1878 during the movement's first phase, giving a jaundiced view of their clientele.[92] Much evidence from the 1880s to 1890s offers a contrary view, underlining how the movement had evolved. In the *Coffee Public-House News*, for instance, coffee public houses advertised premises boasting coffee and commercial rooms for gentlemen and ladies.[93] The Bradford Coffee Tavern Company drew clerks, warehousemen and women as its chief clientele, whose penny- and two-pence purchases generated some £16,000 annually at its thirteen houses. While offering women and other patrons' concerts and entertainments as well as "comfortable, clean, well-furnished houses," the company

[86] *Coffee Public-House News*, 2 Oct. 1882 and 1 Jan. 1885.
[87] Ibid., 1 May 1884.
[88] "No Intoxicants Sold," *Leisure Hour* 31 (1882): 117.
[89] *Coffee Public-House News*, 1 May 1884.
[90] Hall, *Coffee Taverns*, pp. 66, 103.
[91] "Coffee Public-House Movement," *Chambers's Journal*, p. 144; David W. Gutzke, *Women Drinking Out in Britain since the Early Twentieth Century* (Manchester: Manchester University Press, 2014), pp. 16–17.
[92] Hall, *Coffee Taverns*, pp. 66, 103.
[93] *Coffee Public-House News*, 1 Sept. 1883.

returned a respectable 10% dividend.[94] By the turn of the century, women frequented Leicester's coffee public houses, and ordered meals of ham or salmon, bread, butter and tea for 6d. (lunch) or 9d. (dinner). Cycling promoted leisure between the sexes, reflected in growing numbers of sub-urban tea and refreshment rooms. Here and elsewhere, women acting as proprietors emboldened females to patronise their premises.[95]

Respectable women's participation in coffee-house society has been overlooked in other ways. From its opening in 1878, the Princess House, based in Brompton Road, catered exclusively to women, offering not just non-alcoholic beverages but weekly lodgings. Poplar also boasted a women's coffee house, which Miss Phillimore had built and entirely financed in 1900. To encourage interaction between the sexes, she had the coffee house designed with a room for dancing. Several coffee-house rooms for young women were established in Bristol, with a strong overtone of Christianity. None welcomed men, even for Bible reading. As long-standing secretary of the National Coffee Tavern Association in 1893, Joseph Bentley was in a position to know that "in every well-arranged Coffee Tavern accommodation is set apart for the exclusive use of ladies."[96]

Other evidence also suggests that when provided with such accommodation, working-class women found coffee public houses enormously useful. In Liverpool and elsewhere, working-class women "have gladly availed themselves of the advantage," wrote one knowledgeable source in 1880.[97]

A new departure in gender relations and mass catering emerged in the capital in 1887, when philanthropic-minded temperance ladies inaugurated several new coffee houses in the City, offering commercially priced luncheon hot meals aimed at respectable working women. "A stream of young girls' employed at the City warehouses passes in at the door" at 1 p.m., "paying another female manager or superintendent," wrote Benjamin Clarke. Following lunch, diners could attend a brief evangelistic gathering upstairs. Of the 450–500 patrons, young women comprised about twenty.[98]

[94] Bellhouse, "Coffee-House Movement," p. 122.

[95] *Kelley's Directory of Suffolk,* 1896; Elliott, "Leicester Coffee-House and Cocoa House Movement," p. 59; "Coffee-Houses in Great Britain," p. 66.

[96] Lockington and Trickey, "Coffee-house Movement," p. 3; Bentley, "Temperance Coffee Houses," p. 379; H.A. Page, "Coffee Palaces," *Good Words* 18 (1877): 680.

[97] Bellhouse, "Coffee-House Movement," p. 125.

[98] Benjamin Clarke, "Temptations to Temperance," in Rev. Benjamin Waugh (ed.), *Sunday Magazine* (London: Isbister & Co., 1887), pp. 42–3.

Scholars have too readily dismissed the coffee-public house movement as afflicted with numerous fatal contradictions which doomed the flawed concept of philanthropy plus 5%. According to conventional wisdom, the concept succumbed to its own internal inconsistencies within less than a decade of its emergence in the mid-1880s. This interpretation is wrong in several senses. It fails to grasp the many business problems challenging retailing of non-intoxicants and food in late Victorian England, most notably the emergence of the mass market. Coffee houses, far from being a transitory phenomenon, prevailed, notwithstanding the economically difficult times of the late 1870s and 1880s, and successfully recovered. It was not so much the conflicting pressures of philanthropy plus profits, amateurish philanthropists with unrealistic goals, view of poverty as originating in excessive drinking, or even dismissive attitudes of working-class culture, as the inability to conceptualise leisure in a gender-neutral perspective. As long as these reformers focused on integrating classes, not overcoming gender segregation, the movement had minimal prospects for transforming mass leisure. Had the sexes been merged, coffee-house promoters could have embraced women as an uplifting, civilising agency for disciplining as well as instituting new drinking norms antithetical to excessive drinking.

CHAPTER 3

From Philanthropy to Profits in London

No one has previously perceived the link between coffee public houses and the emergence of London's catering on a large scale. John Pearce, together with Robert Lockhart and Ronald McDougall, formed a trio who played important roles in establishing mass catering in late Victorian London. Their religious experiences were exactly the same, and teetotalism shaped their approach to catering. Both Lockhart and McDougall became associated with the coffee public-house movement begun in Lancashire.

This movement afforded a new perspective of how successive caterers would view their role in a different commercial light compared with their predecessors—the philanthropists seeking to reconcile charity with capitalism. From the North came these "disciples of Moody" who started temperance catering in London, one of them having an enduring impact.

Commercialisation became a critical issue for coffee public houses. Originally, "profit was subordinated to … doing a service to the community," remarked the *Coffee Public-House News*. From the late 1870s in the North and soon too in London, coffee public houses introduced striking class differences, offering bourgeois patrons a separate "first-class bar" where surroundings and amenities reflected higher prices.[1]

This inaugurated the process of commercialisation. In Liverpool, the leading centre of coffee public houses, two options confronted share-

[1] *Coffee Public-House News*, 1 Apr. 1884.

D. W. Gutzke, *John Pearce and the Rise of the Mass Food Market in London, 1870–1930*, https://doi.org/10.1007/978-3-030-27095-7_3

holders in the British Workman Public-House Company: retain the original 10% dividends and move upmarket to secure them, or halve the dividends and use profits to establish cocoa rooms in Liverpool's slums. Founded as a philanthropic and commercial enterprise, the company, exactly one decade after its founding in 1875, opted to run its houses on a commercial basis. In an editorial in 1884, the *Coffee Public-House News*—the movement's chief newspaper (and sometimes conscience)—raised the most pertinent question: "How far the Coffee Public-house movement ought to maintain its original relations towards the poorest classes of the community"? Profits were now trumping philanthropy: instead of "service to the community," Liverpool investors were following the dictates of a capitalist enterprise.[2] Two years earlier a coffee public-house manager wrote a letter to the same paper in which he pointed to the early accomplishment of coffee public houses as transforming them into a commercial enterprise, with "many shareholders investing their money solely in the hope of obtaining large dividends."[3]

Generally, solely commercial enterprises, bereft of evangelising as well as conscious efforts of moral improvement, succeeded better than those mixing philanthropy and profit. In a symbolic gesture in 1881, Sheffield's British Workman Public House Company transferred its assets to the Café Co. Putting this change in a larger context, the *Coffee Public-House News* identified a trend in the early 1880s for companies situated in large cities to open houses targeted at the middle class. "The business of the better class of houses is practically that of a restaurant," the paper acknowledged, and then added: "from a commercial perspective middle-class custom simply paid better."[4]

From this trend came restaurant houses specialising in food suitable for bourgeois customers. Both exemplified how entrepreneurs set out to cater for the working class but, having lost their roots, became commercial restaurateurs, the forerunners of mass catering. Companies with the most respected teetotal pedigrees began succumbing to economic pressures.

For those outside London who became most successful, teetotal sentiments did not stand in the way of maximising profits with mass catering.

[2] Ibid., 1 Jan. 1880 and 1 Apr. 1884.

[3] A Manager to the Editor, *Coffee Public-House News*, 1 Nov. 1882.

[4] *Coffee Public-House News*, 1 May 1883; Caroline Oldcorn Reid, "Middle Class Values and Working Class Culture in Nineteenth Century Sheffield" (Unpublished Ph.D. thesis, Univ. of Sheffield, 1976), p. 477.

Instinctively, such entrepreneurs saw the drawbacks of merging philanthropy with profits. In following a marketing philosophy with working-class men as the chief customers, low prices would be imperative, but this strategy imposed serious economic constraints. Two assumptions were made: leasing central sites for houses would be too expensive; and offering cooked food and a wider range of beverages would be uneconomic.

Three individuals formed the vanguard of entrepreneurs establishing mass catering in late Victorian London: Robert Lockhart, Ronald McDougall and John Pearce. Through the American evangelist Dwight L. Moody, these men shared identical religious experiences, while teetotal beliefs influenced deeply their approach to catering.

In 1874, Moody delivered a speech at Liverpool in which he argued that workers frequented pubs and beerhouses not from choice but from lack of alternatives. Along seven miles of Mersey docks, 20,000 men earned their employment. Here, he contended, was ample scope for Christians spearheading temperance initiatives.[5] Responding to the call, leading merchants founded the British Workman Public-House Company, with £20,000 of capital. To feed dockers, within months, the company opened a house capable of seating 500.[6] As one correspondent to the *Coffee Public-House News* remarked,

> Whoever wants anything goes to the counter … obtains his coffee, tea, or cocoa, … chooses his food, and pays for everything at the time, and then is able to eat it sitting. No cries for waiter, no quarrelling; each one is his own servant, the rich as well as the poor.

Several features segregated first- and second-class rooms. First-class patrons drank beverages in larger cups, dined in more spacious and comfortable rooms, and shared the space with females allotted a separate room.[7] The British Workman Public-House Company in Birmingham, in contrast, was more egalitarian; its customers—whatever the class or gender—sat at the same table unselfconsciously.[8]

Moody was pivotal in promoting the emergence of mass catering, inspiring Robert Lockhart's entry into food retailing; Ronald McDougall

[5] E. Hepple Hall, *Coffee Taverns, Cocoa Houses and Coffee Places: Their Rise, Progress, and Prospects* (London: S.W. Partridge, [1878]), pp. 21–4, 39–40.

[6] W. Peskett, "Work in Liverpool," *Coffee Public-House News*, 1 Aug. 1884.

[7] C.C. Smith to Editor, *Coffee Public-House News*, 1 June 1883.

[8] *Coffee Public-House News*, 1 June 1883.

forged close personal ties with the Moody and Sankey mission in Liverpool. John Pearce's experience was altogether different. Becoming an intimate friend of Moody, who launched a crusade in London's Islington in 1874, Pearce responded to the evangelist's promptings to provide dinners, based on temperance doctrines, aimed at workers of diverse class backgrounds.[9] Pearce's career in catering was so long (stretching over 60 years), went through so many stages and had such decisive impacts on central London that he deserves the most historical attention—to which the next chapter, Chap. 4, and subsequent ones are devoted.

Emerging from the Liverpool British Workman Public House Company in which he served as chairman from its inception in 1875, Robert Lockhart conducted his own business as a teetotal entrepreneur with philanthropic instincts committed to aiding the poor, establishing twenty-nine cocoa rooms in the city. Located usually on a separate floor, with higher prices and a dining room, were bourgeois facilities. Eventually, specific provisions for women, a cloak room and lavatory, were included. Through the Liverpool British Workman Public House Company, Lockharts established sixty-five cocoa houses by 1884. Lockhart died in 1880, but his restaurants, having spread to other northern cities, continued, with Newcastle (8), Sunderland (3), South Shields (2) and Darlington (2) the leading centres. Temperance was never far from his business practices. By long-standing custom, friendly societies met on licensed premises, a practice which teetotal Lockhart sought to discourage.[10]

When Lockharts expanded into London in 1883, opening its first shop at Gray's Inn Road/Holborn, followed by branches on Fleet Street and the Barbican in the City, customers knew what to expect: dependable management, inexpensive prices and tastefully presented food. Lockharts enticed customers with a wide array of non-alcoholic beverages, and specialised in light fare, such as sandwiches, sausages, Melton Mowbray pies, pastry and bread. Without joints of meat or vegetables, the firm's "bill of fare is more limited even than an ordinary Coffee Tavern," recorded a *Coffee Public-House News* reporter in 1883. What Lockharts offered still attracted a diverse clientele of workmen, clerks and ladies with business in

[9] See pp. 79–95.

[10] *Sunderland Daily Echo*, 26 Feb. and 18 Dec. 1878; *Salisbury Times*, 21 Apr. 1893; P.T. Winskill and Joseph Thomas, *History of the Temperance Movement in Liverpool and District, from its Introduction in 1829 Down to the Year 1887* (Liverpool: Joseph Thomas, 1887), p. 76; *Coffee Public-House News*, 1 May 1883; *Refreshment News*, 18 Aug. 1888; *Temperance Caterer*, 20 Aug. 1887.

the City. More exclusive customers patronised a separate first-class area providing a ladies cloakroom and lavatory situated on the first floor, an early example of a restaurant chain accommodating both sexes on the same premises.[11] With highly polished urns, an appealing range of cakes and a conspicuous entrance, interiors specially struck customers. "These places of refreshment," remarked the *Coffee House Gazette*, "are always scrupulously clean."[12]

Lockharts offered much the same formula—inexpensive, basic meals of light refreshment served quickly—as would Pearce & Plenty, with six significant exceptions: northern England and Scotland served as the operational base; cocoa rooms jostled for business with pubs literally nearby; joints of meat and vegetables were not on the menu; self-service prevailed rather than waitresses; premises often had separate rooms for women only; and its clientele ranked among the poorest.[13] By design, Lockharts' cocoa rooms were utilitarian: "the fittings are usually plain, the walls bare, [and] the seats not remarkable for comfort." Nor had much changed in the ensuing fifteen years when social observer Helen Bosanquet witnessed "bare trestles and sawdusted [sic] floors."[14]

Liverpool provided a connection with another temperance caterer. A Scotsman by birth but Liverpudlian by upbringing, Ronald McDougall started life from an unpretentious background. Acquiring skills first as a carpenter, he then turned to becoming an undertaker in Liverpool, which made him quite wealthy, "one of the most prosperous tradesmen of his adopted town." This enterprise funded his second career as a temperance caterer. Unlike Lockhart, however, McDougall neither had any connec-

[11] *Temperance Caterer*, 11 June and 20 Aug. 1887; Kathleen Heasman, *Evangelicals in Action: An Appraisal of their Social Work in the Victorian Era* (London: Geoffrey Bles, 1962), p. 143; D.J. Richardson, "J. Lyons & Co. Ltd.: Caterers and Food Manufacturers, 1894 to 1939," in Derek Oddy and Derek Miller (eds.), *The Making of the Modern British Diet* (London: Croom Helm, 1973), p. 163.

[12] *Coffee Public-House News*, 1 May and 1 Oct. 1883, 1 July and 1 Nov. 1884; *Pall Mall Gazette*, 21 Nov. 1889; *Coffee Tavern Gazette*, 22 Jan. 1887; *Temperance Caterer*, 15 June 1901; John Burnett, *England Eats Out: A Social History of Eating Out in England from 1830 to the Present* (London: Pearson Longman, 2004), p. 117.

[13] *Temperance Caterer*, 3 Nov. 1888; Kathleen Joan Heasman, "The Influence of the Evangelicals upon the Origin and Development of Voluntary Charitable Institutions in the Second Half of the Nineteenth Century" (Ph.D. thesis, Univ. of London, 1959), pp. 299–300.

[14] *Coffee Public-House News*, 1 May 1883; Helen D. Bosanquet, *The Standard of Life and Other Studies*, 2nd ed. (London: Macmillan & Co. 1899), p. 17.

tion with the Liverpool British Workman Public House Company, nor placed moral reform above good business practice as the guiding principle. For McDougall, generating self-sustaining profits was imperative to achieving his second goal, the promotion of temperance reform.[15] McDougall joined the Band of Hope when 9 years old, and had participated in the Good Templars, serving as secretary of the newly formed United Templar Order in 1873. Later he became secretary and treasurer of the Independent Order of Foresters, a friendly society. He was not just a temperance advocate, but a total abstainer. His motto, "No Intoxicants Sold," displayed prominently on his shop windows, reassured potential customers about what to expect. An ardent temperance advocate, he contested a council election as a Liberal against a local brewer and defeated him in 1875.[16]

Of all coffee public-house entrepreneurs, he grasped the potential of mass catering, with a clientele far broader than just working-class males. Taking the initiative and entirely at his own expense, he began as sole proprietor, establishing seven popular total abstinence "tea rooms" in Liverpool from 1874, transcending both class and gender boundaries with astonishing results. One audience especially became targeted: "these places of refreshment were fitted upon (sic) in rather a superior manner to suit the wishes and convenience of the middle classes." Women, keen to drink non-alcoholics free of smoky, noisy public houses, formed a significant component of customers. But his tea rooms also drew young male office workers and warehousemen.[17]

Presentation explains why in part he achieved popularity. McDougall had a flair for staging his shops, with "brightness, elegance, and attractiveness of place; the superiority of the provisions; [and] the neat appearance, courteous manners, order and alacrity, of the young lady attendants." Two of the four houses did a brisk trade, one having sales of £200 weekly, while the other catered to 400 middle-class patrons whose purchase of three-course meals for 1s. generated £30 weekly.[18] Pre-eminently, however, "remarkable low charges" impressed patrons most. Some indication of his

[15] "Ronald McDougall," *Biograph and Review* 5 (1881): 118–19; *Western Times*, 7 March 1876; Winskill and Thomas, *Temperance Movement in Liverpool*, p. 75.

[16] "No Intoxicants Sold," *Leisure Hour* 31 (1882): 116–17; *Hartlepool Northern Daily Mail*, 15 Jan. 1908.

[17] "No Intoxicants Sold," pp. 116–17.

[18] *Western Times*, 7 March 1876; [McDougall's interview], "The Originator of London Tea Shops," published in the *Star* and reproduced in the *Temperance Caterer*, 15 Nov. 1912.

success in the ensuing five years was the behaviour of his customers who spent £50,000 in his establishments rather than at nearby pubs.[19]

From his Liverpool apprenticeship, McDougall had acquired much insight into running prosperous restaurants. Coffee could be sold with sugar and milk for a penny a cup, which generated gross profits of 30% and net profits of 6–10% per annum. Property rentals, he recognised, must be kept low, ideally £50 monthly but certainly no more than £100, even when targeting middle-class custom. Higher rents doomed the enterprise, he knew.[20]

Interviewed in the *Leisure Hour*, he gave figures of how he had turned respectable profits (Table 3.1). Serving well-cooked meals to working men had raised altogether new problems. As he himself recognised, working-class men relished most meat from the joint, a quite expensive cut. In fact, this aspect had thwarted catering efforts in London and elsewhere. "No such enterprise has been successful on a large scale south of the [River] Tweed," he stated categorically. So popular was he with his unorthodox marketing tactics that within five years he sold the business, and looked south for another challenge.[21]

Seemingly superb was his timing. Five contemporaneous public companies primarily had promoted coffee public houses. Begun in 1874, the People's Café Co., the first to incorporate on a large scale, had £10,000 of

Table 3.1 Monthly expenses and profits for a middle-class Liverpool teashop in the late 1870s

Rent	£50
Taxes, water and gas	£20
Wages	£75
Repairs/renewals	£15
Coals and sundries	£20
Provisions	£470
Takings	£700
Net profits	£50

Source: "No Intoxicants Sold," p. 116

[19] Winskill and Thomas, *Temperance Movement in Liverpool*, p. 75; "McDougall," pp. 119–20.

[20] "No Intoxicants Sold," pp. 116–17.

[21] Ibid.

capital and the Earl of Shaftesbury as president and Samuel Morley, MP, as a director. To E. Hepple Hall, who wrote an early national survey of the coffee public-house movement, the Café's houses by any measure qualified as enormously flourishing.[22]

Several miscalculations, however, had jeopardised the People's Café Co.'s survival. In refurbishing the Café's first two houses, it laid out £6000, an astonishing sum for a company with just £10,000 in total capital. Rents too complicated matters. Compared to McDougall's low rents in Liverpool, the People's Café Co. had unwisely secured premises with staggering rentals. The Liverpool British Workman Public-House Company paid no more than £100 annually per house, whereas the two London Café houses catering to workers had yearly rentals of £250 and £350, respectively. "To expect to clear such rents out of the profits of selling halfpenny cups of coffee and cocoa was on the face of it an illusion," his Liverpool experience convinced him (Table 3.1). The Café's opening of establishments for dining without offering patrons anything to drink constituted a further shortcoming.[23]

Given his impressive background acquired from Liverpool, McDougall early in 1876 negotiated an agreement with the company in which he arranged to lease for seven years its unprofitable working-class houses, notably at Whitecross Street and Whitechapel, and run ten new cafés. Half would be aimed at working men, the rest at middle-class custom of both sexes, utilising his time-tested philosophy from his Liverpool years (Table 3.2).[24]

Table 3.2 People's Café Co. houses, 1882

Whitecross Street, Shoreditch (1875)	Love Lane, Rotherhithe
Ludgate Circus, Farrington Street/ Ludgate Hill (1876)	143 Drummond Street, Euston Square (1878)
Whitechapel Café, 87 High Street, Whitechapel (1876)	105 Victoria Dock Road, Canning Town (1878)
New Café, 61 St. Paul's Churchyard (1877)	People's Temperance Café, 61 Gracechurch Street (1878)
Marsham Street, Westminster	Jewin Street/Aldersgate Street

Sources: "McDougall," p. 121; *Coffee Public-House News*, 1 Nov. 1878

[22] Hall, *Coffee Taverns*, pp. 21–4.

[23] "No Intoxicants Sold," p. 117; *Illustrated London News*, 15 Nov. 1878.

[24] "McDougall," p. 121; "No Intoxicants Sold," 117; [Interview with McDougall], "Originator of London Tea Shops."

From the start in what seemed a buoyant market, McDougall aggressively pursued a more diverse clientele than had the company's original promoters. "This movement should not be confined to working men; for I already saw [in Liverpool] that there were other classes that those drinking-houses led into wrong ways," declared McDougall. When signing the contract with the company, McDougall promised that the five more upmarket houses would target "men of business, ladies, and that class accustomed to take its refreshment in the old wine-selling restaurants," while lodgers and clerks—young men of the lower middle class with meagre incomes—would comprise the other group.[25]

Class predictably determined takings. At two houses attracting middle-class customers and office workers, St. Paul's Churchyard and Ludgate Circus, McDougall's restaurants offered diners entrées, joints of meat, soups, fish, cakes and bread. Selling primarily tea and light refreshment cost patrons between 6d. and 1s. For beverages the range included not just tea and coffee, but exotic American effervescent drinks, notably Sparking Hygeia and Sparkling Phosphad.[26] Within four years, four houses were making cumulative annual receipts of £40,000. By 1880, St. Paul's Coffee House, the largest and most prosperous, was accommodating some 2000 patrons daily and netting £21,000 in takings annually; Ludgate Circus, its clientele chiefly drawn from the lower middle class, ran a distant second with £10,000 annually. Further down the social spectrum with primarily working-class lodgers and the lower middle class as customers, the People's Temperance Café (Gracechurch Street) and Drummond Street teashop averaged daily takings of just £6. To earn this modest amount, which netted about £1800 annually, meant selling prodigious amounts—almost 3000 cups—of coffee at ½d. per cup. "He is quite an important customer who spends twopence at one visit," he disclosed.[27]

Conscious of the need to expand his clientele across gender lines, McDougall had rooms reserved upstairs for women, such as at Marsham Street (Westminster) and Jewin Street (Aldersgate), where they could choose between 4d. and 6d. dinners. Two Café Co. restaurants as well as

[25] "No Intoxicants Sold," p. 117; *Shields Daily News*, 21 Dec. 1876.

[26] "McDougall," p. 121; *Hartlepool Northern Daily Mail*, 1 Jan. 1908; [Interview with McDougall], "Originator of London Tea Shops."

[27] Hall, *Coffee Taverns*, pp. 21–4; *Coffee Public-House News*, 1 Nov. 1878; "No Intoxicants Sold," p. 117; *Daily News*, 30 March 1878; "McDougall," p. 121.

small dining rooms, housed at the YMCA, fed business women. To lunch, the People's Café successfully drew shop girls, who ordered soup and pudding. In 1878, the *Daily News* reported that to Whitechapel coffee pubs "workgirls (sic) and showgirls (sic) come in great force." For such working females, coffee houses near their work places represented "an absolute necessity" as a convenient, inexpensive place for eating meals.[28]

Exemplifying a new entrepreneurial spirit, McDougall introduced an employee profit-sharing plan in which one-fourth of profits would be divided among his workers, an innovative managerial idea borrowed from his Liverpool days well ahead of any other catering company.[29] There would be a parallel between the Café Co. and the Liverpool British Workman Public House Company: McDougall perceived commercialising catering as an essential prerequisite to survival, anticipating the Liverpool Company's abandoning of its philanthropic beliefs in the next few years.[30] For the Café Co., London's first coffee public-house firm based on limited liability backed with illustrious names from the social and political elite, McDougall's entry as a pivotal managerial figure constituted the initial step in his ultimate takeover in two senses: he alone directed the company's fortunes; and bigger profits with middle-class custom now became the prevailing philosophy.[31]

Nearly four decades later in an interview with the *Star*, McDougall presented himself as "the originator of London tea shops." Inspiration for managing London coffee houses came from Liverpool, the site for developing his catering philosophy. Thus, he introduced teashops into Liverpool in 1874, two years before he arrived in London armed with proven ideas. Throughout the interview McDougall, ever the impresario of new catering experiences, portrayed his entrepreneurial skills as nothing short of brilliant.[32]

McDougall's professed role as the progenitor of London teashops went still further, he boasted during the interview. He cited profit sharing for

[28] *Daily News*, 30 March 1878; Antony Clayton, *London's Coffee Houses: A Stimulating Story* (London: Historical Publications, 2003), pp. 130–31; "McDougall," p. 121; "No Intoxicants Sold," p. 117; [McDougall's interview], "Originator of London Tea Shop"; Heasman, *Evangelicals in Action*, p. 143.

[29] *Coffee Public-House News*, 1 Nov. 1878 and 1 Apr. 1882; Heasman, *Evangelicals in Action*, p. 143; Bellhouse, "Coffee-House Movement," p. 120.

[30] See pp. 49–50.

[31] Hall, *Coffee Taverns*, p. 22; "No Intoxicants Sold," p. 117.

[32] [Interview with McDougall], "Originator of London Tea Shops."

employees, uniformed waitresses, payment at the desk system, removal of standard compartments between seats, separate gender rooms, prohibition of tips, and sale of genuine Scotch scones (made in Scotland)—all borrowed from his Liverpool apprenticeship—as compelling evidence of his claim of having introduced an entirely new business model into catering. It was not just retailing ideas, but personnel too that perpetuated continuity between Liverpool and London. On assuming the managerial role with the People's Café Co., he had in hand, in waitresses transported from his Liverpool shops, a trained staff already available.[33]

After taking control of the People's Café, he maintained that its teashops became "a remarkable success," spearheading what became the "teashop" revolution. Located in the City, the Ludgate Circus shop opening in 1876 on Farringdon Street represented literally the birthplace of London's teashops. "That," he asserted, "was how London got the tea shop habit."[34]

Unaware of this interview, historian Kathleen Heasman half-a-century later still reached the same conclusions in her book, *Evangelicals in Action* (1962), though her evidence is surprisingly thin. Through the People's Café, Ronald McDougall became central to transforming London's catering, she hypothesised. In providing teashops with inexpensive meals and non-alcoholic beverages to accommodate both sexes, the People's Café "made it general for the teashops of the 1890's to accommodate both men and women and so began the modern custom of catering for both sexes."[35]

Yet, the McDougall/Heasman interpretation sits rather oddly with the facts. The striking interval between his entry into the London catering market in 1876 and re-emergence some three decades later had one key cause about which McDougall unsurprisingly remained reticent. In the Edwardian era, he was unmasked as a charlatan, who cleverly inflated his accomplishments, mindful of one apparent goal: to convince his interviewer (and perhaps even himself) that he had once been a great man.

Nothing of the kind could have been further from the truth. He had been bankrupted numerous times—as a restaurateur, winter garden

[33] Ibid.

[34] "No Intoxicants Sold," p. 117; [Interview with McDougall], "Originator of London Tea Shops."

[35] [Interview with McDougall], "Originator of London Tea Shops"; Heasman, *Evangelicals in Action*, p. 143.

promoter and hotelier.[36] Nothing lost more money, however, than his last venture at Liverpool's Washington Hotel, purchased for £40,000 and renovated for another £30,000. Within three years he was bankrupt. His was a career of boom and bust, with much promise followed by devastating disaster.[37] Apparently, his captivating personality persuaded gullible people to back his schemes, disregarding his recurring failures.

Mindful of these facts and McDougall's penchant for exaggeration, was anything left of his claim to being the forerunner of revolutionary change in mass catering in late Victorian London? Dearth of evidence had allowed McDougall to characterise himself as a visionary whose imaginative policies transformed catering with ideas advancing a new business model. Central to re-appraising his career and the basis for a more balanced interpretation are contemporary newspapers, some of them newly digitised.

To evaluate McDougall's assertions, they must be placed in a broader historiographic context. Advent of the mass market in London from the late 1870s drew little scholarly investigation until historian A.E. Dingle's 1972 ground-breaking article in which he identified rising purchasing power, accessibility of consumer goods and stable retail prices for beer as the essential catalysts. Consumer choice widened with imported foodstuffs such as grain, meat, bacon, dairy products and fruit. Many consumer goods industries then belatedly industrialised, enabling inexpensive mass-produced boots, shoes, clothing and food processing to enter the market. Another development—the revolutionising of retailing and distributing practices—fostered falling prices and rises in both real wages and demand.[38] As the range of consumer goods broadened still further, consumer choice burgeoned in the 1880s. Increasingly customers purchased consumer goods as prices fell faster than money wages between 1880 and 1895. Stable beer and coffee prices now seemed relatively more expensive compared to the new consumer goods, so the working class, formerly purchasers of alcohol and coffee, switched to buying consumer durables.[39]

[36] In reconstructing the Palace at New Brighton as a winter garden in 1886, he failed and lost his entire investment of £30,000. Through the British Traders' Guild, he acted as a promoter of the Honey Bread and Flour Company before it went into liquidation in 1899 (*Hartlepool Northern Daily Mail*, 15 Jan. 1908; *Derby Daily Telegraph*, 16 Jan. 1906).

[37] Hall, *Coffee Taverns*, p. 23; *Hartlepool Northern Daily Mail*, 15 Jan. 1908; *Derby Daily Telegraph*, 16 Jan. 1906.

[38] See pp. 9–10.

[39] A.E. Dingle, "Drink and Working-Class Living Standards in Britain, 1870–1914," *Economic History Review* 25 (1972): 608–22.

Amid London's dramatically volatile catering market between 1876 and 1884, McDougall's career must be situated. Coffee public houses nationwide had experienced serious recession from the late 1870s, but the downturn in business hit sooner and harder in London than elsewhere.

Of London's 102 coffee houses in 1879, "most of them pay something; none of them pay a very great deal," confessed the *Liverpool Mercury*. To ensure a meagre profit, price-cutting became mandatory. Abnormally high rents, negotiated when coffee-house companies expanded rapidly in numbers earlier in the 1870s, aggravated the plight of London's coffee public houses. Seemingly thriving with nine coffee houses in London, the Coffee Public-House National Society, for example, put three up for sale in 1881, as several scholars have recognised, but overlooked was a far deeper problem—in that same year, the company began liquidating.[40] In an editorial on London coffee houses the following year, the *Coffee Public-House News* pointed to an unnamed but leading coffee public-house company's recent loss of £3000 as persuasive proof of the movement's weakening business in the metropolis. Meanwhile, the Coffee Tavern Company, founded in 1876, had opened twenty-five houses within four years of founding, but lost half of them in the ensuing eight years (1880–1887). By 1884, ten London coffee public houses had foundered. Of the capital's many coffee public houses, the *Coffee Public-House News* wrote, most had "a very precarious existence," while some of them had actually closed. Formerly solvent coffee public houses doing £70–80 of sales weekly were not now generating even £20. Not one of the London coffee public-house companies, the *News* revealed, could be adjudged thriving using any valid yardstick: not one broke even as a financial concern, much less paid investors stipulated dividends. "Nowhere in the kingdom has there been such an expenditure of capital with such miserable results," complained Thomas Hogben in 1882, who knew personally of what he spoke, having lost £3000 as an investor. One year later the *News* described deepening gloom in which some coffee-house companies were firing employees as a prelude to closing premises altogether; still others appeared desperately ready to sell out at any price.[41]

[40] Robert Thorne, "Places of Refreshment in the Nineteenth-Century City," in Anthony D. King (ed.), *Buildings and Society: Essays on the Social Development of the Built Environment* (London: Routledge & Kegan Paul, 1980), p. 245; Bellhouse, "Coffee-House Movement," p. 119; *Leicester Chronicle*, 11 June 1881; *Liverpool Mercury*, 17 Nov. 1879; *Coffee Public-House News*, 1 May 1884.

[41] *Coffee Public-House News*, 1 July 1882, 1 Feb. 1883, 1 May 1884, and 22 Feb. 1887; Bellhouse, "Coffee–House Movement," p. 119.

For London coffee public houses, the slump deepened in the mid-1880s. A survey of coffee-house owners in 1884 revealed that 20% of respondents were losing money, a figure which undoubtedly underestimated the extent of the problem since two-thirds of the proprietors (160) offered no response, presumably because of grim sales. One year later the proportion of respondents incurring losses rose to 75%. Assuming companies facing dire circumstances comprised the bulk of non-respondents, the actual proportion of proprietors earning profits plummeted to just over one-fourth. This too might have inflated what companies actually were still self-supporting, since indeterminate numbers might have been balancing their books from private donations of philanthropists.[42] London's woes arose from "badly selected sites, unskilful management, bad or indifferent food and absence of commercial principles," contended C.C. Smith (Secretary of the Birmingham Coffee-House Company), in his paper at the National Temperance Congress.[43]

But the broader explanation of why McDougall and so many others succumbed arose from different circumstances. The start of his London career could scarcely have been worse. McDougall's prior experience in the North ill-prepared him for the capital's abruptly worsening catering market.

Had he been less over-confident and more attuned to market trends, he might have intervened quicker and more decisively. Even before McDougall signed his contract with the People's Café Co. in 1876, disquieting signs had appeared. At a shareholders' meeting, directors had disclosed that "the two first cafés had been very successful for the first few weeks, but as soon as the novelty had worn off it was difficult to carry them on at a profit." Worse came early the following year, when the Café Co. declared no dividends. Though middle-class shops (Ludgate Circus and St. Paul's) reported their premises "filled to overflowing," working-class depots experienced growing difficulties. At Whitechapel extensive, expensive alterations generated so little business that it was "barely paying its way"; Whitecross Street, situated in costermongers' quarters, actually incurred a loss. In 1879 the Café Co. passed dividends and in response sold its

[42] C.C. Smith, "The Coffee House Movement in Provincial Towns," *Coffee Public-House News*, 1 May 1884; *Coffee Public-House News*, 1 Nov. 1886.

[43] Thomas Hogben, "Causes of Failure in London," *Coffee and Public-House News*, 1 Aug. 1882; *Coffee Public-House News*, 1 Feb. 1883 and 1 May 1884; C.C. Smith's untitled paper, *National Temperance Congress, 1884*, p. 195.

Whitecross premises. The next year diminishing custom at working-class shops continued, however; both the Canning Town and Rotherhithe cafés were now running at a loss, forcing the People's Café once again to miss dividends. Confronting a rapidly deteriorating catering market, the amateurish Board of Directors unwisely rewarded McDougall another three-year contract. For his part, McDougall became a director of a new concern, Pure Beverage Co., which manufactured non-alcoholic fruit drinks, and signed a contract to sell the beverages to the Café Co. Given the precarious state of the People's Café, this provided yet another example of how McDougall's ambitions outstripped his financial resources.[44]

In control of the troubled People's Café Co. from 1876 in a catering market already past its apex of prosperity, McDougall found that diverse problems—profits declined, mass-produced goods arrived and London catering companies faltered—upended his quest to launch himself as a formidable force in feeding London diners in 1882. Already gross receipts at the two highly publicised middle-class shops—St. Paul's Churchyard and Ludgate Circus (his alleged birthplace of the teashop)—had fallen from £34,000 to £29,000, a decline of nearly 15% in one year.[45] Mounting debts and losses compelled the People's Café to declare no dividends whatsoever in 1882; later that year, before the Liverpool Bankruptcy Court, McDougall acknowledged himself insolvent, his total liabilities reaching £8554. Two years later, the company, forced to liquidate, confessed its premier restaurant, St. Paul's Churchyard, where 20,000 patrons had once generated £24,000 in total annual receipts, was now embarrassingly running at a "great loss." However phenomenally popular he had portrayed himself as a London caterer, McDougall had in fact a transitory career, far too brief to justify a reputation as a pioneer caterer. Nothing more in fact was heard of him in this capacity. His loss-making restaurant at St. Paul's Churchyard, the Café Co.'s jewel, was unloaded in 1884. McDougall resurfaced briefly decades later in 1908 when, while working as manager of a soap combine, authorities arrested him as an "absconding bankrupt."[46]

[44] *Leicester Chronicle*, 11 March 1876; *Norwood News*, 11 Aug. 1877; *Glasgow Herald*, 25 Sept. 1879; *York Herald*, 16 Aug. 1881; *Caterer & Hotel Proprietor's Gazette*, 1 May 1880; Letter to the Editor, 27 July 1876, *Temperance Caterer*, 15 Dec. 1912.

[45] "McDougall," p. 121; "No Intoxicants Sold," p. 117.

[46] *Coffee Public-House News*, 1 Nov. 1878 and 1 Feb. 1884; *Hampshire Telegraph*, 22 Nov. 1882; *Derby Daily Telegraph*, 16 Jan. 1906; *Hartlepool Northern Daily Mail*, 15 Jan. 1908.

Capitalisation, timing, concentration and class together with gender all proved decisive in differentiating the catering careers of McDougall, on the one hand, and Pearce and Lockhart, on the other. McDougall had agreed to run a dozen premises. The People's Café Co., its original prospectus calling for £10,000 of capital, was therefore grossly underfunded, incapable of finding vital capital when the catering market contracted and its depots required updating.[47] Compare the Café with some leading competitors. In eventually running twenty-seven coffee public houses, the Coffee Tavern Company in these same years enlarged its capital from £10,000 to £50,000. Lockharts survived for dissimilar reasons. Well established in the North before moving to London, it had a far-flung base, together with the largest capital of the three, £220,000.[48] Compounding the Café Co.'s problems was that it violated one of McDougall's cardinal tenets, negotiating low rentals.[49] Having paid £6000 for two premises, the company accepted £1400 rental for the most prestigious of the restaurants at St. Paul's. Thus, these arrangements consumed three-fourths of the company's total capital, making it extremely vulnerable to severe economic slumps.

Good timing was vital in overcoming the volatile catering market. McDougall started his London career in 1876 when food retailing sales first began slumping, whereas in Lockharts' case, its first London depot was established in 1883 and escaped the worst economic conditions. Initially, the Co. generated custom with a full complement of beverages—tea, coffee, cocoa, chocolate and milk—ordered with buns, sandwiches and confectionary. Expansion came later with its popular puddings, enabling the company to grow steadily, reaching 54 London houses in 1888.[50]

Dispersed depots became a potent reason, too, for McDougall's failure. He had restaurants widely scattered as far North as Canning Town, due east of the City. The company had rented premises without first assessing how they fitted into an overall business plan, a flaw symptomatic of its inexperienced directors. Supervision of his far-flung depots must have caused difficulties, preventing centralisation of food distribution. Precisely how McDougall served thousands of customers as a basis for his claim as

[47] Depot then described a place where meals were prepared and served. Adding to the confusion was that depots and coffee bars were used interchangeably, eventually being replaced by the term "restaurant."

[48] See p. 52.

[49] *Financial Times*, 30 July 1895.

[50] *Temperance Caterer*, 3 Nov. 1888 and 15 June 1902.

the pioneer of mass catering never earned coverage in his speeches or interviews, much less the press.[51] Thus, McDougall had imaginative but unproven ideas about catering. No other aggregate data appeared publicly indicating how—or even whether—-he established himself as a leader in the mass food market. Lockharts also had widely scattered shops outside London, but in the capital its menu catered for the poorer classes, clerks, working men and ladies undertaking business excursions.[52] Deeper pockets here, too, enabled Lockharts to confront intensifying competition.

Another final factor explains why Lockharts bested McDougall's People's Café Co. Conscious of class as well as gender, Lockharts created first-class rooms on the first or second floors. Of the three caterers—Pearce, McDougall and Lockharts—entering London's market in these years, Lockharts particularly wooed women, for whom it set aside a special room. In its first-class accommodation, the company offered women a cloakroom and lavatory. Nothing so sophisticated rivalled these features at McDougall's shops.[53] McDougall's success really derived from catering to the middle classes, not to those socially below them. Ludgate Circus, home he said of the teashop revolution, and St. Paul's Churchyard—the much publicised teashops with impressive sales—drew exclusively a middle-class custom.[54]

Exaggerating his accomplishments became a recurring feature of McDougall's career, the clever huckster repeatedly marketing his extraordinary accomplishments. His, he argued, were the money-making skills of the gifted northerner: a baker whom he had hired to manage one of his Liverpool teashops stayed for ten years, finally selling out for the staggering sum of £100,000.[55] Such an outlandish claim that he literally sold to the Café Co.'s directors promoted his next venture. At the Café Co., on the one hand, he touted his accomplishments with sales at his leading establishments, both middle class, and on the other, he ignored the fact that as manager of the Co., it passed dividends during four of his six-year tenure (1877–1882). From the outset of his association in 1876, the Café Co. lurched from one crisis to another, scarcely sustaining McDougall's later depiction of it as enormously successful, the forerunner of London's

[51] There was one exception. At the working-class shop on Drummond Street, a press account said it catered to 800 customers daily (*Coffee Public-House News*, 1 Nov. 1878).

[52] *Coffee Tavern Gazette*, 22 Jan. 1887; *Financial Times*, 30 May 1902.

[53] *Temperance Caterer*, 11 June and 20 Aug. 1887.

[54] *Coffee Public-House News*, 1 Nov. 1878.

[55] [Interview with McDougall], "Originator of London Tea Shops."

teashop revolution. His repeated bankruptcies scarcely validated his much vaunted image as London's revolutionary caterer and shrewd entrepreneur.

McDougall did, however, contribute to the emergence of mass catering, but in ways wholly different from what historians have tended to depict. Clearly, he had anticipated to some extent what Pearce and other mass caterers would embrace. Uniformed waitresses, elimination of booth compartments, payment at a cash desk and profit sharing—all these foreshadowed what Pearce soon adopted as part of his Pearce & Plenty business philosophy.[56] Pearce would try payment at a central location, but soon abandoned it as being far too cumbersome and slow to accommodate numerous diners whose short lunch hours compelled service as swift as their consumption of food. Another McDougall innovation, a clientele spanning the class divide, was visionary, though Pearce himself would come to see this as premature early in the 1880s. In this sense, McDougall was ahead of his time, and paid dearly for misreading the market. Some McDougall ideas were never entertained as practicable, such as prohibition of gratuities, gender-segregated rooms and Scotch scones on the menu. Had McDougall embraced a strategy of concentration, his success would have been probably greater. In this regard, he failed partly because he was as excessively ambitious as overly confident, perhaps unable to make the huge transition from two quite disparate catering markets in geographically dispersed parts of the country. That his subsequent history of repeated bankruptcies became a hallmark of his business career attests to serious character deficiencies that thwarted his pursuit of success.

Total abstinence, Evangelist Dwight L. Moody and commitment to feeding vast numbers of London's inhabitants—all these united John Pearce with Ronald McDougall and Robert Lockhart. Careers of the last two were shaped by coffee public houses in Liverpool. McDougall's short-lived catering career in the capital and Lockhart's premature death in 1880 deprived either of recognition as pre-eminent in London's emergent mass food catering market.

Joseph Bentley (editor of the *Temperance Caterer*), who had followed Pearce's career as closely as anyone, was best positioned to appraise McDougall's portrayal as the progenitor of mass catering in late Victorian

[56] "No Intoxicants Sold," pp. 116–17. Compartments, common in the early nineteenth century, were abandoned in the 1850s–1860s as the prelude to the introduction of the restaurant (Thorne, "Places of Refreshment," pp. 237–38).

London. Having reprinted the 1912 *Star* account, Bentley expressed, in a pithy sentence and in a classic British understatement, his assessment of McDougall's claim as the initiator of London teashops: "There is some doubt on this point."[57] The advent of mass catering and its integral feature, the mass market, were closely linked with the retailing revolution, and at its forefront stood John Pearce.

[57] *Temperance Caterer*, 15 Nov. 1912.

CHAPTER 4

From Penny Capitalist to Server of the Multitudes

Unrecognised alike by historians and popularisers, diverse traits contributed to John Pearce's success. Marketing skills, Evangelical religion, advertising, business acumen, innovation, showmanship and class consciousness—all fashioned his character. Pearce also owed his success to business colleagues, who sometimes shared his temperance sentiments or to kindred spirits who wanted to assist the impoverished for philanthropic reasons. He was thus an extraordinary individual whose complex personality diverse influences had shaped.

Various factors contributed to the nature of the capital's eating places. "In London rents are higher, dirt is more abundant, and competition is far greater than anywhere else in the world," remarked a newspaper. Here, too, proprietors, invariably foreigners in central London, ran just their own houses, typically small, airless and cockroach-ridden with vile food and tea. Such establishments "charged four pence for a pot of marvellously bitter tea, which made one ill, twopence for roll and butter, and at least a penny for the waiter."[1]

Foods quickly prepared were unthinkable, save for roast or boiled meat with vegetables and cottage pudding. To cook a steak or chop consumed a half hour, sometimes as much as forty minutes, and meantime, diners confronted tea or coffee of "execrable" quality, "served slopped over into the saucer." Even at mid-day, coffee shops had a limited menu of eggs and

[1] *Coffee Public-House News*, 1 Apr. 1885; *Financial Times*, 10 Aug. 1906, and 21 Aug. 1922; *Temperance Caterer*, 15 Jan. 1909.

D. W. Gutzke, *John Pearce and the Rise of the Mass Food Market in London, 1870–1930*, https://doi.org/10.1007/978-3-030-27095-7_4

bacon or "the humble bloater"; rarely could patrons order a chop and potatoes. Waiters or waitresses reflected the environment in their dress and demeanour—smeared, dirty shirts and aprons, frayed dress coats, and overall slip-shod in appearance.[2]

Mid-Victorian London restaurants—non-existent in the "City" and limited to one or two in the West End—were quite similar, serving British food, "heavy, solid, indigestible, and, for the most part, badly cooked." John Pearce agreed. "There were three sorts of places where you could buy food—the cook shop, the coffee shop and the chop house, but of catering there was very little," he recollected. Here Pearce blurred an important distinction: customers did not so much buy as order food. In the latter case, they consulted a menu and ordered specific items; in the former case—in what would come to be called catering—they bought what had been pre-prepared and quickly consumable.[3]

Whether at chop shops or coffee-houses, Pearce could not forget their having "slovenly attendants in short-sleeves and bare arms." At tables with high-backed boxes sat patrons eyeing linen "more or less soiled—and it was always a question of take it or leave it if any particular dish was worse than usual." Cheap coffee houses in the City, then and for many decades after, catered to customers "penned up in compartments like the stalls of a stable … where dust and dirt seemed to form the chief stock-in-trade."[4] Popular with many workers, public houses offered food, but "it was exceedingly difficult … to get anything which did not carry with it the flavour of bloaters" (Fig. 4.1).[5]

Because fixed meal breaks were virtually unknown at small factories and workshops, food had to be consumed quickly, either on workers' benches or in an improvised affair in a nearby pub. Hastening the devouring of meals was another factor—piece-rates that forced workers

[2] George R. Sims, "Looking Back," *Daily Mail*, 5 Oct. 1921; S.J. Adair Fitz-Gerald, "Chats with Caterers: Interview with Joseph Lyons," *Caterer & Hotel-Keepers' Gazette*, 15 June 1904; *Financial Times*, 10 Aug. 1906; S.J. Adair Fitz-Gerald, "Chats with Caterers: Old Chop Shops: Interview with John Pearce," *Caterer & Hotel-Keepers' Gazette*, 16 Jan. 1905; *Financial Times*, 21 Aug. 1922.

[3] *London Daily News*, 18 Oct. 1911; Clement Scott, *How They Dined Us in 1860 and How They Dined Us Now* (London: Trocadero Restaurant, 1900), pp. 8, 19; Sims, "Looking Back"; Adair Fitz-Gerald, "Interview with Joseph Lyons."

[4] *Temperance Caterer*, 28 Apr. 1888; *London Daily News*, 18 Oct. 1911.

[5] *Coffee Public-House News*, 1 Apr. 1885; *Financial Times*, 10 Aug. 1906; *Temperance Caterer*, 15 Jan. 1909; Adair Fitz-Gerald, "Interview with John Pearce"; *Financial Times*, 21 Aug. 1922.

Fig. 4.1 Men drinking beer with their lunch in a pub (1887) (Benjamin Clarke, "Temptations to Temperance," *Sunday Magazine* (1887): 40) The entrance door in the rear is mislabelled as a private bar, a more select drinking room than the tap room where workers commonly ate food with their beer in rudimentary surroundings

be cognisant of maximising output. Workers began their day with early risings and walking into the City of London, stopping on the way to buy a cup of coffee at a street stall. Clerks and others of the lower middle class came equipped with bulging pockets, replete with two or three sandwiches for lunch, while those socially below them ate at grimy, filthy pubs or coffee houses. The worker destined for pubs visited the most plebeian quarters, the tap room, where he, "having ordered his beer, spread out his handkerchief on an upended empty butt and proceeded to eat his lunch."[6]

Respectable women fared still worse, recollected reporter George R. Sims years later in the *Daily Mail*: "women's place was in the home, and that was where she should take her meals." In pubs, as in the workplace in other public places, such women were not so much inconspicuous as virtually absent. "Women were very rarely seen at any restaurant whatsoever in a public room," Sims emphatically stated. Had they dared defy the unwritten code, they would have incurred opprobrium as "fast" or disgraceful. Exceptions were few, based largely on class. To the top floor in several City houses, he recalled, a lady—quite distinct from a woman—might venture for food at lunch time.[7]

Within this environment, John Pearce competed for custom from the late 1860s, an era before the advent of mass catering.

Second son of an impoverished couple, John was born in 1847 in Hoxton, a slum north of the City full of costermongers, vagabonds, rogues and criminals. There was much poverty in London north and even west of the City, and Charles Booth in *The Life and Labour of the People of London* would later categorise the Hoxton triangle closest to the intersection of City and East Roads as primarily Grades 7 and 8, the very bottom of his 8-point scale with poverty and semi-criminality dominant features. By trade, his father, a Cornishman, was a hat-finisher, who—having developed asthma and a diseased arm—became an invalid, unable to work, which meant "the border-line of starvation was never out of sight." Far more influential as a factor in Pearce's life, his mother, a Welshwoman, inspired deep devotion, respect and love. To support the family, his mother worked in a sweated industry, making the upper part of women's boots, a poorly paid taxing job consuming vast amounts of time. East London was notorious for such drudgery and exploited labour. During these early years, his father died, and, after

[6] [Interview with John Pearce], "ABC Jubilee," *Temperance Caterer*, 15 Nov. 1912; John Burnett, *England Eats Out: A Social History of Eating Out in England from 1830 to the Present* (London: Pearson Longman, 2004), p. 109.

[7] Scott, *How They Dined Us*, pp. 8, 19; Sims, "Looking Back"; Adair Fitz-Gerald, "Interview with Joseph Lyons." Such social distinctions persisted, at least insofar as drinking in pubs and beerhouses was concerned, into the 1930s (David W. Gutzke, "Gender, Class and Public Drinking in Britain During the First World War," *Histoire sociale/Social History* 27 (1994): 388).

brief exposure to rudimentary education, John struck out to find a livelihood.[8]

Three circumstances influenced deeply John Pearce's character, views and attitudes. Deprived of his father at the age of 9, he depended still more on his mother, imbibing her beliefs and relishing her love. No one did more to shape his character, both by guidance and by example, than did she. "If I had no other cause to revere her memory, I should always treasure it for her constant watchfulness of us children in our days of childhood," he later recalled.[9] She did far more for him than perhaps he realised then or later, inculcating her disposition—soft-spoken, kind, even-tempered and loving—into her son, whose great height became a considerable asset. This incongruous mixture of height, projecting his commanding authority, on the one hand, and sympathetic understanding—and where needed compassion—on the other, enabled Pearce to establish an extraordinary rapport with his staff. Other observers later in the decade would note this chemistry remarkable in the catering industry.[10] For lengthy periods, he had known first-hand what it meant to suffer physically and emotionally, character-forming experiences which he shared with many others who became customers or joined his staff.

Nonconformity equally galvanised Pearce. Though he attended several nonconformist chapels, his exposure to the City Road Chapel, where he listened to such prominent Wesleyan preachers as Dr Jobson, Samuel Coley and Dr Beaumont, aroused his interest but not commitment. Two other preachers, however, entranced Pearce. American evangelists Dwight L. Moody and Ira D. Sankey started their London crusade in Islington, ambitiously in a hall with a seating capacity of some 13,000 in 1874. Becoming a friend of Moody, Pearce responded to the evangelists' promptings to provide dinners, based on temperance doctrines, aimed at workers of dissimilar backgrounds. Still more influential was William Carter, an itinerant preacher who started a mission on City Road, accompanied with three "trophies"—a converted thief, a converted burglar and a converted infidel. Pearce responded to the simplicity of their protestations. Through his Southwark mission, Carter developed a remarkable connection with

[8] James E. Ellis, *Pluck, Patience and Power: The Life of John Pearce of "Pearce and Plenty"* (London: H.R. Allenson, 1910), pp. 16, 20–2, 36; Bernard Gainer, *The Alien Invasion: The Origins of the Aliens Act of 1905* (London: Heinemann Educational Books, 1972), pp. 19–20, 22, 25.

[9] Ellis, *Pluck*, p. 21.

[10] See pp. 112–13, 186–87.

what Victorians called the "unwashed." At one of Carter's sermons, Pearce underwent a religious conversation experience and emerged, as his mother later told her son, convinced of his salvation.[11]

Endeavouring to earn enough to support his mother and himself, Pearce held varied jobs, some of them imparting skills of unsuspected but enormous importance later when he became a caterer. From a builder, he acquired knowledge in handling tools as well as design and decorative skills; a pastry shop proprietor revealed the art of making pastry; and a provision merchant provided an informal apprenticeship detailing costs and types of dairy products and sausages.[12] In retrospect, what he assimilated afforded him the vital training necessary to become a caterer. On his mother's death, his wife replaced her in Pearce's affections.[13]

Precisely when he gained insight into his becoming a caterer is unknown, partly because he himself would discuss with interviewers, not what he thought but what he did. To his confidant and future biographer, the Rev. James J. Ellis, Pearce disclosed years later that he "regards his progress from poverty to power as part of a divine plan, and considers that he has a distinct mission in life ... to feed [and] to clothe the sons of toil."[14] Harold Bolce, in a biographical sketch, also saw this religious calling as part of Pearce's success, but expressed it differently. Pearce "literally climbed from 'The Gutter,'" Bolce reflected, "because he visualized, in his daily contact in youth with London's poor, an opportunity for service which others had failed to see."[15]

Demographic changes profoundly affected eating habits. In the two decades after 1875, the population of Greater London increased by almost 50%, while train, tram and bus journeys soared by nearly 300%. No other areas in England and Wales grew faster in the 1880s than four London suburbs. Much impetus for establishing coffee houses was due to the lengthier distances working- and middle-class men travelled to work. Without cheap trains but with early openings for shops, workmen left early

[11] Ellis, *Pluck*, pp. 44, 53; *Temperance Caterer*, 15 Aug. 1895; Kathleen Heasman, *Evangelicals in Action: An Appraisal of Their Social Work in the Victorian Era* (London: Geoffrey Bles, 1962), p. 142.

[12] Ellis, *Pluck*, pp. 44, 47–8, 50.

[13] *Temperance Caterer*, 15 Aug. 1895.

[14] Ellis, *Pluck*, p. 44. Here Pearce was probably speaking generally about his extensive charitable work.

[15] Harold Bolce, "Foreseeing What the People Want: How Initiative, Imagination and a Sense of Value Created an Industry from an Idea," *System* 26 (1914): 154.

for a long walk—Pearce himself would do this. Pubs loomed large in the workman's life, not just for alcohol. "When the old tap-room existed in public-houses, then men did more [often] take their food with them and have their pint of beer with it."[16] Other factors brought workers into pubs. "Wages were pathetic and ... paid in public saloons, and often paid in kind," Pearce remembered. Breakfast itself was customarily taken at pubs, the few establishments open early morning where workers downed rum and milk. Lunch was an improvised affair: "Poor men took their scanty noon-day meal in a red handkerchief or a piece of paper, and the only place they could sit and eat it was in a public house."[17]

Into this dramatically changing commercial context, John Pearce began his career among the residuum, the bottom of the unwashed. Having saved his earnings from various unskilled employments, he outfitted himself with a suit: coat and trousers cost 35d.; and shirt and socks another 14d. Good shoes, vital for tramping long distances while seeking work, struck him as unaffordable, so he economised with a second-hand pair ordered from Kingsland Road poorhouse.[18]

At the intersection of East and City Roads (Hoxton), elderly women running dirty night stalls dispensing indifferent coffee and repellent food formed his competition in the mid-1860s. With £1 in his pocket earned recently as a porter in Covent Gardens, Pearce boldly launched his first pitch in 1866. He bought some coffee beans, and cups and saucers, together with bread and butter, placing these on a rented barrow. On a daily basis, "my initial takings as a caterer were exactly half-a-crown," he confessed in an interview entitled "the Founder of the Famous Poor Man's Restaurants." For six bleak months Pearce ate a daunting diet: "I lived practically on bread and butter and coffee." Time to develop loyal customers and earn money quite apart from his stall for survival came when he found work as a packer, whose thirty-six-hour week earned 10s.[19]

[16] *Evidence of the Royal Commission on Liquor Licensing Laws*, 1897, 36 (Cmnd. 8694), p. 241; Robert Thorne, "Places of Refreshment in the Nineteenth-Century City," in Anthony D. King (ed.) *Buildings and Society: Essays on the Social Development of the Built Environment* (London: Routledge & Kegan Paul, 1980), p. 244.

[17] *Daily Telegraph*, 3 Apr. 1901; Bolce, "Foreseeing What the People Want," p. 156. Also see pp. 70–2.

[18] Bolce, "Foreseeing What the People Want," pp. 155–56.

[19] John Pearce, "'I Started Gutter Hotels': Founder of the Famous Poor Man's Restaurants," *Pearson's Weekly*, 5 Sept. 1914.

His day began at 2 a.m., giving him two hours to prepare his barrow. He walked to Whitecross Street, where he purchased sixty half-quarter loaves freshly baked from the Aerated Bread Bakery (ABC), walked briskly to his headquarters, repeating the journey to get the remaining loaves, to cut it up. Making freshly brewed coffee each morning, he took it and the newly baked bread, called "Tottenham cake," "a long, flat cake in a tin, covered with sugar, sold in big penny piece," to his coffee stall at 4 a.m. where he dispensed these goods for the next four hours. That his patrons would be eating bread also sold in ABC tea shops where middle-class diners consumed it was undoubtedly not lost on working-class Gutter Hotel frequenters. No one else sold freshly baked bread and newly brewed coffee to passer-by customers—these, Pearce felt, constituted "the secret of my success."[20] Tending the stall until 10 a.m., he left for his packing job, a regime that lasted for a year. Pearce then built a stall, selected brilliant red as its colour and, with brass rods for decorations, christened it "The Gutter Hotel."[21] With the motto "Everything new, everything clean," Pearce attracted printers, artisans, mechanics and "swells returning home after a party or a spree" as the backbone of his patrons, but remarkably, few girls or women.[22]

Sufficient capital in hand, he quit his packing job and for the ensuing ten years stood thirteen hours a day supplying customers with coffee and a friendly word at the intersection of East and City Roads. As Pearce himself would put it, customers "could depend on me being there in all weathers." Testament to his commitment was one serious physical consequence, varicose veins, which later required surgery. By the end of this phase, his mornings' earnings had soared from thirty to sometimes as much as 120 pence—"all in coppers," reflecting his customers' poverty-stricken existence.[23]

Pearce was certainly not the first penny capitalist to seek profits with consumables retailed at a coffee stall. Instinctively, he sensed what would

[20] John Pearce, "A Fortune from a Coffee Stall: The Romance of 'Pearce and Plenty,'" *Fortunes Made in Business: Life Struggles of Successful People* (London: Harmsworth Brothers, 1901), p. 42; Marguerite Williams, *John Pearce: The Man who Played the Game* (London: Religious Tract Society, 1928), p. 169; Ellis, *Pluck*, p. 80. Unprepared to emulate Pearce's role as the daily coffee-stall keeper, his successor quickly lost business and closed down. ([Interview with John Pearce], "ABC Jubilee," *Temperance Chronicle*, 15 Nov. 1912).

[21] Ellis, *Pluck*, pp. 74–9.

[22] *Daily Telegraph*, 27 March 1905.

[23] "Coffee-Stall Crisis," *Daily Telegraph*, 3 Apr. 1901; [Interview with John Pearce], "ABC Jubilee."

appeal to his customers, as he recollected decades later when interviewed in the *Star*, and thus rejected outright selling stewed coffee and stale bread. Where he also differed from his predecessors and rivals was in his willingness to undergo great personal sacrifices to satisfy customers.

Personal testimonials afford shrewd insight into why Pearce, though not so many of his predecessors, succeeded. One local observer, who fitted up businesses, had watched as coffee stall proprietors came and went. Pearce, he perceived, was different. "Men would pass others and make their way to him, because they knew they were sure of getting good coffee." Pearce's personality, too, was integral to his progress. Years later he did business with a firm of van builders, its manager relating that his father had habitually purchased coffee from Pearce such as he had never tasted before. "There's no knowing how many you have helped by your kindly talks with them, while they were buying their morning coffee," he told the hard-working entrepreneur.[24]

Class considerations defined his catering enterprises. Averse to disguising his plebeian status, Pearce instead exploited his background as an asset with which his customers could so readily identify. He was one of them, born poor, never too proud (or embarrassed) to acknowledge this. Hence, in dubbing his first venture "The Gutter Hotel," he projected a persona in which he mocked poverty and asked his customers to join him. Turning the propertied stereotype of the indigent on its head, he lampooned the then prevalent concept of self-inflicted poverty. In consuming coffee and other items, patrons recognised their purchases validated the twin Victorian doctrines of self-help and social mobility.[25]

Understanding of his clientele contributed to success. "I know a little about how the working-classes feed," Pearce admitted in a classic understatement. This approach to catering to the impoverished made his stall as distinctive as his subsequent decision to construct an oven for baking his own bread. At the Gutter Hotel, he sold newly baked bread purchasable only in the morning, whereas in his new guise as a baker, he began distributing the bread wholesale as well. He exemplified his own business creed: "Get things right, and keep on keeping them right." Never passing up a

[24] *Coffee Public-House News*, 1 May 1883; Ellis, *Pluck*, pp. 80–1.

[25] J.B. Brown, "The Pig or the Stye: Drink and Poverty in Late Victorian England," *International Review of Social History* 18 (1973): 380–95.

sales opportunity, he sold the surplus to other stall dealers; now, his morning takings exceeded six pounds.[26]

Less well known is that Pearce and contemporaries concealed his wife's role as a caterer in 1868. Two years after he started a coffee stall, his wife began running a "coffee house" on City Road, though we know nothing more about it. Despite John's numerous interviews with the press, his wife's experience as a coffee-house proprietor earned just one brief mention in an 1889 catering journal. Neither then nor for that matter later was anything said about her unsuccessful efforts to expand the family's catering beyond her husband's stall to a fixed depot.[27]

What made Pearce so reticent to acknowledge his wife's contributions? A traditional Victorian male in a catering industry in which men monopolised positions as members of the board of directors and managing directors, he undoubtedly felt inhibited in offering her public respect. Of his twelve offspring, just one was a girl, and like her mother, we know neither her given name nor relationship with the family business from any of Pearce's speeches or interviews, much less his two biographers. Not surprisingly, Pearce's biographers evinced virtually no interest in the Pearce women beyond the mother's role as the matriarch of a huge family.[28] Sexism obviously explains in part this jaundiced perspective, but masculinity loomed large in traditional working-class families. Ironically, Pearce wanted to escape the milieu of the masculine republic of the public house, but replicated it—without the alcoholic drink—in his catering enterprises.[29]

This was not the only episode in his foray into business on a larger scale, but failure distinguished the 1870 attempt.[30] Whether owing to pride, embarrassment, perhaps his loathing of alcohol or even his own vivid self-perception as an honest, God-fearing man of integrity, Pearce studiously engaged in myth-making in which he portrayed himself as the hard-working

[26] J.R. Wintle, "Round the London Restaurants," *Windsor Magazine* 4 (1896): 448; Bolce, "Foreseeing What the People Want," pp. 157–58.

[27] "Mr. John Pearce: The Man and His Work," *British Journal of Catering*, 15 July 1889; [Interview with John Pearce], "Fifty Years of Catering," *Daily News*, 18 Oct. 1911.

[28] His second biographer devoted a short paragraph to her rising at 4 a.m., cutting bread, and spreading butter, jam or marmalade on the slices.

[29] For a discussion of the masculine republic, see David W. Gutzke, *Women Drinking Out in Britain since the Early Twentieth Century* (Manchester: Manchester University Press, 2014), p. 17.

[30] Contemporaries later misdated his entry into catering and misunderstood its outcome (Letter to Editor, *Temperance Caterer*, 15 Dec. 1912).

successful self-made man, the quintessential penny capitalist, a view recounted in numerous interviews over the next four decades. In celebrating his Jubilee in 1911, he (informally) confessed, offering the first truthful account in which he now acknowledged that his rise in the catering industry was far from one of unbroken success. As he recounted to a *Daily News* reporter,

> I tried a temperance coffee-house in 1870 in City-road. ... Its distinctive principle was that I wouldn't send out for beer. I was before my time, and failed. The workers liked my food, but insisted on the beer.[31]

Considerable struggle was thus necessary to establish himself in London's catering business.

Beginning in 1876 Pearce and his older brother, Joseph, subjected their unproven theories about running a viable business to a severe test with their first stationary premises in Finsbury. "If success attended their efforts in a comparatively obscure place like Type Street, they believed that a similar, and perhaps a better, result might be the outcome of an enterprise in a more public and populous locality," recalled the brothers some years later. They devised a business formula in which they personally purchased the best goods and oversaw their cooking and carving.[32]

Pearce and his brother inaugurated what became Pearce & Plenty in 1878, opening a coffee bar at 58 Aldersgate Street, marking his entry into catering in the City of London. They set up "Pearce's Coffee Bar," their first establishment in the City of London, the medieval part that came to be known as the "square mile." Investing savings and profits of £1400 in this new venture, they broadened the menu without abandoning their core customers, working-class men, largely printers and printers' labourers. To them they sold huge quantities of chops, steaks, sausages, potatoes, greens and puddings, averaging 600 meat puddings daily. Patrons got what they wanted. Beef-steak puddings, for which the brothers became famed, gave customers one-half pound of beef with crust for 4d. Sausage, potatoes and bread could be had for 3d.,[33] while the most basic meal, sausage and potatoes, cost 2½d.Catering to the impoverished, the Pearces

[31] [Interview with John Pearce], "Fifty Years of Catering."

[32] "Pearce's Coffee Bar, Farringdon Street, London," *Coffee Public-House News*, 1 Feb. 1883.

[33] The prices were soon raised by 1d. (*City Press*, reproduced in *Coffee Public-House News*, 1 Nov. 1884).

provided tables for those bringing their own food, and made profits from selling half-penny coffee and cocoa.[34]

Into its cavernous dining room they could accommodate 100–150 patrons. No previous business gave diners as much for their money or in such appealing quality. "Prompt service, good food, clean articles and rooms, and pay on delivery, with the personal management of the proprietor, secured patronage," and expanded the Pearce brothers' evolving business strategy. An astonished reporter for the *Coffee Public-House News* recorded the enthusiastic customer reception: "Hundreds of patrons visited the place every day, some taking all their meals there."[35]

Success had little to do with the rudimentary fittings of the premises, but customers were nevertheless delighted with what else he offered them. Several elements constituted the Pearce recipe for catering success: quick service, the lowest tea prices and hot potatoes sold without meat. Pride of place, however, went to home-made steak puddings, which quickly became revered among his patrons. Here, some commentators argued, "Pearce's Coffee Bar" on Aldersgate Street fundamentally transformed the City's catering business.[36]

Keen to live near his shop, Pearce and his wife resided in City Road. Grateful to Joseph for having introduced him to his future wife (and fulfilment of his promise to his mother to look after Joseph), John gave him the Aldersgate depot independently to run on his own before moving to Farringdon Street some years later.[37]

No one has appreciated Pearce's insight into establishing a chain of stalls in the 1870s. Lyons' historian Peter Bird credits Lyons with achieving this marketing feat first in the catering industry in the 1890s, but Pearce was already developing the concept more than a decade earlier. In the 1870s Pearce saw the potential of expanding through satellite stalls, with trained managers hired to man other stalls not surprisingly called "Gutter Hotels." Later, Pearce would apply this same concept to his chain of depots in which his company sold the products it produced, not just coffee but bread. Central to implementing this approach were strict portion

[34] Pearce, "'Gutter Hotels.'"

[35] "Pearce's Coffee Bars, Farringdon St., London," *Coffee Public-House News*, 1 Feb. 1883; Williams, *Pearce*, p. 95.

[36] [Interview with John Pearce], "Fifty Years of Catering"; also see Williams, *Pearce*, p. 90.

[37] Ellis, *Pluck*, pp. 92–3.

control, standardised prices, economies of scale, recognisable shop design and superb service.[38]

Why was London the focus of what one historian has called "new catering institutions"? For a mass market to emerge, numerous people needed to migrate on a daily basis into London, close enough to commute but too far to return home for lunch. Three key occupations—commerce, public administration and professional services—exploded in numbers, increasing from 940,000 (1881) to over 2 million (1911). "These white-collar and white-blouse workers particularly needed light refreshment served quickly in clean, comfortable surroundings," observed John Burnett in *England Eats Out*.[39]

Farringdon Street loomed large in the history of the City's mass catering. There, in 1876, the People's Café Co. had established a depot, which Ronald McDougall began managing the following year as part of the company's coffee public houses. Five years later McDougall, his grandiose vision of transplanting his Liverpool experience to the capital a failure, was declared bankrupt.[40] In 1883, on this very street, the brothers Pearce established a shop.

John Pearce, then 36 years old, assisted by younger brother Henry, opened the first of what would become a highly prosperous chain, branded as Pearce & Plenty, at 84 Farringdon Street, near Ludgate Circus and opposite Fleet Lane, soon "the most successful of all the Coffee Taverns in England." Bigger than the Aldersgate Street depot, with seating for 200, the premises utilised the basement and ground floor. Eventually, the depot encompassed the first floor where a more prosperous clientele paid half penny more for privacy. On the lower floors, workingmen could sit down and buy coffee or tea.[41] With boxes discarded, patrons could sit at open tables (Fig. 4.2). Another big innovation involved serving. "The rule of their Bars," one reporter remarked, "is each person gets at the bar or counter what food he requires, for which he pays on delivery, and takes it to any vacant table he may select." Such was the organisation that diners' experienced minimal delay. Setting his depots apart from competitors,

[38] Peter Bird, *The First Food Empire: A History of J. Lyons & Co.* (Chichester: Phillimore & Co., 2000), pp. 38–9, 42; *Daily Telegraph*, 27 March 1905.

[39] Burnett, *England Eats Out*, pp. 117, 122.

[40] See pp. 56 (Table 3.2), 57 and 59.

[41] *Evidence on Liquor Licensing Laws*, 1897, p. 241; *Temperance Caterer*, 15 March 1902; Pearce, "Fortune from a Coffee Stall," p. 42; Bolce, "Foreseeing What the People Want," p. 158; "Pearce's Coffee Bars."

Fig. 4.2 Eating mid-day at Pearce & Plenty, Farringdon Street, 1902. Boxes still survived at this time, underlining all the disadvantages about getting in and out of a seat. Note the policeman, absence of women seated at tables and minimal numbers of bowler-hatted patrons, signifying the lower-middle class

Pearce selected small marble-topped eating tables as an attractive feature imbuing the décor with a refined look. Even this straightforward organisation had to be modified owing to the crush of customers: "There seems to be a continuous rush of trade all the day long," witnessed one reporter, though the noon lunch hour (mid-day to 2 p.m.) accounted for half of the day's total business. A staff of twenty-seven, dispersed throughout the restaurant, took up positions at designated service points: tea and coffee; pork chops and sausages; and sweets. To Farringdon Street, Pearce now moved with his wife, and here, their first two children were born.[42]

Under pressure, as customers queued outside the shop and down the street, Pearce discontinued patrons retrieving their food as a form of self

[42] "Pearce's Coffee Bars"; Ellis, *Pluck*, p. 94.

service, and pioneered the new concept of mass catering.[43] Pearce, while managing director, put authority (and dignity) aside and delved into the crowds at lunch time, following a man with a huge tray who placed steaming puddings on a hot plate—"quicker than a conjurer can produce an egg from his left elbow"—before passing it to Pearce, who in turn "planted a big spoonful of hot potatoes by the side of the pudding, handed it to the customer, and received fivepence in return." Toiling from noon to 2 p.m., Pearce distributed 3000 potato helpings, or 25 per minute.[44] Over the course of the entire day, some 6000 diners patronised the depot, as these working-class restaurants were then called. Capping the substantial but low-priced meal, diners could hail a circulating boy carrying a huge tray shouting "Jam or Plum! Jam or Plum!" and buy a sweet for a penny. To regulate customer flow, the commissioner of police offered Pearce a much-needed policeman to be positioned at the door (Fig. 4.2). Previously, pandemonium had broken out when working-class "printers' devils" had greeted the arrival of socially superior customers with potatoes flung at the intruders.[45] Even in the rush for food, class differences were scarcely forgotten.

How did this Pearce & Plenty depot appear to its ravenous clientele? One reporter succinctly depicted the eating tables. "All is clean, and though many refinements are absent, and there is little or no pretence to decorations or embellishments, the whole is good, comfortable and thoroughly appreciated." Strapped for cash himself, Pearce knew spotless table tops and food outstandingly priced for the money appealed more to his patrons than anything else.[46] He had not forgotten that once he too relished nutritious food to consume on a perpetually empty stomach.

Speed, space, efficiency and economy of effort—these explained how Pearce dealt with throngs of people who ate quickly and departed promptly. "Every available space is utilised and fitted with every appliance that can add to the rapidity and dexterity of serving," testified one amazed reporter. The goal was to manufacture everything that could be easily undertaken

[43] This had the attendant advantage of avoiding waiters whom customers would be obliged to tip, thereby making meals costlier.

[44] *Evidence on Liquor Licensing Laws*, 1897, p. 242; Williams, *Pearce*, pp. 99–100; Bolce, "Foreseeing What the People Want," p. 158.

[45] Williams, *Pearce*, pp. 99–100, 160; Ellis, *Pluck*, p. 95; *Straits Times*, 29 Apr. 1930.

[46] Edward Callow, "City Taverns, Chop and Coffee Houses, & Co.," *City Press*, reprinted in the *Temperance Caterer*, 15 Jan. 1898.

or, as in the case of brewing tea or coffee, introduce machines that facilitated serving patrons hot, freshly brewed beverages.[47]

Rising profits facilitated his entry into the hotelier business at 84 Farringdon Street.[48] The depot itself consisted of two contiguous shops in which Pearce used just the basements and ground floor for feeding patrons. On the upper floors of the building, he built his next enterprise, the Shaftesbury Temperance Hotel (Farringdon Street), heart of the printing and newspaper district just east of Fleet Street. From its opening in 1882, customer enthusiasm resulted in all sixty beds being taken for a shilling. Running a hotel in conjunction with a depot enabled receipts from patrons to cover the rent of the entire building. At the hotel, billed as "the first poor man's 'hotel' in London," sales of sumptuous beef-steak puddings, a delectable meal for 4d., quickly reached a staggering 6000 daily. Here, Pearce staked his claim for fame. "He can be said to have built up his great reputation on a 4d. steak pudding," pronounced one observer.[49]

As Pearce later recalled, he "had struck oil and was making money fast." From this venture, he was saving previously unimagined sums.[50] Now the penny capitalist earned £1000 yearly, an unthinkable sum to the man who had opened a coffee stall where he stood for hours earning profits counted in coppers. Since over two-thirds of Britain's population paid no income taxes—£250 being the threshold—before the 1914 war, Pearce had been transformed, without formal training or education, from the penny capitalist to the middle class. Armed with this prosperity, Pearce found new premises for his family in Clapton, near Congress Hall.[51]

Sharply contrasting with his competitors who cooked food for meals one day and then sold it the next, Pearce prepared food early in the morning, ensuring his customers ate freshly prepared meals. In another departure, Pearce steamed rather than boiled his meat puddings, convinced this retained "the goodness of the meat."[52]

[47] *Refreshment News*, 12 May 1888 and 16 Aug. 1890; "Pearce's Coffee Bars"; Ellis, *Pluck*, p. 92.

[48] Where Pearce obtained the insight or motivation for this departure remains a mystery.

[49] *Evidence on Liquor Licensing Laws*, 1897, pp. 241–44; Ellis, *Pluck*, pp. 93–5; *Straits Times*, 29 April 1930. By 1914, the hotel was selling 12,000 meat puddings daily (Bolce, "Foreseeing What the People Want," p. 158).

[50] Pearce, "Fortune from a Coffee Stall," p. 42; Bolce, "Foreseeing What the People Want," p. 158; Williams, *Pearce*, pp. 103–04, 120, 160; Ellis, *Pluck*, p. 93; *Straits Times*, 29 Apr. 1930.

[51] Williams, *Pearce*, pp. 116–20; Ellis, *Pluck*, p. 96.

[52] Wintle, "London Restaurants," p. 448; *Financial Times*, 26 Aug. 1926; Ellis, *Pluck*, p. 143.

He fed 6000 mostly working-class men, half of them between noon and 2 p.m., a significant step forward compared with his former premises on Aldersgate Street, where daily sales reached a modest 1200. Staff numbers suggest much about his Pearce & Plenty's business, though figures are extraordinarily difficult to find. We know that his staff numbered twenty-seven (including a policeman) in 1884, expanding to fifty after Pearce & Plenty was established in 1886. Throughout his career, Pearce personally interviewed every person he hired. His female staff, employed typically when nineteen to twenty years of age, received between 9s. and 14s. a week, including food.[53] Ample job applicants for waitress underlined that while Pearce & Plenty paid not the highest wages, their prospective employer more than compensated in their eyes for how he dealt with his staff.[54]

The mass food market and Pearce & Plenty arrived together. Selling meals for 3d., or even 2½d., netted miniscule profits. "It was only by feeding multitudes of people that it paid; it was estimated that six people had to be served to earn one penny for the shareholders," Pearce remarked.[55] To Pearce, accustomed to workers' meagre earnings, this constituted decent profit.

Diverse factors explain Pearce's extraordinary success. An enthused *City Press* reporter presented his informed assessment: "We have never been in a house where superior wares are sold, or where, considering the trade done, the cleanliness is more thorough or where the civility of the staff is more marked." Pearce, himself, fully endorsed this assessment but pointed to other factors too as responsible for growing custom. Assiduous attention to the kitchens, where he daily scrutinised the cooking of beef joints and "watched every detail of the operations," prompted his staff to perform at a high level of efficiency as a way of winning his much-sought approval. Pearce projected his personal reputation with his motto—"Quality—economy—dispatch" and on the restaurant walls where he reminded customers as much as staff of his philosophy: "We serve ourselves by serving others best."[56] Shrewd positioning in an increasingly competitive market likewise secured loyal patrons. Pearce & Plenty attracted customers who sought a menu more substantial than at Lockharts and more flavourful than at the ABCs.[57]

[53] *Evidence on Liquor Licensing Laws*, 1897, p. 244.

[54] See pp. 112–13.

[55] Not all of this meagre return, moreover, went to investors; some had to cover the hefty annual rent of £1025. Pearce, "Gutter Hotels."

[56] "Pearce's Coffee Bars"; Clayton, *London's Coffee Houses*, p. 136; Ellis, *Pluck*, p. 131.

[57] *Temperance Caterer*, 9 Nov. 1889; *Evidence on Liquor Licensing Law*, 1897, p. 242; *Coffee Tavern Gazette*, 8 Jan. 1887.

A fitter-up of catering houses offered his personal insights into Pearce's success. "His opinion," he stated, "was that if the best quality of stuff was sold, and as little money as possible laid out in fitting up the houses of the Company, it would pay." For this individual, Pearce had seen off rivals because they had spent extravagantly in fitting up premises. In one case, for example, a caterer had laid out £150 on a showcase; in another, the proprietor had outfitted the kitchen furnishings for £200. Following the fitter upper's philosophy and providing the "best food and drink only" had set Pearce apart from competitors.[58]

Who purchased Pearce & Plenty's food as the catalyst for steadily expanding numbers of depots? Working-class men employed nearby in print shops and newspaper offices as well as porters and packers constituted the backbone of his clientele, while the rest of his patrons defy easy generalisations.[59] His depots, thought Marguerite Williams, were "the resort of shabby 'penny-a-liners' and other impecunious literary aspirants, as well as of 'printers' devils' and men from the streets, who needed much keeping in order." Labour politician Ramsay MacDonald was an inconspicuous regular, as was an aspiring but anonymous publisher who also attained success later in his career. Likewise, some customers prized their anonymity so much that they purchased food and consumed it privately elsewhere. Smoky environments in his establishments, however, discouraged many women from becoming patrons, despite a special smoke room being set aside.[60]

Clerks, members of the lower middle class socially a step above workers, formed no significant part of Pearce's clientele. "Why a clerk of very limited means cannot dine decently for tenpence without being nauseated by bad and half-cooked meat and dirty table-clothes is the crucial problem," wrote the London correspondent of the *Western Morning News.* In a letter to the editor, one clerk provided enlightenment. To generate the custom necessary for sustaining a caterer economically, the clerk must follow the practice of "bolting his food and making room for someone else," precisely the strategy which Pearce's working-class patrons adopted. Instead, the clerk, having ample time, "sits 'twiddling' his fork" over a lengthy one-hour lunch, consuming "so much time in gossiping that the caterer

[58] *Coffee Public-House News*, 1 May 1883.

[59] The south end of Farringdon Street is the east end of Fleet Street with all the printing work of the period.

[60] Williams, *Pearce*, pp. 97–8; Ellis, *Pluck*, p. 94; Bolce, "Foreseeing What the People Want," p. 159; "Pearce's Coffee Bars"; Clayton, *London's Coffee Houses*, p. 136.

cannot get as many customers as he ought to have."[61] Clerks required dinners with a plate of meat, vegetables, bread and pudding for no more than 7d. or 8d., the maximum which their paltry salaries could afford. Caterers themselves had to generate enough profits to defray the cost of high rents in London's business quarters. Despite these constraints, Pearce ventured into this sector of the food market.[62]

In espousing total abstinence, Pearce had much in common with many late Victorians. His diagnosis of the role of drinking in the alcohol industry focused on the drunk and alcoholic as the chief promoters of societal evils. "It is the man who perpetually drinks that brings the great income to the publican; it is not the man that [sic] has a pint of beer with his dinner or supper." In making this assertion, Pearce expressed a pervasive assumption in late-Victorian England, held even by many brewers. Hence, drunkenness prevailed because the prosperity of the "trade," the broad constellation of industries connected with producing, distributing and retailing alcohol, absolutely depended on excess. "The income of the publican is made out of the degradation of the people, not made out of the legitimate trade of supplying food." Though he had strong prejudice against alcohol and loathed licensed victuallers, he did concede that moderate drinkers who consumed a pint or so daily with their supper or dinner meals hardly constituted a problem.[63]

As a total abstainer, Pearce saw no valid reason for drinking alcohol. Licensed victuallers, he argued, did not "supply a need among the public"; they created one. That the pub seldom sold food, presumably because it competed with alcohol purchases, underlined in Pearce's mind the hypocrisy of calling publicans "licensed victuallers." Without drink as a lure or food available, Pearce reasonably felt that workers would instead buy coffee, cake, bread and butter, hopefully from him. Clinching his dislike of publicans was their reaction to his competition. Viewing Pearce's "Gutter Hotel" as a rival, nearby publicans coalesced and submitted a petition urging police to ban him. Others nearby, however, embraced an entirely

[61] London Correspondent, "Bar and Dining Room to Editor," *Western Morning News*, 24 Sept. 1883.

[62] *Coffee Public-House News*, 1 Oct. 1883.

[63] *Evidence on Liquor Licensing Laws*, 1897, pp. 240–44; David W. Gutzke, *Pubs and Progressives: Reinventing the Public House in England, 1896–1960* (Dekalb, IL: University of Northern Illinois Press, 2006), pp. 97–8.

different perspective, defending him as a "public benefactor," and so, he ultimately prevailed.[64]

Like other temperance advocates, Pearce had rudimentary understanding of alcoholism, a concept that had just begun to emerge in these years.[65] However small the amount consumed, he contended, alcohol had one fateful consequence: "Thirst is created." In his testimony in 1897 to a Royal Commission, Pearce pointed to buyers of goods who conducted business in pubs as alcohol's ultimate victims. Over successive transactions, these moderate consumers of alcohol would treat each other with one predicable outcome: respectable men would "come right down to failure and ruin." With utmost candour, Pearce knew his own efforts at supplying non-intoxicants scarcely "made temperance men" of his customers, but at least he had begun the process of having "weaned men from the public-house."[66]

Pearce's aversion to drinking, publicans and alcohol exemplified standard temperance attitudes. In reviling this trinity, teetotallers subscribed to mid-Victorian beliefs in poverty as a result of individual failings of character and self-help as the promoter of social mobility. Bereft of a grasp of alcoholism as a disease and the role of pubs as centres of socialising, which provided temporary escapes from cramped housing accommodation and which facilitated bonding of males at a site replicating the workplace without the rigours of production, teetotallers occupied an entirely separate world from drinkers. Condemnation stood as a substitute for understanding as well as investigation. Convinced drinking was an unmitigated evil, why bother to explore what was patently so obvious?[67]

His association with William Carter profoundly shaped his attitudes to alcohol. For Carter, alcohol constituted "one of the good gifts of life, which a man might use with safety if he trusted in God." Immersed in his own evangelising efforts, he became overworked, and turned to alcohol as a stimulant, ultimately succumbing to alcoholism. "I never needed anyone to talk temperance to me. I was one of the four who carried Carter to the

[64] *Evidence on Liquor Licensing Laws*, 1897, pp. 241, 244; Williams, *Pearce*, p. 165.

[65] James R. McIntosh, "Alcoholism," in Jack S. Blocker, Jr., David M. Fahey, and Ian R. Tyrrell (eds.), *Alcohol and Temperance in Modern History: An International Encyclopedia* (Santa Barbara: ABC-Clio, 2003), 1: 32.

[66] *Evidence on Liquor Licensing Laws*, 1897, pp. 241, 244.

[67] Brown, "Poverty in Late Victorian England," pp. 380–95; Harrison, *Drink*, 1st ed., pp. 357–58.

grave," Pearce recalled vividly but painfully decades later. "He had been to me a sort of god."[68]

For Pearce, Carter's death from alcoholism culminated a series of harrowing exposures to people who found that alcohol had bested them. To make ends meet following the death of her husband, Pearce's mother took in a gentle lodger whose imbibing of alcohol produced unexpectedly disruptive behaviour in which the man would engage in "sweeping all the ornaments off the mantel-shelf." An uncle also temporarily stayed with the family with no better outcome; drinking made him violent, abusive and terrifying. The frightened young John Pearce thus acquired "a vivid horror of drink that has never left him," recorded the Rev. James J. Ellis, Pearce's first biographer. While employed with a builder overly fond of drinking, Pearce joined fellow workers at a pub where at their urgings he consumed spirits and became intoxicated. On returning home, his mother reproved him, and this, together with his vivid recollection of his mother's destructive lodgers, prompted his repudiating consumption of all alcoholic beverages, a stance known in the late-Victorian era as a total abstainer (sometimes called a teetotaller). Had he any subsequent misgivings about his pledge, future work merely reinforced his antipathy to alcohol. The pastry cook from whom Pearce learnt the trade was a heavy drinker whose work as a result suffered badly. This, together with the ambiance of the popular Eagle pub nearby, compelled Pearce to leave, and finally obtain employment with a provision merchant. Establishing himself as a caterer in Farringdon Street with his first Pearce & Plenty depot, opposite Fleet Lane, Pearce renewed an unwelcome acquaintance with drunkenness. On Saturday nights, he recounted, "we had to keep a fellow there, downstairs, in readiness to come and help me to turn out fellows that were tight."[69]

An impoverished background, premature death of his father, minimal education and unremitting struggle to survive—all predisposed Pearce to respond to Carter's humane appeal and, just as importantly, identify with the downtrodden with whom he shared so many experiences.

Born in Hoxton, Pearce was undoubtedly a Cockney, a term which originally meant someone living within the area where one could hear the Bow Church bells, but which later encompassed all working-class Londoners. By birth and upbringing no less than by temperament and

[68] Williams, *Pearce*, pp. 77–8; Ellis, *Pluck*, pp. 44, 53.

[69] Ellis, *Pluck*, pp. 30–1, 45–7, 50; Williams, *Pearce*, p. 163; *Evidence on Liquor Licensing Laws*, 1897, p. 244; *Temperance Caterer*, 15 Aug. 1895.

outlook, he was a Cockney; none of his customers indigenous to London ever mistook him for anything else. "People know I have come from the working class," and, Pearce added, "that is something in my favour with the working man."[70] Having begun "at the bottom rung of the ladder," Pearce had acquired "an accurate knowledge of the wants of the people," most notably their eating habits. His intimate familiarity with his clientele's lives equally conferred enormous insight into late-Victorian social mobility. From this perspective, Pearce intuitively interpreted class relations.[71]

Both his own suffering as a penniless orphan daily confronting hunger and his unremitting struggles to survive motivated him to provide others with what he had been unable easily to find for himself—inexpensive but nourishing, appealing food prepared to his high standards. Much of the impetus for his pioneering role in mass catering derived from this symbiotic relationship with people of his own class, acute, personal awareness of their struggles, and innate sense of their needs. "One of Pearce's holds on the poor has been the realization on their part that he has never lost his interest in the class from which he sprung," journalist Harold Bolce shrewdly perceived. Instinctively sensing what his customers wanted—indeed, anticipating how these wants were changing—propelled Pearce throughout his remarkable career.[72]

Many aspiring coffee public-house philanthropists in the 1870s had failed, and extensive post-mortem accounts in the press had no shortage of explanations, ranging from retailing practices to business philosophy.[73] None, however, viewed selling coffee from the working-class viewpoint, an insight Pearce derived from his own background of precarious employment, meagre wages and unremitting struggles to make ends meet. Workers distrusted the philanthropist dispensing coffee in part because they were receiving what they saw as demeaning charity and in part because this prevented their grumbling about the product's deficiencies. Pearce's own purpose had nothing to do with philanthropy: "I am strongly impressed with the necessity of keeping business entirely separate from philanthropy," a dictum followed throughout his life.[74] Had holding tem-

[70] Pearce, *"Gutter Hotels."*

[71] "Representative Temperance Caterers: John Pearce," *Temperance Caterer*, 30 July 1887.

[72] Bolce, "Foreseeing What the People Want," p. 156.

[73] See pp. 41–3, 46, 48.

[74] *Temperance Caterer*, 15 June 1894; Williams, *Pearce*, p. 172. For further discussion of this point, see p. 92.

perance meetings on his premises been necessary for financial survival, Pearce would undoubtedly have voiced no objections to their presence. He discovered, however, that customers' patronage carried the Farringdon Street depot financially, while temperance meetings "added little to the takings of the house."[75]

Pearce was as convinced of the reasons for his own success as of the irrelevancy of promulgating temperance. His business was to feed the poor and workers, not spearhead temperance campaigns. Nor did he see himself as a Christian philanthropist, the type who had sought 5% dividends while dispensing biblical lessons exhorting greater effort, discipline and self-denial, together with coffee, tea and other light refreshments as part of the coffee-house movement's philosophy. To Pearce, opening coffee shops were, as one biographer put it, "purely a commercial speculation," so personal ambition drove him to succeed.[76]

No philosophy, such as that of coffee public-house promoters prescribing maximum dividends of 5%, entered into his business calculations. Nothing in his outlook, therefore, prevented his pursuing the greatest profits possible, consistent with his basic principles. Although Pearce wanted to be a moral businessman, he thought it also possible to embrace sound business principles. Failure to turn a profit would in the long run benefit no one; earning a return on sales ensured he could continue to supply workingmen with nutritious food entirely divorced from booze. Embracing this attitude made him true to his total abstinence principles.

An avowed teetotaller, he sought to offer workingmen an alternative to frequenting the pub for breakfast and lunch. Pearce regarded men's excessive consumption of alcohol as the product of dirty coffee houses, on the one hand, and pubs and beerhouses that seldom closed, offering nothing to eat or drink on licensed premises save booze, on the other. In giving workers an attractive substitute, he saw himself as contributing to their temperate habits. Victorian temperance advocates labelled such activities as "counter-attractions." "Catering helps people to be temperate," Pearce asserted, a fundamental article of faith held throughout his life. Strikingly different from coffee public-house philanthropists, he assessed the market as a businessman who saw an unfilled need for good, cheap, speedily served food. Pearce drew customers because of his prices, quality and service, not because of commitment to teetotalism. Only 10% of his customers,

[75] "Pearce's Coffee Bars."
[76] Williams, *Pearce*, p. 90.

Pearce estimated, were teetotallers, though a far greater proportion who drank approved of his hostility to workers' drinking during the day.[77]

In insisting on running his business on acceptable commercial doctrines quite apart from philanthropy, was Pearce simply a hard-headed businessman, consumed with maximising profits? Throughout his life, he used his income, knowledge and pronounced social conscience to aid diverse needy people, from those whom Victorians dubbed the residuum, the base of society, such as orphans, widows and the poverty-stricken, to the unemployed, strikers and even relatives of his own employees. His successful business enabled him to act on his strong Christian convictions, assisting those desperate for help.

Never an outspoken temperance advocate, Pearce regarded his feeding of London's multitudes as an important step towards sobriety. In offering workers nourishing but cheap food without alcohol sold as a beverage, he would later proudly claim distinction as one of "the pioneers of this temperance refreshment business."[78]

Advertising became a hallmark of Pearce's commercial ventures, with spectacle central to his approach. It consolidated his reputation among Cockneys as a popular figure whom they could claim as one of their own. His "Gutter Hotel," painted garish red, transformed the colour itself into a form of advertising. Enormous amusement greeted his next attraction, two convex mirrors positioned at the front and the back of the Farringdon Street restaurant with the first giving an exaggerated thin customer (with a sign labelled "Before dining at Pearce and Plenty's"), while the second an equally inflated well-fed one (with a sign reading "After dining at Pearce and Plenty's"). Capitalising on a newly introduced electrical device that kept Greenwich time, Pearce placed a huge clock over his store window, so workers resetting their watches saw his slogan, "Pearce & Plenty," below. In another form of spectacle, his depot on Farringdon Road installed large electric arc lamps outside the exterior entrances and throughout the interior, the first business on the road with this novel fea-

[77] *Ibid.*, pp. 90, 163–64; *Evidence on Liquor Licensing Laws*, 1897, p. 240; John Nelson Tarn, *Five Per Cent Philanthropy: An Account of Housing in Urban Areas between 1840 and 1914* (Cambridge: Cambridge University Press, 1973), pp. 43, 46; Harrison, *Drink*, 1st ed., pp. 297–98.

[78] *Financial Times*, 10 Aug. 1906.

ture. Pearce fully grasped the role of spectacle in salesmanship. So did the *Coffee Public-House News*: "The brilliancy and coolness of the light have proved a great attraction."[79]

There was another powerful factor in Pearce's personality. Aspiring philanthropist and member of the gentry, Sir Edward Sullivan had endeavoured to feed London's dock workers at Limehouse, spending with friends some £5000 on a sophisticated kitchen equipped with the latest appliances. None of the staff, however, proved up to the task of organising low-priced hot meals, placed in a container, for distribution. Such elaborate effort had netted Sullivan and his friends just two shillings daily![80]

Shared interest in feeding the working class would lead to Pearce meeting the baronet, but first, class differences had to be overcome. A friend of Sullivan had recommended contacting Pearce, so the baronet invited Pearce to his home at Palace Gate to discuss difficulties in feeding Limehouse dock workers. This letter aroused considerable consternation, observed Pearce's biographer, Marguerite Williams. Pearce "was not used to receiving letters from men of a class so different from his own." Nor was his wife accustomed to corresponding with a member of England's social elite. Sullivan's letter (and surname) stirred her suspicions of a Fenian plot to inveigle John into a compromising position: "'I wouldn't go near! They're going to shoot you.'" Mindful of her fears, Pearce declining the invitation instead offered to meet the baronet during the week while at work. Nothing was more important to Pearce's subsequent catering career. In Williams' judgement, the meeting brought about "a great change in the life of the 'pioneer caterer.'"[81]

Each wanted what the other could provide: one had money and social standing; the other had expertise and impeccable working-class credentials. Pearce was probably thinking that Sullivan had failed owing to his ignorance of the Limehouse area, but providing good food without drink was a valid approach, so he thought it should be possible to put it right without too much difficulty. In practice, what this meant was that "putting it right" involved drawing more customers to generate a profit, thereby validating Sullivan's strategy as feasible. But Pearce nevertheless hesitated at the previously inconceivable proposal. "You have the idea I have wanted," the baronet reassured Pearce. The idea was straightforward:

[79] *Coffee Public-House News*, 1 Sept. 1885.
[80] Williams, *Pearce*, pp. 116–20.
[81] Ibid., pp. 116–19.

"Extend it." Dumfounded, Pearce protested: "I don't know anything about companies." Sullivan, a quick admirer and soon friend, was not to be dissuaded: "You don't need to." Sullivan promised Pearce his confidence and support. "All you have to do is to go ahead."[82] So long as Sullivan lived, neither man had cause for complaint.

Drawing on this newly formed friendship, the two co-operated in founding a private limited liability company, Pearce's Dining and Refreshment Rooms, in 1886.[83] Philanthropy motivated most of the twenty or thirty investors, "not at all averse to making a profit," who put up £20,000 in capital. Pearce's pioneering efforts were well rewarded: he received £3000 outright in cash as well as 3000 (£1) shares in the new company, giving him 15% of the company stock.[84] Sullivan along with Sir Henry Oldham and J.P. Hurst, a barrister, served as directors, while Pearce himself acted as managing director.[85] That the market needed this enterprise was revealed when the company soon earned impressive dividends of 14% and thereafter "paid large dividends." "I couldn't go fast enough for them," Pearce recalled. Eager capitalists, "they wanted to spend and increase their money."[86] This partnership had wider implications, inspiring schemes of Lord Iveagh and Lord Rowton to furnish inexpensive dwellings and food to the unwashed.[87]

Born into poverty-stricken mid-Victorian Hoxton, Pearce near the end of his life exhibited how his origins affected his tastes, character and behaviour, becoming indispensable facets of his personality. As an impressionable adolescent, he relished attending the Britannia Theatre, its melodramas of good triumphing inevitably over evil furnishing endless joy. Of the world of better theatres, he was wholly ignorant: "the Britannia was his Paradise." Returning to his birthplace with a friend and second

[82] Ibid., pp. 120–21.

[83] This meant it was registered as a joint stock company, but had no stock exchange quotation (*Evidence on Liquor Licensing Laws*, 1897, p. 244).

[84] Ellis, *Pluck*, p. 190; *Times*, 13 May 1905.

[85] Ellis, *Pluck*, p. 130.

[86] In lieu of balance sheets or annual reports, the new company's prosperity must be inferred from the sole figure for the one dividend and these quotations. *Daily Telegraph*, 25 Feb. 1927; "Caterers for the Common People," p. 523; Burnett, *England Eating Out*, p. 118; Wintle, "London Restaurants," p. 447; Williams, *Pearce*, pp. 116, 121, 129, 148; Ellis, *Pluck*, pp.129–30, 190; *Temperance Chronicle*, 30 Apr. and 30 July 1887.

[87] See, p. 114. Edward C. Guinness, Ist Baron Iveagh (Arthur Guinness, Son & Co.). (David W. Gutzke, "Rhetoric and Reality: The Political Influence of British Brewers, 1832–1914," *Parliamentary History* 9 (1990): Appendix 4).

biographer, Marguerite Williams, the nostalgic Pearce recalled: "I don't go to the theatre now, but when I see that the *Sweeney Todd the Barber*, or *Maria Marten*, or the *Murder in the Red Barn*, is to be played at the Elephant [public house], I always get a thrill."[88]

For Pearce, the impact of his early formative experiences evolved as he aged into enduring personality traits. He held firm to his upbringing, always an unrepentantly humble, modest man who remained faithful to his working-class origins. Nor did his respectful, grateful customers ever forget this. Even when he went up-market in catering to the middle classes, as is explored in the next chapter, he never lost his social compass. "The work of feeding the masses is much more interesting for me" than serving food to the "better-class trade," he declared.[89]

[88] Williams, *Pearce*, p. 15.
[89] *Temperance Caterer*, 15 June 1894.

CHAPTER 5

Advent of the Mass Market

Appearance loomed large in the success of any London catering company. At its beginnings, Pearce & Plenty had thrived, combining competent management with low prices and attractive menu items. Of particular importance was the impeccable cleanliness of the premises.[1]

As managing director, Pearce heeded the Board's advice. Within three years, as three more depots became established, Pearce's Refreshment Rooms expanded into a chain. At each "'a brisk trade is being done,'" Pearce proudly informed a reporter. Its four shops, similar in layout and décor, soon were selling 14,000 meals daily primarily to workmen with a smattering of the lower middle class (Tables 5.1 and 5.2). As the number of depots expanded, sales rose commensurately. Before the decade's end, the company had added eight more depots, enabling its serving some 30,000 patrons daily and qualifying it as a major operator of multiples nationally; a decade later, the number reached 40,000.[2] By the mid-1890s, its forty-six shops were selling 65,000 meals to workmen. Within two

[1] *Coffee Tavern Gazette*, 22 Jan. 1887.

[2] "Representative Temperance Caterers: No. 1, Mr. John Pearce," *Temperance Caterer*, 30 July 1887, 23 March 1889 and 15 June 1897; G. Shaw, "The Evolution and Impact of Large-Scale Retailing in Britain," in John Benson and Gareth Shaw (eds.) *The Retailing Industry*, vol. 2: *The Coming of the Mass Market, 1800–1945* (London: I.B. Tauris, 1999), p. 251. In mass market national sales, Pearce's Refreshment Rooms easily outstripped the Liverpool British Workman Public House Co, the biggest and oldest of the coffee tavern companies. Compared with the 25,000 meals daily sold in the latter's sixty-two houses

D. W. Gutzke, *John Pearce and the Rise of the Mass Food Market in London, 1870–1930*, https://doi.org/10.1007/978-3-030-27095-7_5

Table 5.1 John Pearce's mass catering, 1879–1905

	P&P	*P&P hotels*	*BTT*	*BTT hotels*	*Total depots*	*Employees*	*Capital*
1879	–		–		1[a]	15	
1882	–	1	–		2[b]	15	
1887	4	1	–		4		£20,000
1889	11	3			11	306	
1896	22	12	24	2	46		£39,400
1897	23	12	27	2	50	800	
1898	23	14	29	2	52	900	£300,000
1899	24		33				
1901					74		
1902	26		50		76		
1905	26		58		84	1500	

Source: Williams, *Pearce*, pp. 159, 167, 169; Bolce, "Foreseeing What the People Want," p. 155; Wintle, "London Restaurants," pp. 447–48; "Caterers for the Common People," p. 523; John Pearce, "A Fortune from a Coffee Stall: The Romance of 'Pearce and Plenty,'" *Fortunes Made in Business: Life Struggles of Successful People* (London: Harmsworth Brothers, 1901), p. 43; Kathleen Heasman, *Evangelicals in Action: An Appraisal of their Social Work in the Victorian Era* (London: Geoffrey Bles, 1962), p. 142; *Temperance Caterer*, 30 July 1887, 23 March 1889, 10 Aug. and 15 June 1894, 15 Aug. 1898, 15 May 1901, 15 June 1903, 15 Feb. 1904, and 15 Sept. 1908; Pearce, "Gutter," *Pearson's Weekly*, 5 Sept. 1914; "Pearce," *British Journal of Catering*, p. 9; *Evidence on Liquor Licensing Laws*, 1898, pp. 241–42; *Daily Mail*, 19 June 1902; *Financial Times*, 11 May 1901 and 9 May 1905; Ellis, *Pluck*, p. 93; *South London Chronicle*, 26 May 1905

[a]Aldersgate Street
[b]Farringdon Street

decades, the company had established twenty-six Pearce & Plenty "depots" throughout central London.[3]

At Farringdon Street, two bakeries centralised the preparation of bread and pastry for all the depots, cutting costs as an indirect means of increasing profits. As one journalist concluded, centralisation and in-house food as well as beverage preparation made the firm extremely competitive in a

(1887), Pearce's dispensed 30,000 meals daily in its 11 depots (1889) ("Representative Temperance Caterers: No. 2, Mr. W.H. Peskett," *Temperance Caterer*, 3 Sept. 1887).

[3]"Caterers for the Common People," *Review of Reviews* 14 (1896): 523; John Burnett, *England Eating Out: A Social History of Eating Out in England from 1830 to the Present* (London: Pearson, 2004), p. 118; W.J. Wintle, "Round the London Restaurants," *Windsor Magazine* 4 (1896): 447; Rev. James J. Ellis, *Pluck, Patience and Power: The Life Story of John Pearce of "Pearce and Plenty"* (London: H.R. Allenson, [1910]), pp. 130, 190; Anthony Clayton, *London's Coffee Houses: A Stimulating Story* (London: Historical Publications, 2003), p. 136; Marguerite Williams, *John Pearce: The Man Who Played the Game* (London: Religious Tract Society, 1928), p. 121; *Temperance Caterer*, 30 July 1887.

business with small profit margins.[4] One amazed reporter recorded his impression of the lunchtime hour at one of the new depots: "At one o'clock the whole energy of the house is taxed to meet the hungry mortals who swarm the stairs, fill the benches and pour themselves like a wave of ink over the many floors."[5] Another reporter regarded the menu—"the most varied yet publicly exhibited in London"—as especially noteworthy.[6]

From the start the new company's floatation was successful. Shareholders received a 14% dividend, quite impressive in the mid-1880s.[7] Pearce had an intuitive sense of changing market conditions, while his directors warily watched a market filled with failed new catering companies. This owed nothing to lack of capital. Since eighteen catering companies had been formed before the Royal Commission on Liquor Licensing met in 1897, Pearce noted that "London is very well provided for now during the last ten years" with working-class catering.[8]

By the late 1880s, Pearce came to see that with the market, at least in the City, saturated with his depots, he ought to go upmarket catering to a higher social stratum, but class consciousness made the pronounced proletarian Pearce & Plenty's unsuitable for such a socially diverse clientele (Fig. 4.2). Of this fact Pearce had convincing anecdotal evidence. An erstwhile patron, outfitted in a frock coat and his head adorned with a silk hat, had improved his lot in life, but not so much as to permit spending money more freely on food. Having joined the petty bourgeois as a black-coated worker, he then had avoided Pearce & Plenty, lest he embarrassingly meet employees of his firm. Though he could ill-afford paying twice as much for tea elsewhere, he had no other alternative as he informed Pearce: "I must not associate with my [social] inferiors." Another class-conscious diner, a journalist, remarked that "I always send [out] to Pearce and Plenty for my dinner." For him, the reason was obvious: "I daren't be seen there, but there's no better food in the City, and it's so cheap." Another man told Pearce that he had missed him. "Look here," the erstwhile customer con-

[4] Wintle, "London Restaurants," p. 448; *Financial Times*, 26 Aug. 1926; Ellis, *Pluck*, p. 143; S. J. Adair Fitz-Gerald, "Chats with Caterers: John Pearce," *Caterer and Hotel-Keepers' Gazette*, 16 Jan. 1905; *Temperance Caterer*, 15 June 1897; *Refreshment News*, 15 July 1889.

[5] "Mr. John Pearce: The Man and His Work," *British Journal of Catering* 3 (15 July 1889): 9.

[6] *Refreshment News*, 5 May 1888.

[7] Williams, *Pearce*, p. 148.

[8] *Financial Times*, 1 Nov. 1889; *Evidence of the Royal Commission on Liquor Licensing Laws*, 1898, 36 (Cmnd. 8694), p. 243.

fided, "I could do with coming there all right, but I've been promoted, and our packers come to you."[9]

Pearce thought his original customers had developed more exacting and delicate tastes, but surely a more compelling explanation derived from changes in the nature of work and who primarily undertook it. People doing manual labour—construction work on new buildings or refurbishing existing ones, or print work which involved moving the metal around or just running a linotype machine—remained a substantial part of the City work force, but did not increase at all quickly. They were likely to remain faithful to Pearce & Plenty, forming the core of his clientele. But clerical workers, especially female ones, expanded at a distinctly faster pace, so had no need for one-half pound of beef pudding or other substantial foods to keep one going at manual labour. This leads to the hypothesis that Pearce's move upmarket with the British Tea Table Company (BTT) did well out of the new clerical workers who found that a ham sandwich and a cup of tea easily sustained them throughout the day.[10]

Indeed, these bourgeois workers formed the pivotal group motivating market changes in the City. In the half century from 1861, national numbers of female office workers rose by 400 times, while their male counterparts increased five-fold. So impressed was historian Lee Holcombe that he argued "the advent of women clerks as a new class of cheap but efficient workers" fostered a "revolution" in clerical work. By World War I, female clerks ranked third behind shop assistants and teachers as the leading groups employing most middle-class women in Britain.[11]

Several key skills—shorthand and typewriting—together with the invention of the telephone, massively transformed the nature of work. Of these the typewriter—made more generally available in Britain from 1882—most directly affected employment because it mechanised office work. An influx primarily of middle-class women needing accessible,

[9] Harold Bolce, "Foreseeing What the People Want: How Initiative, Imagination and a Sense of Value Created an Industry from an Idea," *System* 26 (1914): 160; Williams, *Pearce*, pp. 148–49; Ellis, *Pluck*, pp. 138–40; *Refreshment News*, 11 Jan. 1890; [Interview with John Pearce], "Fifty Years of Catering," *Daily News*, 18 Oct. 1911.

[10] I want to thank Trevor Lloyd for the interpretation on which this paragraph and the following one are based.

[11] Lee Holcombe, *Victorian Ladies at Work: Middle-Class Working Women in England and Wales, 1850–1914* (Newton Abbot: David & Charles, 1973), p. 141.

gender-neutral, respectable and inexpensive places to dine propelled Lyons and the ABC into the forefront of changes in dining for light refreshments.[12]

In response to what he perceived as rising aspirations of customers eager to enjoy social mobility, Pearce decided to move upmarket with a new chain of outlets, significantly called restaurants, not depots. His titled backers baulked at this proposal, fearful that "he would lose caste with the poor whose millions of mites were making them all rich." "Don't get proud" warned Sullivan as chairman of the company. "Let's have all we can of a good thing," he urged his managing director. Pearce's rejoinder was that though he remained unchanged, "the social position of thousands of his old customers had changed for the better." Adopting a conciliatory tone, Pearce implored Sullivan: "Let me have one shop. It will not cost much to fit it up. If it fails we can make it into a Pearce and Plenty."[13]

At what point did Pearce perceive other crucial changes in the catering market? The press might have offered him guidance, though whether he read "The Coffee Tavern Movement in London" by A. Jepson (director of the London Coffee Tavern Co.) is unknown. Published in the *Supplement* to the *Temperance Caterer* in 1887, Jepson's article made the telling point that few coffee public houses catered to clerks and other lower-middle-class workers. Coffee taverns and ABC depots served as substitutes. Pearce himself, some years later, pointed to increasing distances London workers had to commute between home and work as a key factor fostering demand for food.[14] Again, John Pearce's reading of marketing trends was more accurate than his understanding of the underlying causes.

Directors struck a shrewd compromise: Pearce could establish one place as an experiment at 28–29 Aldersgate Street, a location wholly unaccustomed to the tea table restaurant he envisaged opening. One of Pearce's sons, an artist, would design the premises with more refined décor and furnishings, denoting higher social status than the typical Pearce & Plenty depots. From the outset, with the opening of this first tea table restaurant in 1892, Pearce continued to display his flair for advertising. In the

[12] Gladys Carnaffan, "Commercial Education and the Female Office Worker," in Gregory Anderson (ed.), *The White-Blouse Revolution: Female Office Workers Since 1870* (Manchester: Manchester University Press, 1988), pp. 78–80, 82; Holcombe, *Ladies at Work*, pp. 142–44.

[13] Ellis, *Pluck*, pp. 139–40.

[14] A. Jepson, "The Coffee Tavern Movement in London," *Supplement* to the *Temperance Caterer*, 10 Sept. 1887; *Temperance Caterer*, 15 June 1894.

front, visible from some distance, "was suspended a large table of the bamboo pattern, set ready with teapot, cups and saucers."[15] "Its success was instantaneous," wrote journalist Harold Bolce. Sullivan exclaimed: "It is the very thing … that is wanted." An overwhelmed deputy chairman J.P. Hurst bestowed on Pearce the ultimate accolade, dubbing him "the Spiers and Pond of the Masses." What the latter did for the propertied classes, he contended, Pearce had done for workers.[16]

Untrained though he was, his uncanny insight into what potential customers would want stunning even his own directors as well as close friends, Pearce believed in himself enough to press his Board into adopting a new direction altogether. Not surprisingly, the existing profits on Pearce & Plenty depots remained encouraging and overall sales continued rising. Early in 1891 the company had opened another Pearce & Plenty depot outside the City on Tottenham Court Road, earning impressive returns with 6800 customers daily, compared with not quite 2500 average customer sales at existing outlets. Contributing to success was Pearce's relentless pursuit of efficiency. "Every available space is utilized and fitted with every appliance that can add to the rapidity and dexterity of servicing," the *Refreshment News* enthused.[17]

Pearce's epiphany led to the forming of a separate firm, the British Tea Table Company (BTTC), with a modest capital of £39,400 in 1892. Aimed at city clerks and other clerical workers, what advertisements called "a better class of customers," it specialised in summer dishes of eggs on toast and ham salad, while heartier winter fare featured soup, chops and steaks. Here, Pearce moved socially upwards to cater to individuals previously outside his standard working-class base, with "superior arrangements to Pearce & Plenty" offered without higher prices.[18] His most recent biographer succinctly described what transformation the BTT had wrought: "It suited the man who couldn't sit down with the bricklayer and the carman (sic)." Hurst contrasted the clientele of the two companies in this revealing way: "Patrons of the BTT room wore black coats and top hats, while

[15] *Temperance Caterer*, 15 Oct. 1892; Ellis, *Pluck*, p. 140.

[16] Bolce, "Foreseeing What the People Want," p. 160; Williams, *Pearce*, pp. 148–49; Ellis, *Pluck*, pp. 138–41; *Refreshment News*, 11 Jan. 1890. For Spiers and Pond, see Bryan Morgan, "A Short History of Spiers and Pond," in Bryan Morgan, *Express Journal, 1864–1964: A Centenary History of the Express Dairy Company Limited* (London: Newman Neame, 1964), pp. 134–35.

[17] *Refreshment News*, 16 Aug. 1890 and 14 March 1891.

[18] For lunch, Pearce & Plenty patrons spent 3d. eating two eggs with a mug of cocoa during winter, while at dinner, they laid out 6d., consuming steak pudding and potatoes (*Evidence of the Royal Commission on Liquor Licensing Laws*, 1898, 36 (Cmnd. 8694), p. 243).

"Pearce and Plenty's" customers revelled in fustian and corduroys." Essentially, Pearce had opened "a fashionable shop in that neighbourhood." Given this more upmarket clientele, Pearce knew he must avoid his own name because of Pearce & Plenty's association with working-class customers, lest potential lower-middle patrons be deterred. "We would not get the clerk in if Pearce's was put on over the door," he later revealed to the Royal Commission on Liquor Licensing Laws, disclosing his shrewd understanding of class relations.[19]

Soon Pearce had serious competition. J. Lyons & Co. expanded its catering business with teashops from 1894, long after the mass food market had "revolutionised" catering in London. Whether in establishing multiple branches, selling massive numbers of meals, generating a working-class clientele or featuring substantial hot meals with meat, John Pearce had unquestionably assumed the pioneering role as the City's mass caterer. By the time Lyons opened its first teashop, Pearce and his companies were

Table 5.2 John Pearce's daily meal sales, 1879–1908

	P & P	*Daily sales*	*BTT*	*Daily sales*	*Total daily customers*
1879	–		–		600
1883	–	6000	–		6000
1887	4	14,000	–		14,000
1889	11	30,000	–	–	30,000
1894			18		30,000–40,000
1896	22	50,000	24	15,000	65,000
1898	23		29		70,000
1903					80,000
1904	26	40,000			
1905					120,000
1908					33,000

Source: Williams, *Pearce*, pp. 159, 167, 169; Bolce, "Foreseeing What the People Want," p. 155; Wintle, "London Restaurants," pp. 447–48; "Caterers for the Common People," p. 523; John Pearce, "A Fortune from a Coffee Stall: The Romance of 'Pearce and Plenty,'" *Fortunes Made in Business: Life Struggles of Successful People* (London: Harmsworth Brothers, 1901), p. 43; Kathleen Heasman, *Evangelicals in Action: An Appraisal of their Social Work in the Victorian Era* (London: Geoffrey Bles, 1962), p. 142; *Temperance Caterer*, 30 July 1887, 23 March 1889, 10 Aug. and 15 June 1894, 15 Aug. 1898, 15 May 1901, 15 June 1903, 15 Feb. 1904, and 15 Sept. 1908; Pearce, "Gutter," *Pearson's Weekly*, 5 Sept. 1914; "Pearce," *British Journal of Catering*, p. 9; *Evidence on Liquor Licensing Laws*, 1898, pp. 241–42; *Daily Mail*, 19 June 1902; *Financial Times*, 11 May 1901 and 9 May 1905; Ellis, *Pluck*, p. 93; *South London Chronicle*, 26 May 1905

[19] *Daily Mail*, 17 Nov. 1900; *Evidence on Liquor Licensing Laws*, pp. 241–42.

selling 30,000–40,000 meals daily in the City, primarily to workers but with growing numbers of the lower middle-classes (Table 5.2).[20]

Like board executives at Pearce & Plenty, those at Lyons were unaware of how economic changes had transformed London through the mass market. According to Joseph Lyons in a 1904 interview, "Not only were the so-called restaurants dirty, but the table cloths were soiled and greasy and the waiters wore unclean shirts and aprons, and their general appearance was slovenly." This quotation strongly suggests that Lyons proprietors had a mistaken idea of the competition, later endorsed by the official company historian, Peter Bird, who, in *The First Food Empire: A History of J. Lyons & Co.*, depicts London's late-Victorian catering world as divided broadly but rather simplistically into two periods: the bleak pre-Lyons years of disgusting catering and the Lyons era of teashops conferring enlightened culinary civilisation. Lyons' competitors, so went the official Lyons interpretation, catered exclusively to just the working class: they were amateurs, inept and unwisely preoccupied with minimising costs, wholly incapable of attracting new clerical workers of the lower middle classes. In seeking to expand their markets, catering companies had failed dismally in whatever direction one might look—food, service, menus, prices and presentation. Into this untapped market, according to Peter Bird, came Lyons in 1894, fostering a "Teashop Revolution" in which it offered light refreshments of better quality at lower cost to a neglected group—the lower middle classes—than had hitherto prevailed.[21]

Lyons' portrayal of catering companies was in fact anachronistic. Recalling the late 1870s and early 1880s, not the late 1880s and early 1890s, as Bird would have it, Edward Callow thought Lockharts' City depots "all were ghastly failures financially and practically." One reason for the company's inability to thrive owed to its serving coffee and cocoa of strength and flavour no different than the typical "coffee tavern standard."[22] Soon taken over by Winthrop & Baker, striking for its enamelled and white-lettered signboard advertising, Lockharts' new management turned the firm around. Of Lockharts, the *Coffee Tavern Gazette* wrote in 1887: its "secret of success lies ... mainly in giving really excellent and well-cooked provisions for the money." In these same years, Charles Booth, chronicler of London's late-Victorian poor, characterised Lockharts as "the best and

[20] See pp. 11–16 for further discussion of this point.

[21] Peter Bird, *The First Food Empire: A History of J. Lyons & Co.* (Chichester: Phillimore & Co., 2000), p. 38.

[22] Edward Callow, "City Taverns, Chop and Coffee Houses, & C.," *City Press*, reproduced in the *Temperance Caterer*, 15 Jan. 1898; *Coffee Public-House News*, 1 May 1883.

most numerous" of the chain catering companies. Prosperity continued into the 1890s, its gross profits rising tenfold and dividends fluctuating between 7% and 12%, both respectable given the competitive catering market. Lyons' entry into the City had thus not cast the gloom over one of London's major catering firms as represented by the company itself.[23]

Different interpretations have been advanced for Lyons' "teashop revolution" in the 1890s, focusing chiefly on what patrons were being offered—superior ambience, wider selection of light refreshments and competitively priced Lyons food. Regardless of these attractions, demand as a central factor is entirely overlooked. In fact, growing numbers of clerical workers—predominantly females—provided the impetus for Lyons' introduction of its teashops.[24]

Seen as part of a wider context, Lyons' teashops marked an evolutionary first stage as prelude to preparing for the company's grander plans, the opening of bigger and more profitable restaurants, built on a truly palatial scale, spanning the class divides in dining. In this sense, Lyons' teashops served as a testing ground for reconfiguring the dining habits of Londoners.[25]

Women assumed a vital role initially in this process. According to the *Temperance Caterer*, "There is no refuge for the girl who wants her dinner out, and rather than face the ordeal of going into a restaurant full of men, she has recourse to an 'ABC' or some kindred eating place, where she cannot possibly get a satisfying hot meal."[26]

Even the ABC, "an essentially feminine institution," made little headway in appealing to women in the City. Public space for women diners became highly contested. Editor Joseph Bentley in the *Temperance Caterer*

[23] Charles Booth, "Pubs and Cocoa Rooms," *Life and Labour of the People in London*, vol. 1 (London: Williams and Norgate, 1889), p. 116; Winskill and Thomas, "British Workman Public Houses," *Temperance Movement in Liverpool*, p. 75; B.F. Babcock, "The Liverpool Cocoa Rooms," *Methodist Temperance Magazine* 9 (1876): 221–23; Heasman, *Evangelicals in Action*, pp. 142–43; *Temperance Caterer*, 3 Nov. 1888; *Coffee Tavern Gazette*, 8 Jan. 1887; *Edinburgh Evening News*, 17 June 1897; *Economist*, 21 May 1898, and 26–27 May 1899.

[24] See pp. 60, 100 for demand as a factor. For an overview, see Anna Davin, "City Girls: Young Women, New Employment, and the City, London, 1880–1910," in Mary Jo Maynes, Birgitte Søland and Chirstina Benninghaus (eds.), *Secret Gardens, Satanic Mills: Placing Girls in European History, 1750–1960* (Bloomington: Indiana University Press, 2005), pp. 209–23.

[25] See Bird, *Lyons*, pp. 47–55.

[26] *Temperance Caterer*, 15 Nov. 1900; Lynne Walker, "Vistas of Pleasure: Women Consumers of Urban Space in the West End of London, 1850–1900," in Clarissa Campbell Orr (ed.), *Women in the Victorian Art World* (Manchester: Manchester University Press, 1995), p. 79.

pointed to some popular restaurants in which proprietors reserved tables just for women. Such matters became so serious that "in certain parts of the City woman has so crowded man out at his luncheon hour that he has had to be protected by having tables marked 'for gentlemen only.'" Writing to the paper, an anonymous male correspondent grumbled at how women commandeered the best seats near the door, discouraging men looking in for available seats from entering. The correspondent continued his litany of complaints, stressing "a *clientele* of women does not pay" because they spent less on meals than men did. Mindful of this gender difference, restaurateurs "set apart, in a prominent place, tables for men only."[27] Expanding numbers of female clerical workers who became conspicuous diners in the square mile just before the war thus engendered new attitudes towards women as suitable patrons.

But Lyons was scarcely alone in catering to women from the early 1890s. Refreshment rooms in large department stores, such as Liberty and Whiteley's, accommodated females, as did ABC shops, especially in Bond, Regent and Oxford Streets and around Piccadilly. The newly opened ABC's Pall Mall shop in 1898 offered women separate coffee and smoking rooms. "Ladies can and do go to these restaurants without reproach; their presence has made a great alteration; there is always an atmosphere of cheerfulness, if not of exhilaration," wrote Walter Besant. Low prices, appetising food and exceptional service, all drew women patrons.[28]

Peter Bird, in contrast, looks to external factors, particularly weak competitors, as a major factor in the "teashop revolution." Dismal, boring menus, inferior food, inept presentation and prices prohibitively high that excluded the growing lower-middle classes concentrated among office workers—these he cites as placing Lyons' rivals at distinct commercial disadvantages. Explosive growth of Lyons' teashops crested in 1910, when the company opened twenty-four new establishments, nineteen of them in London. "Increasingly challenged by variety and excellence of lunchtime choices" at Lyons' teashops, both Pearce & Plenty and Lockharts—specialists in working-class breakfasts and dinners—struggled to protect their market share,

[27] *Temperance Caterer*, 15 Oct. 1910; Mrs. C.S. Paul, "Lunch for Ladies in London," *Hearth & Home* No. 578 (12 June 1902): 274; Dora Greenwell McChesney, "The World of the ABC," *Daily Mail*, 15 Apr. 1903. Similar hostility to women encroaching on traditional male space occurred in the West End ("Female Poaching on Male Preserves," *Westminster Review* 129 (1888): 293).

[28] Paul, "Lunch for Ladies," p. 274; *Refreshment News*, 30 Aug. 1890; *Temperance Caterer*, 15 Apr. 1898.

thinks Bird. Lyons' success in attracting an untapped market, working-class women, a segment of the market to which Pearce & Plenty depots had not appealed, perhaps because of their smoky environments, drove in part this soaring expansion.[29]

Under-performing catering companies as an explanation for Lyons' "teashop revolution," however, sit oddly with the facts. For Slaters, business soared in the 1890s: turnover rose five-fold as did profits, capital tripled and dividends averaged 11–12%. This heady expansion caused a boom in new depots, which increased from one to thirty-eight. "The management had been asked to open establishments in almost every quarter of London," enthused Chairman John Crowle in 1900.[30] Far from the ABC struggling with unpopularity, its dividends reached 30% and even 40% early in the 1890s. In the decade 1896–1905, the ABC declared astonishing total dividends of 387.5%. Notwithstanding Lyons' teashops appearing throughout London, the ABC saw off this competition, serving 1,579,240 more customers in 1905 than in the previous year.[31]

Bird's portrayal of class is likewise flawed, blurring differences between working- and lower-middle-class customers. He misrepresents John Pearce's coffee stalls as "restaurants" having a lower-middle-class clientele in the 1870s. Neither statement was true. Only unfamiliarity with surviving materials of these firms could explain Bird's appraisal. Not until Pearce went upmarket with the British Tea Table in 1892 would its newly established "restaurants" cater primarily to the lower middle class with substantial meals, depending on the season (Tables 5.1 and 5.2).[32] Lockharts and the ABC were likewise targeting such a clientele, though admittedly their menus were limited to light refreshments.[33]

By appealing to a broader sector of the public wanting better food offered at "value for money," on the one hand, and instituting economies of scale with its teashops, on the other, Lyons changed catering in the

[29] Bird, *Lyons*, pp. 37, 42; Burnett, *England Eats Out*, p. 124.

[30] *Financial Times*, 12 June 1900 and 1 Dec. 1902.

[31] Ibid., 7 Nov. 1905; *Temperance Caterer*, 15 Jan. 1909.

[32] Bird, *Lyons*, p. 38. Patrons could select heavier meat meals in the winter.

[33] *Coffee Tavern Gazette*, 7 Aug. 1886 and 8 Jan. 1887; *Temperance Caterer*, 15 June 1901 and 15 June 1902; Bird, *Lyons*, p. 37–8. See, pp. 11–14. Ye Mecca, for example, served just sandwiches, buns and pastry.

light refreshment sector, though not to the extent Bird suggests.[34] A better perspective for analysis would be the Edwardian era in which Lyons' weathered one of the worst catering crises since the mass market's arrival far better than its competitors as a result of its greater market diversity, deeper financial pockets, broader network of stores and concentrated nexus of supplies.

It was not so much Lyons' teashops as changes in the catering market that prompted Pearce to reappraise his strategy. Between 1896 and 1904, Pearce & Plenty sales began slumping badly and falling by 20%, while new BTT outlets apparently steadily grew. The geographic dispersal of the branches widened. In 1895, at Tottenham Court Road and Oxford Street, miles from the City, the company opened a new restaurant. By the end of this period, BTT restaurants were responsible for nearly half of the overall total sales. Between 1898 and 1902, the number of BTT outlets soared from fifty-two to seventy-six, while Pearce & Plenty restaurants relatively declined as a proportion of the whole as depots grew from twenty-three to twenty-six. By 1902, BTT restaurants accounted for two-thirds of the company's establishments (Tables 5.1 and 5.2).[35]

Had Pearce not shown such remarkable perspicacity as managing director into how the market was evolving, the BTT's performance would have faltered severely. In 1898–1899, the company opened seven new depots, just one of them a Pearce & Plenty outlet. In the forthcoming Edwardian debate among catering companies on the respective roles of general managers versus managing directors, Pearce's foresight deserved recognition as the indisputable sage of the thrifty working-class catering market for those who qualified as knowledgeable observers.[36] Pearce's personality, popularity and reputation, however, carried far more weight with small and modest investors than with huge shareholders whose voting power could (when combined with some smaller shareholders) counter whatever sentiment Pearce might mobilise at shareholder meetings to impose the Board's views, policies and decisions on a managing director.

At the BTT's twenty-four houses, 15,000 meals were consumed daily, a modest number compared with Pearce & Plenty because customers

[34] Bird, *Lyons,* p. 38.

[35] Sales at BTT restaurants must be inferred from the company's overall figures and the respective numbers of outlets for the Pearce & Plenty and the BTT. *Temperance Caterer*, 15 Oct. 1895.

[36] *Financial Times*, 25 May 1899.

came from a higher social class, but patrons ate lighter meals than those at Pearce & Plenty.[37] Cumulatively, the two private companies did an enormous trade, declaring dividends of 5%, 20%, 30% and 10% in the years 1894–1897, the only ones for which such figures survive, vindicating Pearce's perceptive understanding of the catering market.[38] Profits likewise soared: the £9500 earned in 1893 more than doubled within two years, and topped £25,000 in 1896.[39]

Amid growing competitive pressures, BTT depots were carefully positioned, offering customers food comparable in quality to competitors but at half the price. This meant, of course, that BTT profits would not compete with their bigger rivals, but the company had two offsetting assets. As the managing director of BTT restaurants, Pearce came to appreciate the most important: "it was doubly difficult for others to compete with them." Pearce's colleague, J.P. Hurst, the company chairman, identified the second: "The receipts from the hotels attached to the depots kept up in a miraculously steady way."[40]

Pearce now had the support of Sullivan and other leading Board members, such as Lord Iveagh (representing the Guinness brewery in the House of Lords) and Colonel Sir Henry Oldham, who together with some 1500 others invested £300,000 in a new company, (confusingly named) the British Tea Table Co., merging the existing British Tea Table Co. and Pearce's Dining & Refreshment Rooms. Investors bought both companies for £226,750 in 1897, creating a new company, the British Tea Table Company, with almost £60,000 of capital. Again the newly formed concern prospered, its daily meal sales topping 70,000 at twenty-nine restaurants (Tables 5.1 and 5.2).[41]

[37] Wintle, "London Restaurants," p. 448.

[38] *Temperance Caterer*, 15 June 1898. Dividends ultimately reached 35% (*Times*, 31 May 1910).

[39] *Financial Report of Auditors for Pearce's Dining and Refreshment Rooms and British Tea Table Co., 15 June 1897, Daily Mail*, 16 June 1897.

[40] *Morning Post*, 25 May 1898; *Financial Times*, 25 May 1899; *Temperance Caterer*, 15 June 1898.

[41] *Financial Report of Auditors for Pearce's Dining and Refreshment Rooms and British Tea Table Co.*, 15 June 1897, *Daily Mail*, 16 June 1897; *Report by the Comptroller of the Companies Department for the Year Ending 31 Dec. 1909*, Board of Trade, p. 16; Heasman, *Evangelicals in Action*, p. 142; Fitz-Gerald, "John Pearce"; Burnett, *England Eats Out*, pp. 117–18; *Evidence on Liquor Licensing Laws*, p. 240; Williams, *Pearce*, pp. 153–54; Bolce, "Foreseeing What the People Want," p. 160.

Each company, however, retained its own separate public identity: on windows of the British Tea Table restaurants appeared "BTT," while the original Pearce depots continued with their "Pearce & Plenty" name. With this infusion of money, rapid growth soon permitted the opening of fifty-eight restaurants. Replicating the success of the first shop, the BTT targeted "a superior class of customer at the lowest possible rates" and for the first time drew substantial numbers of "young people of both sexes in business ... people shopping, and visitors to London" whose patronage generated staggering dividends of 35%. In the company prospectus, Pearce boasted that the BTT "combined the best characteristic of the London 'bread shop' with those of the Paris Restaurant Duval." The BTT predominately catered to the lunchtime trade, with business much smaller for mid-afternoon tea, even when augmented with young people of both sexes as well as female customers shopping in nearby districts.[42]

Of the new shareholders, Pearce qualified as a major investor, holding some 7000–8000 shares, but the company's greater capital meant that the new votes radically diluted his influence, placing him indeed at the mercy of principal shareholders. In the original company, Pearce held 3000 shares, just over 7.5% of the capital, whereas in the newly floated, more substantial company, his 8000 shares represented merely 2.7% of the shareholdings. Unbeknownst to him, the influx of shareholders with bigger investments would shift decisively the locus of power from Pearce as the managing director to the Board of Directors as a whole.

Based primarily in the City of London, the company also had depots as far north as Upper Street, Islington. Depots especially dotted the St. Pancras borough: Euston/King's Cross and Holborn areas accounted for twelve depots. For shoppers, the company had restaurants on Oxford/Bond Streets, Charing Cross/New Oxford Street and Tottenham Court Road. Elsewhere outlets were overwhelmingly in working-class neighbourhoods. Some indication of the new BTT's size can be inferred from its fifty-six cafés, running its own bakeries as well as confectionery and mineral water departments.[43] In the ensuing years, restaurants became dispersed between Oxford Street and New Cut, broadening the firm's "appeals to a very wide range of customers."[44]

[42] *Times*, 31 May 1910; *Evidence on Liquor Licensing Laws*, p. 244.

[43] *British Tea Table Depots, 1908* (London: BTTC, 1908); Burnett, *England Eats Out*, p. 118.

[44] *Financial Times*, 9 May 1905.

Both the type of London rentals and the business undertaken favoured BTT depots over those of Pearce & Plenty. BTT restaurants required less space, so the company rented the shop and basement or shop and first floor as adequate for its needs, whereas Pearce & Plenty restaurants—dependent on quick, large-scale turnover of customers—required the whole building for doing business.[45]

Pearce's enterprises exemplified the new concept of mass catering. At his first chain, Pearce & Plenty, he centralised baking at the Farringdon Street depot, where forty bakers prepared food. Eight vast steam ovens occupied the top of the house as the pudding kitchen. To visitors, the scene represented "a living factory composed of industrious bees." From 6 a.m., bakers began their daily routine of preparing 1500 beef-steak puddings, together with hundreds of jam and plum puddings. Separate floors were devoted to preparing vegetables and joints for grilling. Pearce & Plenty ran other bakeries for cooking bread and pastry and elsewhere bottled its own mineral waters, allowing the firm to cut costs and produce items as cheaply as possible. Eventually, the company centralised these functions (and later added a laundry) for Pearce & Plenty outlets, acquiring two attached buildings on Farringdon Road, joining four others there to act as firm headquarters. To cope with expanding numbers of restaurants in the City, Pearce had eleven vans dispatch food to them, supplying some 40,000 meals daily.[46] Erratic control of hot foods at BTT houses, however, prompted the company to centralise cooking at one location, where food was placed in sealed jars before being immersed in hot water and then dispatched to restaurants. As a result, the firm could expand considerably its offerings of hot foods, an innovation to which the public responded enthusiastically.[47]

Vigilantly overseeing another vital dimension of the company, Pearce undertook to purchase all of its chief goods.[48] Because he monopolised this vital activity while managing director, Pearce guaranteed not just the quality of the company's food but the cheapest wholesale prices. With such knowledge he put orders out to competitive bidding. As the

[45] *Temperance Caterer*, 15 June 1899.

[46] Ellis, *Pluck*, p. 143; Fitz-Gerald, "John Pearce," p. 15; *Temperance Caterer*, 15 June 1897 and 15 June 1899.

[47] *Temperance Caterer*, 15 June 1903.

[48] *Evidence on Liquor Licensing Laws*, p. 244; Williams, *Pearce*, p. 150.

managing director, he ordered just what goods were needed, thereby reducing waste.[49]

Pearce alone interviewed, hired and fired workers. Coming from a higher social status, women saw work as servants or shop assistants as inferior to that of refreshment houses. His closest business competitors—Lockharts and ABCs—paid waitresses more than he did. As the *Temperance Caterer* noted, however, Pearce "has the reputation of being a thoroughly just and kind employer." He gave the staff respect; they reciprocated with loyalty. "On an average," Pearce told a reporter, "we have twelve fresh applicants for positions as waitresses every day, most of them from domestic service."[50]

Critical to staff morale, performance and loyalty was Pearce's compassionate relationship with his employees. Summoned to account for her breaking company rules that resulted in costly losses, one waitress approached the meeting with considerable foreboding, particularly given Pearce's commanding height of 6 feet 4 inches. "He was so tall, and I felt so frightened of him, but when he talked all my fears went away. He spoke so fatherly, that I felt as if I could kiss him." In another instance, an unemployed domestic servant, daughter of an impoverished, disabled tailor, wanted to live with and assist her parents. Rebuffed when approaching numerous firms for employment, she turned desperately to the BTT for an interview with Pearce: this was denied her. Intervening at this vital juncture, the Rev. James J. Ellis (and first biographer of Pearce) arranged for a life pension for the miserable tailor and presented her case to his friend John. Typically empathetic and understanding, Pearce replied promptly: "let the girl come up, with your card, and I will find her a job." This, as promised, he did, solving the anxious daughter's problems.[51]

"The Governor," as his employees respectfully and affectionately dubbed John Pearce, exercised firm but fair control over his handpicked employees. "'The old Governor,'" confessed one staff member, "'used to

[49] *Morning Post*, 12 May 1906; *John Bull*, 4 July 1908. See pp. 175–76 for discussion of what problems arose when Pearce no longer controlled the entire process of buying goods.

[50] *Evidence on Liquor Licensing Laws*, p. 244; *Temperance Caterer*, 15 Apr. 1895, 15 Feb. 1898 and 15 June 1902; H. Dendy, "The Position of Women in Industry," *National Review* 1616 (1894): 811. Unlike most other caterers, Lyons paid waitresses no salary, but allowed them to keep commissions, from which 1s. 9d. was deducted for weekly washing.

[51] Ellis, *Pluck*, pp. 141–42.

have us on the carpet and give us a wigging, but we knew it was all for our good.'" He earned workers' respect, loyalty and gratitude—with integrity, even-handedness, genuine personal concern, compassion and pre-eminently humility.[52] Paying tribute to his "kindness and generosity," branch managers presented him with a silver cup in 1890.[53] Ever-mindful of his staff and obligations to them, he later started a benevolent fund, with Pearce as its leading contributor donating £1000.[54]

Pearce oversaw the running of all the outlets, no detail too small for his scrutiny. As Pearce himself acknowledged, he "really loved and worked in the interests of the business." Each morning at 4 a.m., he "made a careful round of his shops," a habit never lost on his employees. Known throughout the company by staff was his philosophy: accept no employee's testimony without investigation. On an ongoing basis, Pearce personally "inspected the kitchens, looked at the joints, and watched every detail of the operations." Evident to his biographer was the result: "with such minute and incessant toil this business increased." Indeed, unremitting attention explained Pearce's commercial success. As one biographer recorded, meticulous oversight of behaviour afforded Pearce "knowledge of every man's worth, and kept every servant alert to win approval." Like the benevolent paternalist, he presided over a work force of some 800, praising those who performed well, while chiding others to improve and reach higher standards.[55]

Easily overlooked was Pearce's shrewd role in hiring and then promoting experienced, responsible and dedicated employees upwards through the ranks of the hierarchy—unskilled worker, cook and then moving into managerial positions. Admittedly, without company records, memoirs or indeed biographies, little is known of such individuals, and for this reason, Charles Cann's career is quite suggestive. Like Pearce, a Cockney by birth and total abstainer by choice, Cann worked his way from the entry level, starting as a "washer-up" at the coffee stall on Bethnal Green Road of Joseph Pearce, brother of John, before doing the same work for John. Having proved himself, he became a pudding maker and then general cook. When forming Pearce's Dining and Refreshment Rooms in 1886, Pearce made Cann manager of the Lambeth Hill branch, its eclectic

[52] Ibid., p. 131.
[53] *Temperance Caterer*, 18 Jan. 1890.
[54] *Financial Times*, 25 May 1899; *Temperance Caterer*, 15 June 1899.
[55] Ellis, *Pluck*, pp. 131, 138, 142; Williams, *Pearce*, p. 150, 152.

clientele of top-hatted clerks, fish porters and boot blacks testing his managerial skills. Pearce's promotion of Cann was certainly justified: this depot became remarkable for having men and ladies eat together and, for twelve years, serving 3000 meals daily. Rewarding this effort, Pearce promoted Cann to the Minories, a much bigger house.[56]

Pearce and Cann exhibited similar traits, notably identical managerial styles: "The smallest detail never escaped notice, yet he had such a kindly way of correcting faults that the employees always looked up to him with confidence." Both imbibed the company philosophy in which patrons got priority: "Our customers: no matters of what degree are our friends, upon them we depend for the success of our business." Unswerving dedication to Pearce and the company culminated in Cann being appointed superintendent of all Pearce & Plenty depots. Like Pearce, Cann instinctively grasped that at day's end the business must pay for itself, making customers' needs of paramount importance.[57]

As managing director, Pearce recognised that he had a broader responsibility to his employees as well as to the wider community. Given the working-class background of his workers in which tight family budgets prohibited extravagances, annual holidays simply did not exist as an option.[58] Workers' lives attracted his attention as a concerned sympathetic employer. Finding affordable working-class lodgings he discovered could create considerable hardship. One of his employees arrived late for work one day, having overslept in a doss house, a place where indigents sought cheap accommodation. Aware of a huge building, its 700 rooms equipped with beds and floors with baths and a washhouse unoccupied, Pearce saw his opportunity to help men like his employee find respectable lodgings. Keen to transform the building but bereft of the sufficient funds, he approached Sir Edward Sullivan, who regarded the plan as overly ambitious. Having discovered that Lord Rowton, Sullivan's friend and formerly Benjamin Disraeli's private secretary, was entertaining similar ideas, Sullivan put Pearce in touch with the peer. Impressed with Pearce's plan, Rowton donated £30,000 to the building of what became Rowton House (Vauxhall), capable of accommodating some 400 men in separate cubicles. While officially unassociated with this project, Pearce had played a significant part in its fruition.[59]

[56] *Temperance Caterer*, 15 Aug. 1900 and 15 Aug. 1907.

[57] Ibid.

[58] *Coffee Public-House News*, 1 Dec. 1885; *Temperance Caterer*, 9 Nov. 1889, 15 Aug. 1896 and 15 Feb. 1898; Burnett, *England Eats Out*, p. 126.

[59] Williams, *Pearce*, pp. 125–27; [Interview with John Pearce], "Fifty Years of Catering."

In an entirely different context, Pearce displayed compassion on recalling emotional ties established long ago with customers who now needed his help. Amid the bitter London dockers' strike in 1889, he organised company vans to feed 2000 strikers and their families for ten days with heavy pea-soup and bread, for which many waited hours. Some of them were "his old Gutter Hotel customers" who had moved geographically from Clerkenwell, and with whom he "exchanged reminiscences of those so different days." His support was far from symbolic: "If I'd been a docker I'd have been one of the ring leaders."[60] This ability to identify with the oppressed reaffirmed in the eyes of so many Pearce & Plenty customers that his social conscience had not diminished, much less disappeared, with economic success.[61] As the *Temperance Caterer* recorded, "These hundreds of men, had work been possible, would have felt it a humbling position to have waited upon the generous gift of the man who thus proved himself their friend."[62]

Sometimes appeals for assistance came to him directly. Struggling with a faltering mission in a London poverty-stricken district, the Rev. James J. Ellis sought Pearce's advice and help. Pearce responded promptly, reorganising the staff, offering astute counsel and dispensing free meals to the male mission workers and women employed at nearby factories. Having put the mission on its feet, he joined its Board of Management and took an active part in activities, which he also helped financially sustain. Impressed with Pearce's behaviour—"kind, shrewd, clear, and absolutely straight"—Ellis became a life-long friend and Pearce's first biographer.[63]

Much of the impetus for other philanthropic acts stemmed not from a calculated strategy to ingratiate him with the masses, but from his deep Christian faith to help those in need or less fortunate than he. Pearce arranged for 2000 children, London's most destitute, to travel to Epping Forest, where provisions from his shops fed them. Dispensed each month for eighteen years, some 200 board-school students received free suppers, dishes laden with steak pudding, potatoes, jam or plum pudding and cocoa. He also instituted annual excursions to Kentish seaside resorts for

[60] Ellis, *Pluck*, pp. 125–27; Williams, *Pearce*, p. 246.

[61] *Coffee Public-House News*, 1 Dec. 1885; also see *Temperance Caterer*, 9 Nov. 1889, 15 Aug. 1896 and 15 Feb. 1898.

[62] *Coffee Public-House News*, 1 Dec. 1885; *Temperance Caterer*, 7 Sept. and 9 Nov. 1889, 15 Aug. 1896 and 15 Feb. 1898. For another example, see *Reynolds's Newspaper*, 27 Nov. 1892.

[63] Ellis, *Pluck*, pp. 125–27, 133, 137–38; Williams, *Pearce*, pp. 136–37, 246.

4000 people, whom he fed on their arrival. Profits from sale of special low-priced tickets were divided between a police orphanage and a railway benevolent agency. At the other end of the age continuum, Pearce gave 100 needy, worthy widows and young families, hefty Christmas gifts weighting some twenty pounds and had them delivered to their doorsteps. For them, he also dispensed meat and groceries for a feast on Christmas Day. Ensuring the day's success, he furnished coal for cooking and contributed 1s. for buying trifles.[64] Nothing about this charity was calculating. Pearce, commented biographer James E. Ellis, "likes to do good quietly, and does not parade his kind deeds."[65]

Another revealing form of his philanthropy involved Pearce's "Drift Children," the most neglected, ignored and despised of adolescents. "No person cares for them, and there are thousands of them," lamented one newspaper. Pearce contradicted this generalisation. Beginning in 1896, he and his wife entertained such waifs at an outing at Epsom Downs, serving pies and tea before giving each child twopence. To the society's outcasts, he confessed: "'I was a poor boy, but by sobriety, industry, and trust in God, I have prospered.'" This indeed was his formula for leading a successful, godly life.[66]

Of the many factors contributing to Pearce's success, one of the most critical derived from his flair for showmanship, displaying his clever sense of spectacle that attracted throngs of patrons to his premises (Fig. 5.1). Pearce fully understood the role of spectacle as part of his business persona. "The brilliancy and coolness of the light have proved a great attraction," pronounced the *Coffee Public-House News*.[67] Another dramatic display and testament to the emergent mass food market was a placard outside his Farringdon Road shop. Higher public profile for Pearce came when the Old Vic Theatre was placed under a new trust in 1891. At the front of the house, Pearce ran a Pearce & Plenty restaurant, which inevitably served no alcohol (Fig. 5.2).[68]

Sometimes other entrepreneurs allied with Pearce for mutual commercial benefit. George Newnes, for instance, had pioneered the concept of popular penny weeklies with his *Tit-Bits*, making it a resounding northern

[64] *Temperance Caterer*, 21 Dec. 1889.

[65] Ellis, *Pluck*, pp. 133–34; *Coffee Public-House News*, 1 Dec. 1885.

[66] *Coffee Public-House News*, 15 Feb. 1903.

[67] Ibid., 1 Sept. 1885.

[68] George Rowell, *The Old Vic Theatre: A History* (Cambridge: Cambridge University Press, 1992), p. 76.

Fig. 5.1 John Pearce personally endorsing his popular steak puddings, 1890 (Reproduced by permission of the Mary Evans Picture Library/ The National Archives, London, England)

success. When he came to London to expand his base, he sought out Pearce and negotiated an arrangement in which they inaugurated another form of advertising. Measuring ten foot high, its arresting gold letters advertising *Tit-Bits*, London's first sky-sign appeared above Pearce's shop.[69]

Of the foremost influences in his life, evangelical religion and teetotalism ranked first and second, with his wife and business following respectively in importance. Reflecting in middle age on his life, he pointed to his mother, "a genuine Christian," as the inspirational figure who had shaped

[69] Bolce, "Foreseeing What the People Want," pp. 158–59; Williams, *Pearce*, pp. 101–03, 107–09; Pearce, "Coffee Stall," p. 43; Ellis, *Pluck*, p. 132.

Fig. 5.2 Old Vic Theatre, with a Pearce & Plenty operating on the ground floor, 1926–27 (The Print Collector/Alamy Stock Photo)

most his attitudes and behaviour. This typified working-class sons, who esteemed their mothers and showed this strong bond in residing no more than streets away from them after marriage. Certainly sons respected, sometimes even loved, their fathers. Mothers, however, occupied an exalted position, earned from fierce commitment to protecting their children whatever the physical sacrifice, avoidance of heavy boozing and—unlike so many fathers—never abandoning them. From Pearce's mother, he revered honesty and integrity: "I must go through life straight."

He disappointed neither her nor himself. For Pearce, religion and temperance thereafter became embedded in every aspects of his life. "If it hadn't been for religion, I should have gone to the bad again and again," he confessed later in life. "Only God and I know what temptations I've come through."[70]

Pearce understood that the working poor resented charity as strongly as the philanthropic impulse to improve those at the social base of society. In a fair, justifiable, humane arrangement, he dispensed tasty food in exchange for money at rock bottom prices. His customers, Pearce remarked, "are independent and they come in, and … feel they are paying for all they have."[71] He knew that "I have given working men honest value for their money, and in return they have given me success and fortune." Pondering further on his silver wedding anniversary, Pearce saw that he had enabled their moving socially upwards, emulating his own career path. Their relationship was reciprocal, with mutual respect the dominant factor.[72]

While temperance played no direct role in the running of the business, it loomed large as a principle which Pearce promoted through temperance bodies. From 1889 he participated in the National Temperance Caterers' Association, and also worked with the National Coffee Tavern Association (1870–1895), serving as chairman of the London Executive with a seat on the Board. His was not a symbolic presence. At the annual conference in 1894, Pearce delivered a paper, "What the Movement is doing in the Way of Providing Cheap Meals in Hard Times." He also served as director of the Temperance Caterers' Journal Co.[73]

In Pearce's mind, temperance was integral to his becoming a caterer: his chosen career represented his ultimate commitment to temperance. "Catering," he often said, "helps people to be temperate." Looking back over changes in catering during his career, Pearce took great pride in—and claimed some responsibility for—the fundamental shift in which businessmen sealed a deal over a cup of coffee rather than toasting each other with alcohol. Pubs thus ceased to be the only venue for transacting business.[74]

[70] *Temperance Caterer*, 15 Aug. 1895; Carl Chinn, *They Worked all their Lives: Women of the Urban Poor in England, 1880–1939* (Manchester: Manchester University Press, 1988), pp. 21–7, 164–65; John Burnett (ed.), *Destiny Obscure: Autobiographies of Childhood, Education and Family from the 1820s to the 1920s* (Harmondsworth: Penguin, 1984), p. 237.

[71] *Evidence on Liquor Licensing Laws*, pp. 244–45.

[72] Pearce, "Coffee Stall," p. 43; *Temperance Caterer*, 15 Aug. 1895.

[73] *Temperance Caterer*, 15 June 1894, 15 Dec. 1895, and 15 July 1907; Williams, *Pearce*, p. 164.

[74] Williams, *Pearce*, p. 164.

His pronounced social and moral beliefs, products of his deprived upbringing, empathy with the oppressed and influences of such evangelicals as Carter and Moody—all over time transformed Pearce into a public figure whose reputation became inextricably part of London's poverty-stricken districts as a result of his altruism. "Unintentionally, Pearce regularly facilitated this personal rapport with customers in visiting one of his own houses daily while customers ate lunch or dinner, when many addressed him affectionately as "Sir John" or "Old John.""[75]

For Pearce, philanthropy profoundly affected working-class perceptions of him. "His unostentatious acts of kindness," reflected the *Temperance Chronicle*, "have gained the affection of those who know him personally." His was a genuine response and so recognised as such. "His unfailing rectitude has won universal respect," reassured the newspaper.[76]

Having come from a humble background and, from the age of 9, having led a life of unremitting struggle as an orphan, Pearce developed a character striking in its modesty, sincerity and compassion for those who suffered as he himself had done. A devout and strong Baptist, he assumed a leading position as a deacon in the Chatsworth Road Baptist Chapel.[77]

Late in the 1890s the editor of *Figaro*, a London newspaper, castigated caterers of the poor as "dirty, dear, and indifferent," who followed the motto, "Anything is good enough for the poor." Recalling Pearce's early years, Daniel F. Powell responded with a letter, recollecting his installing electric lights at Farringdon Street, its premises impressing him, especially with their spotlessness, sound organisation and meat quality. Pearce, Powell argued, "was the first in London to provide the working man with liberal supplies of good food in well-appointed rooms." *Figaro*'s editor agreed, noting that Pearce's claims were exceptional in an industry in which the working poor were duped with misleading advertising that promised but never delivered inexpensive, quality meals.[78]

Testament to Pearce's role in elevating his customers' lives came from an unexpected quarter, the "enemy." No one had more of a salutary impact on the working class than John Pearce and his Pearce & Plenty depots, attested one former publican. "Pearce and Plenty," he declared, "was the most perfect effort in the City to gladden the hearts of the

[75] Ibid., p. 226.

[76] *Temperance Chronicle*, 15 Dec. 1895.

[77] Ellis, *Pluck*, pp. 110–19.

[78] *Figaro*: 20 and 27 Aug. 1898; Daniel F. Powell to Editor, undated, 27 Aug. 1898.

working classes." By the late 1880s, both the *Temperance Caterer* and *Refreshment News* agreed that Pearce's coffee bars and depots earned his distinction alone as having "revolutionized the catering trade in London."[79]

Pearce's remarkable career as a prophet and practitioner of mass catering was coming to an end with the BTT. Critical were changes to the Board of Directors: Sullivan, chairman of the Board and ally since the early 1880s, died in 1899; another staunch supporter, Sir Henry Oldham, retired; and Pearce's son, Arthur Charles, with the company for a decade, now received a seat on the Board and promotion to Assistant general manager. The new chairman, J.P. Hurst, with whom Pearce had quarrelled often and heatedly from Pearce & Plenty's formation in 1886,[80] drastically diminished the Pearce family influence, father and son, on the Board. Their "opinions were set aside, their plans overruled, and their conduct subjected to criticism," recorded one of Pearce's biographers.[81] In negating the well-tested beliefs of the mastermind of the Pearce catering empire, his social superiors on the Board of Directors subverted the prevailing commercial formula promising success. In retrospect, the origins of escalating boardroom strife were rooted in the new company's floatation, diminishing Pearce's shareholdings relative to the much enlarged firm.

[79] *Temperance Caterer*, 9 Nov. 1889; Williams, *Pearce*, p. 90; *Refreshment News*, 14 Apr. 1888.

[80] See pp. 156–57 for development of this point.

[81] Ellis, *Pluck*, p. 205; Williams, *Pearce*, p. 147; *Financial Times*, 4 Jan. 1899.

CHAPTER 6

Catering Crisis in Edwardian England

Changing customer taste immensely complicated the business of caterers. Formerly, patrons had ordered relatively straightforward meals, but in the previous ten years, catering companies had introduced savoury dishes, featuring meat, fish eggs and vegetables. More sophisticated menus cut profit margins considerably, causing plummeting profits. Light luncheons had cost 1s. 2d., whereas in the Edwardian era, they fell by 8d.—over 50%. Shorter work hours of labourers meant declining demand for meals. In part this was due to the shift from a 6- to a 5.5-day work week, enabling workers on Saturdays to return home for lunch. Competition intensified in yet other ways—catering companies as well as night stalls stayed opened longer until 7:30 or 8 p.m.; big companies started catering facilities for their own workers; and transportation improved (particularly underground extensions and tramways), enabling workers to move beyond the area in which they worked.[1]

Other factors also affected customers. Per capita income fell almost 10% below its 1903 level, a loss not fully regained until 1913. Since the general price level was rising, though very slowly, price-cutting would be very hard to achieve without sacrificing quality or quantity, which might turn out to lose customers. Another complicating factor was that as real wages increased from 1900, workers shifted purchases from consumer durables

[1] *Financial Times*, 18 June 1908 and 15 Aug. 1914; *Temperance Caterer*, 15 Sept. 1914; *Morning Post*, 16 May 1907.

D. W. Gutzke, *John Pearce and the Rise of the Mass Food Market in London, 1870–1930*, https://doi.org/10.1007/978-3-030-27095-7_6

to beer, reflected in rising beer consumption.[2] Attitudes too were changing towards catering. Because of declining retail prices, thought Horace Pearce, "people are not so satisfied to pay fancy prices as they were 20 years ago." Corroborating his case, he compared prices for a cup of tea with newspapers. In the 1890s, each item cost three pennies, but years later in Edwardian England, the half-penny newspaper and tram rides resulted in pressure for corresponding catering prices. For 7s. a week, workers now could get an appetising breakfast of eggs and bacon for breakfast, and a joint or entrée with a sweet for dinner.[3]

For the BTT, as for other catering companies, these were demanding trading years, "especially those who worked on a small margin," observed the *Financial Times.* Quite simply, customers had less money for food. Though leading catering companies declared respectable, sometimes even impressive, dividends, financial returns on investments were modest at best. Of the £5.6 million invested in five leading companies, the *Economist* calculated that this had earned a financial return of not quite 3% in 1898–1899.[4] From the workingmen's popular 4d. plate of meat, caterers derived no profit whatsoever, prompting pressures to charge an extra penny. Beverages too drew attention. Charging customers a half-penny for a cup of tea, coffee or cocoa earned no profit for sellers, so Pearce & Plenty and Lockharts spearheaded the drive for higher prices in 1900. Economic conditions, however, deteriorated further, inducing Thomas Jenkins, chairman of Cabins, a small catering company, to observe in 1905 that "not for a long time has there been so bad a trading year as the last in the City of London." Newly opened branches, the Annual Report conceded, "have met with non-success."[5]

The chief problem, however, was hardly new: "there were too many catering companies." Informed estimates put the number of coffee and tearooms in the metropolitan area at 7000. In the City itself, thought the managing director of a small catering company, Ye Mecca, total numbers were not so much the difficulty as excessive light refreshment houses. This sector had undergone an "extraordinary increase," observed the *Economist* in 1899. Ten years before, just ABC shares had been listed on the stock exchange, whereas now four more had been added, more than doubling

[2] A.E. Dingle, "Drink and Working-Class Living Standards in Britain, 1870–1914," *Economic History Review* 25 (1972): 608–22.

[3] Interview with Horace Pearce, *Morning Leader*, 3 Sept. 1910.

[4] *Financial Times*, 21 June 1905; *Economist*, 27 May 1899.

[5] *Daily Telegraph*, 20 Nov. 1900; *Financial Times*, 14 March 1905; *Temperance Caterer*, 15 Apr. 1905.

Table 6.1 Share capital of major catering companies, 1899

Aerated Bread Co.	£2,532,531
Lyons	£1,525,000
Slaters	£837,500
British Tea Table Co.	£495,000
Lockharts	£240,625

Source: *Economist*, 27 May 1899; *Financial Times*, 17 Aug. 1898

the share capital (Table 6.1). In the three-year period of 1897–1899, the quoted companies, which "practically constitute the whole of the cheaper catering businesses in London," had steadily rising dividends.[6]

Curiously, optimism about the continued prosperity of this sector of catering still persisted. Though in 1902 the Express Dairy Company noted competition in London was "becoming very keen," it continued expanding its numbers of refreshment depots. Amid the heady atmosphere of one company declaring ordinary dividends of 16% again in 1904, the *Financial Times* expressed its belief that "restaurant companies which cater reasonably for the public and make their depots attractive and comfortable are as able to do well now as in any other time during the last ten or fifteen years."[7]

Eating habits, meanwhile, noticeably altered, contributing to market instability, which in turn accentuated business acumen as a vital factor in earning dividends. Electric trams played a vital role in this change. First introduced in London in 1901, they exploded in popularity, with journeys on LCC trams soaring from 117 million (1903) to 505 million (1910). To this latter figure should be added another 250 million journeys with other operators.[8] "Customers by the hundreds of thousands are speedily and cheaply carried to their suburban homes to lunch and dinner who were formerly the caterer's customers," observed the *Temperance Caterer*. Loss of the afternoon tea-cup business proved quite harmful to small companies, such as the Express Dairy Co. and Ye Mecca, because profit margins were greater on this transaction than on other sales.[9]

[6] "Gold in the Tea-Cup," *Daily Mail*, 9 Nov. 1904; *Financial Times*, 7 Dec. 1909; *Economist*, 27 May 1899, 19 May 1900 and 1 Jan. 1910.

[7] Annual Report, Express Dairy, Museum of English Rural Life, TR EXP/5/2, 1902, p. 2; *Financial Times*, 25 May 1899, 17 Nov. 1904, and 24 Nov. 1906.

[8] Michael Ball and David Sunderland, *An Economic History of London, 1800–1914* (London: Routledge, 2001), pp. 251–53; *Temperance Caterer*, 15 Feb. 1904.

[9] *Temperance Caterer*, 15 Feb. 1904 and 15 Jan. 1909; "Gold in the Tea-Cup"; *Financial Times*, 17 Nov. 1904 and 24 Nov. 1906. Both the Express Dairy Co. and Ye Mecca had £100,000 of issued stock.

To understand the turbulent history of the BTT, explored in the following chapter, experiences of its large competitors—Lyons, ABC, Slaters and Lockharts—will merit examination to place the BTT in a broader, meaningful context. Examining two smaller firms, the Express Dairy Co. and Ye Mecca, will provide insight into how well they survived compared to the principal concerns.

The nature of these catering companies defy easy generalisation. Lockharts, Ye Mecca and the ABC, each concentrated on doing business in the "square mile," while Slaters spread into the West End and Strand. Diversifying business became an asset in a depressed economy. "Their own profits in the West-end were excellent, and on them they could pay 15 per cent; but unfortunately business had fallen off in the City," admitted the chairman of a small catering firm, W. Hill and Company, in 1906. For another small-scale company, the Express Dairy, catering ranked as a subsidiary business. The newest arrival to the catering business, Lyons opened restaurants not just in the City, but Westminster and the West End. Its approach to the new venture contrasted sharply with the existing companies. With huge capital, sophisticated advertising, lighter and more varied menus, and from the beginning, a female clientele, Lyons positioned itself as the most sophisticated business among catering companies. Lyons not merely encompassed different classes as part of its clientele, but spanned catering categories. Supplementing its profits were the manufacture and delivery of bread, outdoor catering, high-class restaurants and bakeries undertaking wide-ranging activities.[10]

Amid heightening competition, Lyons commenced its first phase of teashop expansion in these years. More geographically dispersed than most catering companies, it chose to site four-fifths of its new shops in the City, Westminster or the West End. Five shops, for instance, appeared in the City, already overstocked with depots.[11] From the outset, Lyons established itself as an enormously profitable company, earning average dividends of 31% in its first two decades. Profits likewise steadily increased, topping £300,000 in the immediate years before World War I.[12]

[10] *Economist*, 7 Apr. 1906; J. Lyons & Co., London Metropolitan Archives, J. Lyons first Annual Report, 1895, Acc. 3527/2.

[11] Peter Bird, *The First Food Empire: A History of J. Lyons & Co.* (Chichester: Phillimore, 2000), p. 42, Appendix 4, pp. 348–50; Robert Leon, "Rise and Fall of the Aerated Bread Company," *Camden History Review* 25 (2001): 48.

[12] Compiled from Bird, *Lyons*, Appendix 6.

Originating as retailers of tobacco under the trading name of Salmon and Glucksteins, the two families turned to catering, becoming involved as a contract exhibition caterer in Newcastle in 1887. Here they tested new catering ideas, with Montague Gluckstein and, to a lesser extent, his brother, Isidore, the masterful guiding forces in founding a teashop chain.[13]

Numerous factors explain the phenomenal success of what became Lyons. Drawing on extensive experience in the tobacco trade, the Glucksteins applied their knowledge of shop siting and personal service to catering. A second reason stemmed from their vast capital savings which, as historian D.J. Richardson notes, permitted "them to experiment with new ideas and support infant projects" as well as sustain their ever-expanding catering business. Two other interrelated advantages derived from their tobacco sales: pricing and publicity. Tobacconists Salmon and Glucksteins had used price reductions as a shrewd marketing strategy encapsulated in the slogan "The more you smoke, the more you save," which had garnered widespread publicity. This flair for publicity, displayed at their tea pavilion where they hired a Hungarian orchestra at the lavish fee of £150 weekly, shocked contemporaries. Respectability, quality, cheapness, speed and cleanliness—these traits all defined what Lyons wanted to project as a corporate identity and account for its success, argues Richardson. Lyons' company historian, Peter Bird, stresses other factors, most notably "conformity of pricing" in its teashops which he contends Lyons borrowed from Lockharts. Under this rubric, he points to economically priced temperance fare, appealing surroundings and courteous service as fundamental causes of Lyons' extraordinary expansion. So too was Lyons' impressive menu of some sixty-seven items, "a far greater selection than offered by competitors." In centralising food production at Olympia, the company supplied customers with a wider array of items. None of these was more popular than mutton pie, priced at 7d.[14]

Neither of these explanations, however, recognises that Lyons' teashops embraced Lipton retail shops' pioneering of an entirely new concept, "place-product-packaging," an innovative marketing strategy in which a company marketed products throughout its chain of retail outlets. Integral to this goal was strict control of food portions of exact size and

[13] D.J. Richardson, "J. Lyons & Co. Ltd.: Caterers and Food Manufacturers, 1894 to 1939," in Derek Oddy and Derek Miller (eds.), *The Making of the Modern British Diet* (London: Croom Helm, 1973), p. 164.

[14] Bird, *Lyons*, p. 40; Richardson, "Lyons," pp. 165, 168.

price, facilitating economies of scale as well as exemplary service. Trained female staff, dressed in identical black uniforms, served items from a standardised menu. Outside each teashop, the new concept aimed at total design with "clear corporate images projected onto landscape." Advertising was integral to the concept. Lyons developed a distinctive decorative house style of gold on white as easily recognisable as its building designs. In essence, Lyons sought to embed a message in building structures readily decipherable by passers-by. "There is something about their style of doing business which attracts the public," acknowledged the *Temperance Caterer*.[15]

Central to Lyons' successful formula would be expanding numbers of catering customers, better meal quality and—through strict portion and price controls—economies of scale, an entirely novel concept in catering. Of utmost importance was standardised, competitive pricing throughout the teashops, a smart ambience and superior staff, none of which Lyons' competitors supplied.[16] One of the original partners, Montague Gluckstein, characterised the teashop influence as involving

> conformity of pricing ... in all Lyons teashops wherever they might be located, and a commitment to giving the public what they [sic] wanted. This he perceived to be good temperance fare at economic prices, in attractive surroundings and with a polite and dignified service—factors missing or neglected by other refreshment providers ...[17]

Several catering companies became offshoots of related trades, notably milk delivery and baking. One of the smallest in terms of both capital and depots was the Express Dairy Company.[18] For these reasons, its economic performance was an anomaly compared with the other catering companies.

[15] For discussion of how this concept emerged in brewing in Britain and other industries abroad, see David W. Gutzke, *Pubs and Progressives: Reinventing the Public House in England, 1896–1960* (DeKalb: Northern Illinois University Press, 2006), pp. 187, 190–93; John A. Jakle and Keith A. Sculle, *The Gas Station in America* (Baltimore: Johns Hopkins University Press, 1994), pp. 18–47; Philip Langdon, *Orange Roofs, Golden Arches: The Architecture of American Chain Restaurants* (New York: Alfred A. Knopf, 1986), Chaps. 2–3; *Temperance Caterer*, 15 Apr. 1895.

[16] Bird, *Lyons*, p. 38.

[17] Gluckstein quoted in ibid.

[18] Of the Express Dairy Company's early history, little is known. As a small concern in the Strand in the 1870s, Nell Gwynn's Dairy began providing customers with a glass of milk during the morning. Over time they and others came to regard this as a well-established

Earning its reputation for delivering milk to customers' houses, the company sold other dairy products—cream, butter, cheese, eggs and meat—from its delivery vans. Its teashops sold milk and several staple items such as cakes and buns. Such thriving London suburbs as Blackheath and Hampstead became sites of the firm's first teashops, which sold light refreshments and dairy products from the late 1880s. This side of the business flourished, and total numbers reached thirty-three (1904), a figure that doubled by the war. Notwithstanding the disruptive World War I, the firm still established eleven more teashops.[19]

Overall, the Edwardian years were difficult but not certainly devastating for the Express. Between 1895 and 1902, the firm prospered, earning solid dividends of 5.5–6% while putting £3000 in reserve. For three years thereafter, no dividends were earned, but it recovered in 1906–1908, with average dividends of 6%. Perhaps sensing the fragile catering market, the firm put £15,000 in reserves, bringing the overall total to £35,000. Following a bleak 1909, the company declared modest dividends of 2.5%. By the war, the company annual reports recorded rising profits.[20]

Another small catering company was Ye Mecca, with £100,000 of capital. Founded in 1898 after the Pure Coffee Trading Association was liquidated, Ye Mecca catered to City male clerks, a narrow but devoted clientele drawn from the lower middle class. As chairman G.H. Brougham Glasier recalled, Ye Mecca was "the pioneer company in connection with smoking cafés and coffee restaurants in the City of London." Located in the square mile were twenty of its twenty-one cafés. In the years 1897–1903, it recorded impressive dividends of 8–10%.[21]

custom, particularly when the company supplemented this with a currant bun as a prelude to serving sandwiches and cakes. Thus, evolved the Express Dairy's involvement with light lunches ("History of the Express Dairy Co.," Museum of English Rural Life, Univ. of Reading, Express Dairy Company TR EXP/5/9, [n.d.], p.4).

[19] Bryan Morgan, *Express Journey, 1864–1964: A Centenary History of the Express Dairy Company Limited* (London: Newman Neame, 1964), pp. 33, 40, 43, 138–39; John Burnett, *England Eats Out: A Social History of Eating Out in England from 1830 to the Present* (London: Pearson Longman, 2004), p. 120; Annual Reports, Express Dairy Company, Museum of English Rural Life, Univ. of Reading: 1887 Annual Report, TR EXP/5/2, p. 2; 1911 Annual Report, 1911, TR EXP/5/2, and 1913 Annual Report, TR EXP/5/3; *Pure Food: The Record of a Great Public Service* (n.p., [1929]), p. 11, TR EXP/5/9).

[20] *Financial Times*, 5 Apr. 1909; Express Dairy Company Annual Reports, 1911 and 1912, TR EXP/5/2-3.

[21] *Financial Times*, 17 and 19 Aug. 1898; *Temperance Caterer*, 15 March 1902.

Table 6.2 Ye Mecca's number of depots, 1898–1911

Year	*City of London*	*Provinces*
1898	20	1
1902	21	11
1906	21	14
1911	20	11

Source: *Financial Times*, 25 Aug. 1906, and 23 Feb. 1911

For Ye Mecca, Edwardian England was altogether different (Table 6.2). No new depots were opened, and symptomatic of a crisis was Ye Mecca's declining dividends from 8% to 3% (1904–1905). As a stable but limited clientele, male clerks who drank coffee while smoking cigars had disappeared, leaving the company without a viable constituency of customers. Sales of coffee and cigars, the two mainstays of the company, had plummeted sharply. Compared with 1904, Ye Mecca used 12% fewer coffee beans, while selling almost one-third fewer luxury cigars (6d.) and nearly one-fifth cheaper cigars (4d.) one year later. Much of the company's early prosperity was due to the efforts of Mrs DeLong, a lady superintendent for eleven years.[22] Gender constituted a powerful inhibitor to the company's growth in another sense. Female clerks smoked no cigars, while coffee was readily available at numerous and expanding numbers of restaurants and teashops. Critically, Ye Mecca needed to target as part of its new clientele explosive numbers of women entering clerical positions, but its basic formula of cigars and coffee had decreasing appeal overall among City clerks and other female employees.[23]

Disgruntled shareholders appointed an Investigative Committee in 1906 that interpreted dwindling profits primarily as a result of several factors: bad management causing poor supervision; and the retirement of Mrs DeLong, who had been charged with visiting all the London depots. The company sorely needed firm, experienced direction from management. Reviving the appointment of a lady superintendent charged with overseeing all the London depots was seen as absolutely imperative. This woman would institute strict supervision of catering manageresses, systematic instruction and guidelines for expected gross profits.[24] The

[22] *Financial Times*, 21 Feb. and 17 Aug. 1898; *Temperance Caterer*, 15 March 1906.

[23] See above pp. 110–11.

[24] *Financial Times*, 23 and 25 Aug. 1906.

Committee also cited a third less important factor: "the loss of spending power in recent years by the general public." But the Committee ignored other possibilities, such as people spending their money on different things, or on the same things provided by different people.[25]

Yet, none of these constructive ideas revitalised Ye Mecca's fortunes, firmly stuck at 3% dividends. Proposals to enter the catering market received scant support, lest the company alienate many former customers averse to interacting with diners. Shareholders also baulked at closing marginally profitable or loss-incurring depots because this might injure the company's reputation in the City. In the provinces, where many depots had generated no profits, a different policy prevailed, the shutting of such outlets where leases could be cancelled. Another untested strategy—cutting menu prices—was rejected.[26]

Unable to solve its problems, Ye Mecca lurched from crisis to collapse. In 1911, its lowest trading profits (£5190) in six years, it made an average profit of just £168 per depot. This grim news again prompted calls for closing uneconomic depots, but, as the *Financial Times* stressed, there was "extreme difficulty of disposing of leases at the present time without heavy loss." Two years later, Mrs Sampson, voicing the disquiet of other investors at the halving of dividends to 1.5%, queried why other catering companies doing a similar trade had achieved success, but not Ye Mecca. This criticism culminated in her making the unwelcome but not unreasonable request that "the directors ought to give place to someone who knew something about the catering business."[27] By 1914, Ye Mecca faced dire conditions as dividends hit zero.[28]

More than twice as large as Ye Mecca but with many similar problems, Lockharts drew patrons almost exclusively from the working classes.[29] Throughout the late 1890s, Lockharts' Board of Directors declared robust dividends, fluctuating between 7% and 12%.[30] Given intensifying competition in the catering market—"restaurants have sprung up in every direction"—the company decided tardily to expand its customer base, repositioning itself to appeal to "a higher class of trade." Lockharts had no

[25] I am grateful to Trevor Lloyd for this point.

[26] *Financial Times*, 3 Dec. 1908, 24 Feb. 1909, and 23 Feb. and 4 March 1911.

[27] Ibid., 23 Feb. 1911 and 12 March 1913.

[28] *Temperance Caterer*, 15 March 1913; *Financial Times*, 28 Feb. and 4 March 1914.

[29] *Financial Times*, 10 and 18 June 1908.

[30] *Edinburgh Evening News*, 17 June 1897; *Economist*, 21 May 1898, and 26–27 May 1899.

viable choice. Exploding numbers of catering shops "would not have been in existence had the old firm taken up the dinner trade earlier," reproved the *Temperance Caterer*. To compete with Pearce & Plenty, Lockharts, previously specialists in puddings, turned to offering customers of "the better classes" meat cut from the joint as an entirely new venture into late afternoon meals. What Pearce had done obviously impressed the company in yet another sense. To cater specifically for a more prosperous working-class clientele, Lockharts envisaged opening an upmarket line—County Cafés (1901), its equivalent of Pearce's BTT shops. Existing Lockharts' depots, their interiors redecorated, modernised and repainted with lighter colours, aimed to move socially upwards, but not compete directly with Slaters, ABC or Lyons in this overcrowded sector of the catering market. Among the first of the new chain located in the "heart of the city," a Cheapside café featured a three-course meal, oxtail soup, leg of mutton and two vegetables and apple pudding, for a competitively priced 11d. in an area with onerous rents.[31] Its original base of working-class patrons was not, however, forgotten. To cater to vast numbers of young women working in warehouses, who commuted between 4 and 12 miles daily to work, Lockharts opened a depot in the Barbican in 1900.[32]

For some years, this new chain remained an unfulfilled aspiration because Lockharts lacked funds sufficient to undertake necessary renovations and remodelling. To present a new image attracting a higher class of trade, Lockharts concluded, "the blue enamelled signs would have to go: they savoured too much of the ha'penny mug and penny bun.'" Its new general manager recalled assuming his new duties in 1905, with the shops still "comparatively empty" and laid out in the traditional design. Remodelled shops "would fit them for a higher class of trade," "where there were not so many competitors," observed the Report of the Investigative Committee. Shortage of funds hurt the company in another way, disqualifying it from gaining wholesale discounts. Placing purchases on credit cost the company £500 annually in extra fees.[33]

Short-sighted financial policies immensely weakened the company's long-term financial strength. To sustain growth and earn shareholder

[31] *Financial Times*, 28 Jan. 1905; *Temperance Caterer*, 15 June 1901, and 15 March and June 1902.

[32] *Temperance Caterer*, 15 May 1900. Lockharts later reconstructed a depot on City Road, where it built a separate room for young women (*Temperance Caterer*, 15 Nov. 1905).

[33] *Temperance Caterer*, 15 June 1901, 15 Feb. 1905, and 15 July 1911; Report of the Investigative Committee, *Financial Times*, 28 Jan. 1905.

gratitude, the Board thought as little about building up a reserve as about upkeep and writing off cost of leases as they depreciated. Reserves stood at £6000 in 1902, not strikingly increased to £6200 two years later. Most of this, the company invested in LCC stock and consuls. For a company with nearly a quarter of a million pounds of capital, an inability to envisage possible market downturns seemed remarkable. Profits, however, were precarious, dependent on thin profit margins on each sale with thousands of transactions producing modest gains. Without deep pockets, managerial mistakes could neither easily nor quickly be remedied. In retrospect, admitted Chairman C.B. Thring, Lockharts "took too much profit from its customers, while repairs and the cost of equipping the depots were not sufficiently dealt with." Lockharts, he further admitted, followed the customary strategy of closing uneconomic shops, but some of them remained unlet and a continual drain on profits.[34]

Directors had ample forewarning of an impending crisis as ordinary dividends tumbled from 11% (1897) to 2% (1902). For seven straight years from 1903, Lockharts paid no ordinary dividends whatsoever. Net profits equally plummeted by one-third, with the company incurring a loss of £160 in net profits, despite overall trading profits of £5506 in 1905.[35]

Two factors explained Lockharts' financial crisis. According to one analysis, the depressed economy forced workers to cut expenditure drastically. "A man that [sic] used to be able to spend 6d. [could] now only spent 2d. or 3d.," remarked Arthur C. Tessier, chairman of Lockharts, in 1904. There was, however, another factor. The *Financial Times* warned the company against sacrificing quality to maintain present prices: "The remedy would almost certainly be worse than the disease." Nevertheless, Lockharts unofficially ignored this advice. Patrons discovered numerous staple articles "inferior in quality and dearer in price than the same article sold by its competitors."[36]

Frustrated shareholders took action, appointing an Investigative Committee that ousted Tessier as chairman and installing Christopher B. Thring as his replacement. In reappraising the company's performance, the Committee's report pointed to Lockharts' managerial system as a criti-

[34] *Financial Times*, 30 May 1902 and 5 June 1907; *Temperance Chronicle*, 15 June 1902 and 15 July 1908.

[35] *Financial Times*, 5 June 1907.

[36] Report of the Investigative Committee, *Financial Times*, 25 May and 1 June 1904.

cal factor in the firm's lacklustre performance. In response, Lockharts summarily fired its managing director, and substituted, instead, a Board of Directors under whom a general manager, experienced in overseeing restaurants with a frugal clientele, would work. To compete with rivals, the Committee expanded the number of articles on the menu.[37]

More significantly for the company's long-term recovery, the Committee effectively abolished the shop-fitting department, an ill-timed move when most depots "were in a dirty and uninviting condition."[38] Long-standing neglect of shops hurt custom, placing them at a competitive disadvantage. Even something as basic as serving food hot eluded managers, in part, because depots often lacked hot plates! These difficult years had forfeited "the confidence of the public," acknowledged Arthur Pearce later. In 1907, Lockharts "had to expend colossal amounts on repairs and redecorations to improve the shops," sometimes having to shut them while the work was being completed. To maximise profits, Lockharts' shops ran three working shifts, enabling business for 22 hours of the 24-hour day. So desperate were these years for Lockharts' Board of Directors that sympathetic observers "advised them to take down their sign boards and trade under another name," a radical strategy symptomatic of a grave financial crisis.[39]

Lockharts embraced an aggressive policy in difficult trading years when it declared no ordinary dividend, continued spending on alternations and improvements, and incurred £12,000 in losses that led it to terminate uneconomic leases. In 1907, for example, it spent £13,000 on such matters, comparable to 12% of the company's capital. In addition, £6200 had been earmarked for reserves.[40]

Underlining the gravity of the company's weakening situation, the Committee appointed Arthur Pearce, eldest son of John Pearce, as the new general manager. Deeply confident of his abilities, the Investigative Committee gave Arthur Pearce "a free hand," something which neither his father John at the BTT nor brother Horace at the ABC enjoyed.[41]

[37] *Financial Times*, 1 June 1904, and 28 Jan. 1905.

[38] Ibid., 1 June 1904 and 13 June 1907.

[39] *Temperance Caterer*, 15 Oct. 1905, 15 June 1906 and 15 July 1911; *Financial Times*, 13 June 1907; *Daily Mail*, 2 Oct. 1912.

[40] *Financial Times*, 5 June 1907.

[41] *Temperance Caterer*, 15 Apr. 1913.

Thring as well as Arthur Pearce grasped the roots of the company's financial crisis: the reserve fund needed enlargement, while goodwill must be written down. Failure to write down leases of freehold and leasehold properties principally contributed to inflating the company's value. The Board gradually closed unprofitable depots, accounting for almost one-fifth of the total number and underlining the extent of the firm's crisis. Since equipping each depot required at least £500—sometimes as much as £2000—closing 14 of them in the span of less than a decade caused immense financial problems, largely because the cost of equipment and depreciation of the value of leases had not been written off. Between 1904 and 1907, Lockharts incurred costs of £11,000 in closing shops and another £2000 in modifying and upgrading premises. Existing reserves were altogether insufficient to cover costs of closing four more shops, forcing the company to continue passing dividends and defer both vital repairs and redecorating remaining shops. Dividends owed preference shareholders steadily accumulated, likewise obstructing plans to update depots. These interrelated problems culminated in a crisis in 1909 in which the company wrote off not just nearly £60,000 of the value of leases and furniture, but £28,000 of goodwill. Shares plunged disastrously from £1 to 5s. in value. With the company stock vastly overvalued, the Board could bring the reduced capital into alignment with realisable assets. The adjusted capital was now £137,000, nearly 40% lower than the previously stated value.[42]

Arthur Pearce provided the motivation, knowledge and insight for introducing sweeping but overdue organisational changes. Christopher Thring pointed to Arthur's "very fertile brain and sound judgment" as responsible for resuscitating Lockharts. As Arthur told the *Temperance Caterer*, "the whole system of the management and conduct of the restaurant business had been reorganized." Central to instituting "an extended and improved system of catering" was modernising twenty-five restaurants, nearly 40% of the total. When leases allowed enough time, he had the depots entirely tiled, a more modern, easily cleaned decor that recouped investments. Some of the restaurants originated from his own imagination in creating another new line of more upmarket depots, Ideal Restaurants, founded in 1909, though only now belatedly getting

[42] *Financial Times*, 5 June 1907 and 18 June 1908; *Temperance Caterer*, 15 June 1906, 15 July 1908 and 15 Jan. 1910. Two years earlier, Cabins likewise reduced its capital from £100,000 to £62,348 (*Times*, 19 Oct. 1912).

managerial attention.[43] The first one opened at the Monument in 1910, and three more followed in as many years. These became effectively "supper restaurants" with seating capacities of about 1000. Overall, his efforts led to soaring business at depots, which had "regained their lost trade and the confidence of the public." Painstaking attention to detail characterised the Pearce family's approach to management. Upper floors of restaurants were either vacant or let to clubs at modest rents, so Pearce had them modified for other purposes and sublet at competitive fees. Given this approach, he remarked, all now generated "good revenue." In 1911, the first time in eight years, Lockharts declared not just dividends but impressive ones of 15%—the biggest in the company's history. Having learned the lessons of the past, the company declined to declare dividends up to the hilt; now, the Board withheld some funds to meet diverse needs of the business. The *Financial Times* enthused in an editorial that "prospects would seem to have a more rosy look than for a long time past."[44] This forecast was accurate, with similar dividends for two more years, before falling to 5% once World War I began, a typical fate of other catering firms. Without Pearce, Lockharts might not have recovered so quickly or even fully. In assessing Pearce's overall contribution, it is vital to recognise that there was, by 1911, an upswing in the economy, which undoubtedly assisted his efforts. Without Pearce, Lockharts might not have been able to benefit, but he did have general economic conditions on his side.[45]

In diversifying into temperance hotels, Lockharts had emulated its competitor, Pearce & Plenty. Rosebery Hotel (Pentonville Road) marked the start of this venture in 1905, offering working-class patrons "increased sleeping accommodation upon temperance lines for travellers."[46]

Arthur Pearce's nearly nine years at Lockharts had turned the firm around, literally bringing it back from imminent collapse. In assessing his impact, nothing short really of revolutionary in the catering trade, Joseph Bentley at the *Temperance Caterer* paid him impressive tribute: "the houses were modernized, the show windows were artistically set out, the service was reorganized, the latest and most approved methods of management were introduced, and the Ideal Restaurants were started to meet the requirements of classes above those previously catered for."[47]

[43] *Financial Times*, 27 Sept. 1909; *Temperance Caterer*, 15 July 1910 and 15 July 1911.
[44] *Temperance Caterer*, 15 July 1911 and 15 Apr. 1913; *Financial Times*, 8 June 1911.
[45] I want to thank Trevor Lloyd for this observation.
[46] *Temperance Caterer*, 15 Aug. 1907.
[47] Ibid., 15 Apr. and 15 Nov. 1913.

Upheaval at Lockharts had significance for John Pearce in three vital senses. First was the downgrading of the managing director with a seat on the Board into a mere subordinate—a general manager without board representation. Second, the company ironically turned to Arthur, son of John Pearce with whom he had gained considerable experience of the catering trade—especially as assistant general manager since 1899—as the new general manager. Arthur assumed his new role in June, 1905.[48] Finally, since Lockharts catered to much the same clientele as the BTT, it set a precedent not lost on John Pearce's critics.

The war years resulted in a major setback to sustained recovery. Negative net profits were earned, with no dividends declared. Chairman Thring expressed the pessimism afflicting the catering industry. Turning a profit was, he confessed, unthinkable. "It would be quite easy to increase their prices so as to cover the increased cost to themselves, but within a week … they would have emptied their shops, and might close their doors."[49] Lockharts shuttered four unremunerative depots in response to two developments. First, there was an inability to pass along higher food prices to customers. Second, shortage of meat cut from the joint drove many customers away. Patrons, said the chairman, "were suspicious of curry, hashes and stews." Other alternatives—vegetarian meals and egg and cheese substitutes—likewise found few takers.[50] Not until 1919 did the company earn £179 in net profits and declare dividends of 5.5%, though preference shareholders earned nothing from 1912 well into the 1920s.[51]

Much larger than Lockharts, Slaters faced dissimilar catering problems, despite being diversified, with fishmonger, butcher and florist shops opened in the West End. Of these businesses, fish was of foremost importance. Slaters operated, so the *Financial Times* thought, "the largest high-class fishmongers in London." In the late 1890s, its restaurants too reached beyond the "one square mile," as Slaters' depots appeared on the Strand, Piccadilly Circus and Oxford Street. The *Financial Times* was bullish. "Nothing," it remarked late in 1902, "seems to pay so well as the catering business."[52] Rejecting the concept of running multiple shops, Slaters prided

[48] *Financial Times*, 28 Jan., 9 May, and 21 June 1905.

[49] *Temperance Caterer*, 15 July 1916.

[50] *Financial Times*, 20 June 1916, 17 June 1917, and 11 July 1918.

[51] *Economist*, 12 July 1919 and 17 Jan. 1920. Typical company regulations said ordinary shareholders should not get any dividends until preference shareholders had been paid first. It is unclear why the company deviated from this norm.

[52] *Temperance Caterer*, 15 March 1896; *Financial Times*, 14 June 1897, 15 Nov. 1902, and 11 Sept. and 1 Dec. 1905.

Table 6.3 Performance of Slaters, 1889–1912

Year	*Profits*	*Depots*	*Capital*	*Dividends*
1889	£8000	1	£100,000	11.5%
1899	£44,000	38	£300,000	12.5%
1906	£52,000	61	£355,000	12.5%
1912	£24,000	21	£355,000	7%

Sources: *Financial Times*, 12 June 1900, and 25 July and 25 Nov. 1908; *Temperance Caterer*, 15 June 1912

itself on possessing autonomous shops that prepared their own food (Table 6.3).[53]

Slaters grew enormously in the 1890s, with the size of profits, numbers of depots and amount of share capital, each increasing. According to John Crowle, its chairman, "the business was in great demand by the public, and the management had been asked to open establishments in almost every quarter of London." Given the tripling of capital in one decade, Slaters moved from being a small concern to becoming a powerful catering company, the third largest in the country. Though never a huge supplier of luncheons, the firm had four City houses serving altogether 2000 meals daily. To achieve this turnover, six patrons, in turn, occupied each seat over the two-hour luncheon period (1–3 p.m.). Expansion into the ice trade, likewise, grew at a remarkable pace, increasing 3.5 times in five years. Slaters, its restaurants concentrated in the "one square mile," now spread into the West End, with a large depot accommodating 220 people opening at Piccadilly Circus (Fig. 6.1). These were extraordinarily prosperous years for shareholders. One woman saw her £6000 investment in the company grow to £30,000–35,000.[54]

This phenomenal expansion, however, did not last. Between 1899 and 1905, Slaters confronted an unprecedented crisis, losing 75% of its share value, easily surpassing Joseph Lyons, which had dropped about 25% in value.[55] The former's ordinary dividends, apparently immune to these developments, began a delayed long-term decline, more than halving over six years (1905–1911).[56] Examination of receipts revealed the culprit.

[53] *Financial Times*, 8 Dec. 1914.

[54] Wintle, "London Restaurants," pp. 447–48; *Financial Times*, 1 Dec. 1899, 12 June 1900 and 15 Nov. 1902; *Temperance Caterer*, 15 March 1896.

[55] *Temperance Caterer*, 15 March 1896; *Financial Times*, 3 March 1910.

[56] *Financial Times*, 9 May, 21 June, 1 and 7 Nov., and 1 Dec. 1905, and 3 March 1910; *Economist*, 14 Dec. 1918.

Fig. 6.1 Slaters' Restaurant (Piccadilly) (Reproduced by permission of the Mary Evans Picture Library)

Housewives, themselves confronting tighter budgets, spent one-fifth less per visit. Slaters was also being squeezed in another direction—rising food prices, which with small profit margins on each transaction could not be passed on to customers. These pressures, coupled with proliferating numbers of middle-class restaurants that had saturated the market, prompted the Board's slashing of prices at its restaurants. To generate the same turnover, the company needed to attract 15–20% more customers. Desperate to hold its existing custom, Slaters lowered prices still further in 1907, continuing the existing ordinary dividends of 12%. But the respite was temporary, as both net profits and dividends slumped in the ensuing years.[57]

Dividends fell sharply from 1905, in part, because Slaters transferred money normally earmarked for shareholders to maintaining and upgrading outlets. "We thought it better to be lavish rather than to be niggardly

[57] *Financial Times*, 1 Dec. 1906, 3 Dec. 1907, 10 June 1908, and 7 Dec. 1909; *Economist*, 14 Dec. 1918.

upon expenses," commented John W. Reacher, its new chairman. In other strategic moves, the company continued opening more outlets, drawing funds from augmented share capital, which reached £355,000 in 1906. Expansion came at a hefty price for a choice location. Opening sumptuous premises on Oxford Street, "the finest position in the whole of the West End," remarked the *Financial Times*, Slaters spent an astonishing £10,000 acquiring a 999-year lease. Perhaps the success of adding a large ladies room in what one paper characterised as "the most comfortable and reasonably priced restaurant in the West End" warranted the huge outlay in a difficult financial period.[58]

Notwithstanding its diversified interests, Slaters created a reserve fund, as the company's articles directed. To prevent shareholders clamouring for directors to maximise dividends, company articles specified that shareholders would receive a flat 10% with the rest (25%) being placed in reserve, an amount comparable to one-fourth of its capital. Slaters' reserve fund grew from £61,000 (1902) to nearly £89,000 (1904), a sizable amount among catering companies.[59]

Slaters defined goodwill in its own unique way. Goodwill represented the amount Slaters had paid for restaurants. Rejecting a policy of posting erratic dividends, Slaters instead opted to declare steadily rising ones. Chairman John Crowle viewed money allocated to reserves as a basis of business stability. To keep pace with establishments' ever-growing in numbers, the company increased its goodwill commensurately.[60] It had also paid high dividends. Unfortunately, the goodwill, having progressively accumulated since the company's formation, stood at over £124,000 in 1911. The new chairman, Sir David Burnett, had proposed a different strategy in which Slaters would pay lower dividends as a way of writing off goodwill. Declining dividends from 1907, however, forestalled this needed change, amid shareholder unhappiness about the company's loss of over one-third its net dividends in just seven years. Slaters also had placed sizeable sums, some £24,000, in leases reserve.[61]

To offset tightening competition, Slaters implemented a two-fold new marketing strategy, reaching out to clerks—part of the lower middle class—as customers and starting depots in the more upmarket West End.

[58] *Financial Times*, 3 Dec. 1907 and 7 Dec. 1912.
[59] Ibid., 1 Dec. 1902.
[60] Ibid., 3 Dec. 1898, 1 Dec. 1902 and 1 Dec. 1904.
[61] Ibid., 1 Dec. 1904, 7 Dec. 1911 and 3 Dec. 1913; *Economist*, 14 Dec. 1918.

Both approaches seemed successful. Notwithstanding stiff competition, Slaters' West End depots were holding "their own."[62]

By 1908, the Edwardian trade depression hit catering companies with working-class customers as their backbone particularly hard, especially those such as Slaters, which catered to patrons wanting substantial lunches and dinners, rather than less expensive teas and cakes.[63] Slightly higher prices as well as strict economy were now Slaters' twin motivating factors. Companies similarly placed to Slaters followed a common survival strategy: reduce prices, shut unprofitable restaurants and economise on decorations of those remaining. Following this philosophy, Slaters abandoned expansion from 1908, but when forced to open new outlets, the chairman promised to "spend less money on them" than usual.[64]

To cope with the business crisis, John W. Reacher, chairman of Slaters, offered a stark appraisal of what the firm must do to survive: "If others were willing temporarily to forgo profits for the sake of retaining old and perhaps obtaining new customers, this company must be prepared to do the same." Such dire measures had profound consequences. Reducing prices cost Slaters £20,000–£25,000 in net profits, driving down its ordinary share capital by 8–10%. Worse came in 1909, when Reacher admitted that "a desire to spend as little as possible induces growing numbers of people to patronise the teashops and restaurants of a cheaper class to ours." Anxious to stabilise—if not reverse—plummeting profits, Slaters inaugurated an entirely new policy in which its restaurants henceforth offered patrons the choice of ordering a half-portion at commensurately lower prices. Again, a relieved Reacher reassured shareholders that "this movement meets with much satisfaction and leads to an increase in our trade." His optimism was unfounded: the company experienced continuing financial problems.[65]

Slaters, like some other catering companies, had refused to write off leases in which sales had been declining. In the long run, this was disastrous. When depots had to be closed with lengthy periods left on the lease, the company had no choice but to write off the entire initial expenditure.

[62] *Financial Times*, 1 Dec. 1905 and 24 Nov. 1906.

[63] Ibid., 7 Dec. 1909.

[64] Ibid., 3 Dec. 1908 and 7 Dec. 1909.

[65] Ibid., 3 Dec. 1908, 7 Dec. 1909 and 29 Nov. 1911.

As Slaters' chairman knew so well, "this had absorbed money urgently required for repairs and redecoration of other shops."[66]

In the immediate pre-war years, Slaters' performance reached a plateau, with dividends at 7%. Trade was reviving in these years, so Slaters was doing less well than its competitors. As profits fell by one-fifth between 1909 and 1914, the stock market delivered a vote of no confidence: Slaters' stock prices fell from £4 to less than £1 per share within the twelve months of 1911.[67]

Amid these disturbing results, Sir David Burnett had replaced Reacher as chairman. Organisational structure was partly blamed for the company's dismal performance, so the Board enhanced the power of the new chairman. Formerly, two men served as managing directors, with seats on the Board. Now, one managing director resigned, while the other was demoted to the rank of general manager without a seat on the Board. Burnett thought Managing Director William Kirkland, downgraded to general manager, "had not sufficient energy and initiative and that the restaurants were suffering in consequence." Age was a factor in his decision: "A younger man and more active should undertake the control."[68]

The Aerated Bread Company (ABC), likewise, exacerbated rivalry when it inaugurated a new policy in the 1890s, in which it disposed of outlying outlets and focused on the City. Competition naturally intensified. Within short order, its City shops more than tripled in number and accounted for half of the company's total. Here, the surrounding businesses accounted for the frenetic tempo of what passed for lunch at a typical restaurant: "At the witching hour of one, it is thronged by hurried-looking men, intent on getting through their meal."[69]

"The World of the ABC," Dora Greenwell McChesney's article in the *Daily Mail*, conveyed vividly the ambiance of teashops at the turn of the century. Except in the City, women dominated them (Figs. 6.2, 6.3, and 6.4). In the vicinity of Regent Street and Piccadilly, suburban mothers, their daughters in tow, gave such shops a distinctive atmosphere, retiring for tea after shopping expeditions or cultured galleries. That the ABCs followed strict temperance policy also shaped the pervasive respectability which the "celebrated 'beef cup'" reinforced. Whether in the West End or

[66] Ibid., 16 Dec. 1909.

[67] Ibid., 7 Dec. 1911.

[68] Ibid., 6 Dec. 1910, 29 Nov. 1911 and 11 March 1916.

[69] Dora Greenwell McChesney, "The World of the ABC," *Daily Mail*, 15 Apr. 1903.

Fig. 6.2 ABC Teashop, Wilton Road, London (Author's Personal Copy)

Fig. 6.3 Interior of ABC depot (Ludgate Hill), mid-day, London (Reproduced by permission of the Mary Evans Picture Library)

An Aerated Bread Shop.

Fig. 6.4 Interior of an ABC teashop, 1920 (Mrs E.T. Cook, *Highways and Byways in London* (1920), p. 321)

further afield, "the place in all its varying forms is featureless, modern, unadventurous, and it subdues its frequenters to its own image."[70]

Of London's catering companies, perhaps only Lyons could match ABC's incredible financial performance in the years 1896–1905. Investors received 387.5% in cash dividends, equivalent to £681,000 in cash and bonuses of shares. Over a seventeen-year period (1884–1901), the share capital had increased 100%, while profits easily outpacing this had soared almost 500%. Such success arose from ever-growing numbers of custom-

[70] Ibid.; Edward Callow, "City Taverns, Chop and Coffee Houses, & C.," *City Press*, reproduced in *Temperance Caterer*, 15 Jan. 1898.

ers. It served 1,579,240 more customers in 1905 than the previous year; its 130 depots dispensed 100,000 meals daily in 1908, second only to Lyons, which served about 250,000 meals daily in 120 depots. Breakfast meals of eggs and bacon or hot or cold fish were served at nearly all of the company's depots. Typifying the more upmarket patrons, ABC's meals normally cost between 3d. and 1s. each, but offered no vegetables and little hot food. Chairman George Edwards pointed to the "catering for the higher-class public"—including members of the establishment (notably the Royal family and the Archbishop of Canterbury)—as one of two factors responsible for the company's astonishing growth. The other factor derived from ABC's developing its own manufactured goods.[71]

In the Edwardian era the company's performance changed substantially. Financially troubled like other catering firms, the ABC saw its share value plunge by almost one-third and net profits fall by one-fifth in 1903–1904.[72] Paradoxically, the ABC's balance sheet sat oddly with its popularity: more customers patronised the firm's 122 shops than ever before. In putting aside £10,000 in reserves in 1906, the company opted to protect itself from deteriorating economic circumstances, but sacrificed declaring high profits and dividends.[73]

From 1907, its dividends slumped, falling from 37.5 % (1907) to 22.5% (1911). Its shares, quoted at £15 around the turn of the century, had likewise dropped, not even reaching £3 a share in 1911. Its turnover too had risen modestly, while net profits had fallen by over a third. Never again would its dividends reach the extraordinary heights of 30% and more, much less the 40% of the years 1898–1903.[74]

Such mounting financial problems arose from serious underlying business problems, which neither George Edwards (ABC chairman and managing director) nor the Board of Directors fully comprehended.

[71] *Temperance Caterer*, 15 Nov. 1901, 15 July 1903, 15 Sept. 1908 and 15 Jan. 1909; *Financial Times*, 30 Oct. 1891, 7 Nov. 1905 and 6 Nov. 1906. City teashops did not cater to the Establishment; popular with these individuals was the Oxford Street depot (*Temperance Caterer*, 15 Nov. 1912).

[72] Annual Reports and ABC meetings, the only sources for the company's financial performance, stopped disclosing dividends in the years 1904–1906. Extrapolating from net profits of £59,500 and £61,400 (1904–1905) suggests dividends fell into the 30–34% range (*Financial Times*, 7 Nov. 1905 and 31 Oct. 1907).

[73] "Gold in the Tea-Cup"; Robert Leon, "Rise and Fall of the Aerated Bread Company," *Camden History Review* 25 (2001): 48; *Financial Times*, 6 Nov. 1906.

[74] *Financial Times*, 20 Dec. 1909 and 15 Nov. 1911; *Times*, 19 Oct. 1912; *Economist*, 11 Nov. 1911; *Temperance Caterer*, 15 Nov. 1911.

Appointed at an extraordinary general meeting in 1909, a Shareholders' Committee "portrayed directors as a casual group, without any of the special knowledge necessary for managing the business, relying on out-of-date methods, and content with an unsatisfactory system of organisation." Castigating Edwards as bungling and the Board of Directors as inept, it recommended that he resign and be replaced with a general manager.[75]

Retail sales of tobacco epitomised the ABC's misguided business strategies, charged critics. Shareholders challenged the Board's priority in selling tobacco, "now one of the most unremunerative businesses in London." Impressed with profits that Salmon & Gluckstein had made from its 67 tobacconists, directors beginning in 1906 had invested in opening 10 tobacco shops, their profits "under the most favourable conditions" reaching no more than a meagre 4%. Ye Mecca's similar disappointing trade with cigars provided critics with much ammunition. Given the company's commitment to catering and refreshment, "the most lucrative form of retail business known" and paying 30% dividends, shareholders demanded the Board reappraise its business strategies.[76]

Disagreement between dissident shareholders, on the one hand, and George Edwards and the Board of Directors, on the other, pivoted on one issue—the authority, duties and power of a general manager. Determined only perfunctorily to accommodate shareholders' demands, Edwards wanted a general manager without a seat on the Board. "The Company," he contended, "was not managed by the General Manager but by the Board, and the General Manager's duty was to carry out the instructions of the Board." Thus, asserted Edwards, the general manager would lack any independence whatsoever. The Board equally emphasised the manager's subordinate status in another way, directing that he also assume the administrative role of company secretary.[77]

The Shareholders' Committee opposed ABC leadership, reaching outside the firm for an altogether different business approach. For their part, angry shareholders sought a general manager capable of exercising authority entirely free of the old guard's intervention, criticism or opposition. Horace Pearce was hired to assume the new role of general manager without a seat on the Board in 1910 at the behest of the Shareholders'

[75] *Economist*, 4 June 1910.

[76] Shareholder circular, *Financial Times*, 20 Dec. 1909; *Temperance Caterer*, 15 July 1906 and 15 Jan. 1910.

[77] "Interview with Horace Pearce," *Financial Times*, 15 Nov. 1911.

Committee, with the unstated expectation that he wield independent control in implementing "more progressive ideas" than those of Edwards. Given both his background as John Pearce's son and experience as managing director of JP Restaurants, the Committee felt that he alone possessed insights into the formidable difficulties confronting the ABC's recovery. Pearce described succinctly his own understanding of his position: he must be "given a free hand."[78]

Edwards' archaic business methods, Pearce discovered, had led to depots being shorthanded, causing much customer discontent. Still worse, "I found a number of houses in bad condition." Some neglected depots had become so "dilapidated" that Pearce had no choice but to spend considerable sums of money bringing them up to the standard expected of ABC restaurants. His policy of improving depots, which had increased financial outlays, had justified itself. Although shareholders were unhappy because the interim dividend had declined, Pearce noted that some of the dividends lost had been regained over the course of the year.[79]

According to Pearce's diagnosis of ABC's precipitate decline, the company desperately needed to modernise its business strategy that reflected recent changes in catering as well as heightened public expectations of what dining had come to represent in Edwardian England. In this view, he had the Shareholders' Committee's complete support. In an interview with the *Temperance Caterer*, he warned that "the Company today is existing upon its past reputation, and unless some drastic reforms take place, its position is one of peril."[80]

Personality differences aroused deep animosity between the men. Having Pearce forced upon him and resentful of what he saw as a shareholder rebuke, Edwards blocked any changes which the new general manager advocated. "Edwards," Pearce exasperatedly declared, "*strongly objects to the sight of anything new.*" In an interview with the *Financial Times*, Pearce derided the policy of Edwards in which the general manager would "only be allowed to do what was done before." Pearce fully understood the

[78] Ibid.; *Financial Times*, 14 Oct. 1911. Lack of clarity obscures the difference between a general manager and a managing director, a problem insolvable without company records. What motivated shareholders to give a general manager a "free hand?" How would his activity differ from that of a managing director? Was this "free hand" idea relatively common, or was it just that the Pearce sons were able to insist on it? So many pertinent questions must remain unanswerable without company records, reminiscences or memoirs.

[79] "Interview with W. Horace Pearce," *Temperance Caterer*, 14 Oct. and 15 Nov. 1911.

[80] Ibid., 15 Nov. 1911; *Economist*, 4 June 1910.

appropriate but radical solution: Edwards must be deposed. So too thought the *Economist*. But it was not Edwards who capitulated. Resigning after just a year of this unworkable arrangement, Pearce expressed his discontent in a *Financial Times* interview. "Nearly every reform I proposed was from the first opposed and ultimately frustrated," he protested. Turning his wrath on the chairman, Pearce castigated Edwards, whose "influence is greater than his knowledge of modern catering conditions warrants."[81]

Shareholders shared Pearce's frustration. Following his resignation, they attacked the Board at an ordinary meeting in October 1911: "Are we, fools," inquired one outraged investor? "It's about time some of the old fossils who are absolutely unfit should be sent off the Board." To this tirade, fellow shareholders responded with glee, giving him "loud cheers and stamping of feet." Another shareholder focused on the ABC's long-term decline. "The Company is steadily going down year by year," he complained, and pointed to the fact that "at one time the shares stood at £15, now they are under £3."[82]

Few in the catering industry really appreciated what underlay the acrimony of Edwards and the Board of Directors, on one hand, and Pearce and shareholders, on the other, more than Joseph Bentley, editor of the *Temperance Caterer*. Astutely interpreting the quarrel, he stressed that "What would do in the catering trade even five years ago, won't do today." Quickly changing norms and assumptions in catering transformed retailing food and what customers had come to expect, requiring that the ABC's governing body embrace a more informed and enlightened approach in guiding the firm. Clearly, the old guard running the company resented and resisted ideas that questioned their authority, especially from a younger man whose father epitomised the importance of constantly improving catering as a time-tested way to maintaining and expanding market share.[83]

The upshot of ABC's managerial crisis was that George Edwards survived as chairman, but critically in exchange for concessions. Pearce offered to withdraw his resignation if given greater authority and freedom to act as a managing director, but the Board declined this.[84]

[81] "Interview with Horace Pearce," *Financial Times*, 14 Oct. 1911; *Temperance Caterer*, 15 Nov. 1911; *Economist*, 4 June 1910.

[82] *Temperance Caterer*, 15 Nov. 1911.

[83] Ibid. See pp. 189–90.

[84] "Interview with Horace Pearce," *Financial Times*, 15 Nov. 1911.

The "reform party" of shareholders nevertheless had achieved some significant concessions from a Board which held a good deal of power and had already defeated one general manager:

- The company agreed to lease its tobacco depots.[85]
- The post of managing director, created in 1874 and combined with that of the chairman, was now abolished and a general manager instead appointed.
- The Board of Directors was increased from four to six. Unable to find someone qualified to act as a general manager, the Board appointed Charles E. Davies, who lacked experience in catering but had wider expertise in business and organising skills.[86]

Various factors had fomented the crisis. Shareholders had become accustomed to the ABC earning high profits and declaring comparable dividends. What they chose not to recognise was "the power of competition to diminish profits." As the *Economist* remarked late in 1911, "the most serious factor in the company's affairs is its inability to meet the competition of its prosperous rival."[87]

But at a deeper level, the acrimonious debate was a struggle over authority, between an old guard that projected its influence through a chairman who also held the post of managing director, on the one hand, and shareholders, who viewed the policies, priorities and powers of ABC leadership as utterly unacceptable, on the other. In this shareholder rebellion, neither side vanquished the other, though each had to relinquish some cherished goals: without acting as a managing director, the chairman was less powerful, while shareholders asserted their attitudes through a general manager, who as a non-member of the Board had subordinate status. Perhaps as a pyrrhic victory, shareholders could console themselves with having ended the ABC's promotion of tobacco retailing.

Of the six catering companies relying primarily on working- and middle-class custom examined in this chapter, only the Express Dairy Company avoided internal upheaval in Edwardian England, largely because its restaurants contributed modestly to overall profits. Boards of Directors at Ye

[85] *Economist*, 11 Nov. 1911.

[86] *Temperance Caterer*, 15 Nov. 1911; *Economist*, 11 and 18 Nov. 1911; *Financial Times*, 15 Nov. 1911.

[87] *Economist*, 1 Jan. 1910 and 11 Nov. 1911.

Mecca, Lockharts, Slaters, the ABC and the BTT in turn confronted disgruntled committees of inspection in the years 1904–1909 and 1915. Each company had similar problems—declining profits, dividends and gross sales, together with unremunerative shops. Three of them—Ye Mecca, Express Dairy and Slaters—had periods of missed dividends,[88] while Slaters and two others (ABC and Lockharts) had plummeting share values. Whether the companies had set aside reserves or declared some or no goodwill seemed to matter not at all in terms of long-term financial health (Tables 6.4 and 6.5). What mattered most in restoring a company to stability were skills of the general manager, as Arthur Pearce demonstrated at Lockharts.

Table 6.4 Performance of catering companies in Edwardian England

	Share capital	*Declining dividends*	*Reserves*	*Goodwill*
Ye Mecca	£100,000	1898–1913[a]		£46,470
Express Dairy	£100,000	1903–1905,[a] 1911–1914	£35,000	
ABC	£2,532,531	1903–1912	£10,000	0
Lockharts	£240,265; £137,000 (1909)	1903–1909	£6200	£65,532

[a]None declared

Table 6.5 Stock prices in leading catering companies, 1899–1909

Company	*1899*	*1909*
ABC	15 13⁄16	3 ½
BTT	3 1⁄8	Liquidated
J. Lyons	8 1⁄8	5 ¾
Lockharts' Preference	1 7⁄16	11⁄16
Slaters	3 15⁄16	15⁄16

Source: *Economist*, 1 Jan. 1910

[88] Even smaller firms such as Cabins missed dividends. Of the eleven years (1902–1912) for which information survives, it declared no dividends in five of them, despite having half of its depots located in other parts of London than in the City (*Times*, 19 Oct. 1912; *Financial Times*, 18 March 1902).

Excluding the BTT, Slaters encountered by far the worst economic crisis of all the major firms based chiefly in the City. Two chairmen and the entire Board of Directors lost their positions, signifying the failure to reverse the company's headlong slide into disaster. Certainly Slaters embraced creative solutions to its weakening financial position, from instituting structural changes in oversight of the company and diversifying its business into the West End to radically cutting menu prices (at the expense of profits and share value) and bolstering amounts placed in reserve. Too late did the company propose paying shareholders' lower dividends as a strategy for writing off goodwill. Economising on depot upkeep, a logical interim step, had long-term serious consequences, the loss of business reputation and mounting future costs for modernising outdated premises.

Lockharts likewise jettisoned a chairman and managing director, owing to serious miscalculations with earmarking ample reserves and writing off depreciating assets. Struggling for years with missed dividends and depressed, off-putting depots, Lockharts hired Arthur Pearce who provided shrewd leadership, seeing the company through the worst years in its entire history.

Serious economic woes among catering firms in Edwardian England provoked struggles to assert greater control over management. ABC, Slaters and Lockharts—three of the largest firms—eliminated the position of managing director, substituting instead, a general manager. This liberated the chairmen and Boards of Directors to pursue policies independently of another rival source of authority and potential criticism as well as conflict. In focusing on organisational structure rather than expertise, managerial skills, experience or talent, the Boards of Directors were in many ways seeking a scapegoat to placate unhappy shareholders. These difficult years required imaginative, tenacious, shrewd and insightful leaders with wide practical experience. Such men were in short supply, except in the Pearce clan.[89] As distinguished clan leader, John Pearce grasped fully those traits necessary for leadership.

The crisis ultimately engulfing the BTT must be seen amid catering woes at the Aerated Bread Company. From 1907 its dividends slumped, falling from 37.5 % (1907) to 22.5% (1911).[90] Since the mid-1870s, the ABC had combined the posts of chairman and managing director, but in 1909 an Investigative Committee castigated George Edwards, holder of

[89] *Financial Times*, 1 May 1910, and 6 and 14 Oct. 1911; *Economist*, 4 June 1910.

[90] *Financial Times*, 15 Nov. 1911; *Times*, 19 Oct. 1912.

both positions, as incompetent and the Board of Directors as weak. In its strictures, the Committee "portrayed directors as a casual group, without any of the special knowledge necessary for managing the business, relying on out-of-date methods, and content with an unsatisfactory system of organisation." It thus recommended that Edwards be replaced with a general manager. To stifle dissent, the ABC Board of Directors appointed Horace Pearce as general manager. This well-meant arrangement proved soon untenable. Familiar with the catering business, he protested at not having "a man of more progressive ideas" than Edwards as chairman, whose antiquarian views thwarted any innovations. In an interview with the *Financial Times*, Pearce derided the policy of Edwards in which the general manager would "only be allowed to do what was done before."[91] Treated humiliatingly as a mere cipher, Horace Pearce predictably resigned. That the ABC had turned to another of Pearce's sons for expertise and guidance again underlined the family reputation: John stood as the patriarch of the much-respected clan.

[91] *Financial Times*, 1 May 1910, and 6 and 14 Oct. 1911; *Economist*, 4 June 1910.

CHAPTER 7

Collapse of the British Tea Table Company

"It is only another instance of the old, old story," reflected journalist Joseph Bentley. "One man by patient toil builds up a business, and then those who think they know, but don't, come in and wreck it."[1] For John Pearce, the Edwardian years marked the most serious financial and personal crisis he faced in his entire career. Manoeuvred into resigning from the company he had founded and carefully managed, he watched sadly as it collapsed into bankruptcy and disappeared altogether.

For the first decade of the company's history beginning in 1886, the economy expanded gradually. Although few records survive for these early years, the company's growth can be inferred thereafter from total sales figures as well as the auditor's report issued on the eve of the new company's formation. These suggest quite prosperous years, with total weekly sales of meals soaring from 275,000 (1892) to 400,000 (1898). Aggregate profits paralleled this increase, more than doubling from under £10,000 (1893–1894) to over £20,000 (1895–1896). Just before the new company's flotation in 1897, profits were projected to exceed £25,000, a 250 percent increase in four years.[2] Cumulatively, the two companies did an enormous

[1] *Times*, 1 June 1907; *Temperance Caterer*, 15 Dec. 1909.

[2] *Financial Report of Auditors for Pearce's Dining and Refreshment Rooms and British Tea Table Co., 15 June 1897, Daily Mail*, 16 June 1897.

D. W. Gutzke, *John Pearce and the Rise of the Mass Food Market in London, 1870–1930*, https://doi.org/10.1007/978-3-030-27095-7_7

trade, declaring dividends of 20% and 30% in 1895 and 1896.[3] While dividends declined in the next three years, they still remained respectable, ranging between 10 and 12%, matching the performance of Slaters and exceeding those of Lockharts.

Predictably, prosperity generated consensus on the Board of Directors at the British Tea Table Company, Pearce, his ally and the chairman, Sir Edward Sullivan, at his elbow, working harmoniously with John Hurst, the apparent successor as chairman. Pearce must have left some aspects of finance to Sullivan and the Board, with Pearce perhaps saying, "We need money for new developments," but leaving the directors to decide if the money should be raised by a loan from a bank, debentures, unsecured bonds or issuing new shares: the Board would have to agree about general prospects for development. This was relatively easy for most of the eleven years that Pearce and Sullivan worked together in the company, because the economy was expanding gradually until it reached a peak about the beginning of the Boer War. Optimism, the natural product of the later 1890s, pervaded the outlook of the company's governing board.

Amid this buoyant context, the two constituent companies merged in 1897, forming a new limited liability company, confusingly called the British Tea Table Co.[4] How promoters of the BTT calculated the amount of goodwill, representing over one-fourth of the total purchase price, had long-term significance. According to the government's subsequent Liquidation Report in 1910, the amount allocated for goodwill had been equivalent to six years' purchase of the profits, deemed in hindsight to be an "excessive amount for businesses which depended for their success upon the management at the time of the company." A critical appraisal in the *Economist* one year after the company was founded had raised this same issue. "The distribution [of dividends] is larger … than the profits justify, for nothing has been written off from the cost of goodwill, which stands at the large amount of £130,000," the journal argued. In the ensuing years, shareholders periodically raised the

[3] *Temperance Caterer*, 15 Jun 1898. Pearce himself recalled that in the company's best years, dividends had reached 40% (*Financial Times*, 30 July 1908).

[4] The company owned fifty branches: twenty-three (Pearce's Dining & Refreshment Rooms with twelve hotels attached), and twenty-seven British Tea Table Company depots with two hotels. These were appraised altogether at £19,763 (*Financial Report of Auditors for Pearce's Dining and Refreshment Rooms and British Tea Table Co., 15 June 1897, Daily Mail*, 16 June 1897).

subject of goodwill at annual general meetings, though the Board of Directors largely ignored it altogether.[5]

The struggle between Pearce and the Hurst faction must be understood as part of a broader trend in which the chairmen and Boards of Directors of some major catering companies sought to exert authority over managing directors through various tactics—dismissal, demotion to general managers without seats on the Board or even eliminating the position altogether.

John Pearce and J.P. Hurst as managing director and chairman respectively became engaged in a power struggle in which the winner would secure unfettered control running the BTT. They came from different parts of the social spectrum, pitting the resourceful, talented "player" against the acknowledged "gentleman."[6] Born in London's East End, Pearce was the uneducated but gifted working-class penny capitalist who had an intuitive grasp of retailing food, grounded on extensive experience, and strong sympathy with the struggles of the underclass. Sensing changes in catering in 1892, Pearce had advocated going upmarket with a new chain, ultimately named the British Tea Table Company. In earning an astonishing dividend of 35%, impressive even when compared with larger competitors, the new company confirmed his reputation as the foremost caterer to those with limited funds.[7] Hurst, in contrast, came from the privileged elite, university-educated, moderately wealthy and convinced of his own innate class superiority. It infuriated Hurst to be forced to cede authority over practical managerial details to Pearce, his social inferior. Hurst the gentleman, instinctively felt any intelligent, well-bred person could run the company, especially someone who had gleaned much insight from watching Pearce conduct affairs for over a decade.

Given these vast dissimilarities, Hurst and his allies naturally regarded Pearce as overpaid, drawing substantial but undeserved compensation as the managing director. Under BTT rules, each director received £1500

[5] *Temperance Caterer*, 15 Feb. 1910; *Economist*, 28 May 1898; *Financial Report of Auditors for Pearce's Dining and Refreshment Rooms and British Tea Table Co., 15 June 1897, Daily Mail*, 16 June 1897.

[6] D.C. Coleman, "Gentlemen and Players," *Economic History Review* 26 (1973): 108–09; John F. Wilson, *British Business History, 1720–1994* (Manchester: Manchester University Press, 1995), p. 116; also see David W. Gutzke, "Sydney Nevile: Squire in the Slums or Progressive Brewer?" *Business History* 53 (2011): 961–62.

[7] *Report by the Comptroller of the Companies Department, Board of Trade, for the Year Ending 31 Dec. 1909*, p. 16.

annually as salary, with an additional percentage awarded when net profits surpassed £15,000. As a managing director, Pearce received naturally the pre-eminent sum, more than twice as much as the then chairman of the Board, J.P. Hurst:

John Pearce	£23,550
J.P. Hurst	£11,600
Col. S.H. Oldham	£6970

That Pearce had an astonishing record in directing the company in an intensely competitive market apparently mattered not at all. Relentless unjustified criticism convinced Pearce that "he was looked upon as a man who was taking a large sum that was not honestly earned." Overlooked in this appraisal was the fact that in terms of overall profits, Pearce, entitled to receive 10%, opted to forgo 2.5% as sign of his fairness. Under his contract, moreover, directors had the power to terminate his position once he fulfilled his five-year agreement, but far from exercising this option, they urged Pearce to remain as managing director.[8] In light of these circumstances, Pearce, aware of being resented, acquitted himself well, placing the company's interests before his own personal feelings.

Class outlook likewise divided them. The Hurst faction disliked Pearce—humble, modest, sensitive, ingenuous, candid and the Board's only teetotaller—as much for his transparency as for his evangelical moorings. Given his social origins, perhaps his own disinclinations as well, Pearce was reluctant to assert his views to those he saw as his social superiors. "Small minds resent a difference of opinion as a personal slight," observed the shrewd Reverend James J. Ellis, Pearce's first biographer, fellow philanthropist and long-time acquaintance.[9]

Sullivan had successfully diffused hostility between John Pearce, talented founder of the company, the player, and J. D. Hurst, member of the Board of Directors since Pearce & Plenty became a joint stock company[10] in 1886, who exemplified traits of the gentleman. Not surprisingly, Pearce

[8] *Financial Times*, 20 May 1905; *Times*, 11 Feb. 1910; *Temperance Caterer*, 15 Feb. 1910.

[9] Rev. James J. Ellis, *Pluck, Patience and Power: The Life Story of John Pearce of "Pearce and Plenty"* (London: H.R. Allenson, [1910]), pp. 162, 195; Marguerite Williams, *John Pearce: The Man who Played the Game* (London: Religious Tract Society, 1928), p. 154.

[10] The company was registered as a joint stock company, but not quoted on the stock exchange (*Evidence of the Royal Commission on Liquor Licensing Laws*, 1898, 36 (Cmnd. 8694), p. 244).

recoiled from Hurst's distasteful, disagreeable and disheartening demeanour. Within six months of Pearce & Plenty's establishment, Pearce thus declared the situation unbearable: "I went to see Sir Edward Sullivan and told him I wanted to be released." In this instance, Sullivan dissuaded him from resigning, but this merely postponed, not resolved, confronting the roots of their disagreements.[11]

Of the directors, two—Sullivan and Col. H.H. Oldham—acted as a cohesive team, sympathetic to Pearce's insights and grateful for his gifts.[12] Throughout his first thirty years as a London caterer, Pearce, the quintessential penny capitalist, had—with both unstinted hard work and business sagacity—transformed his coffee "Gutter Stall" into a catering enterprise of impressive size. Sharing a mutual interest in philanthropy, he and Sullivan—from different ends of the social spectrum—had forged a dynamic relationship which propelled Pearce & Plenty into a major late Victorian catering company. When Pearce had confessed to his limited understanding of business, Sullivan, ever the confidant, loyal friend, admirer and conciliator, reassured him of steadfast support. Nevertheless, Pearce found his freedom of manoeuvre considerably restricted, but not, fortunately, entirely negated. With Sullivan as a staunch ally, Pearce received the authority to develop his ideas in creating a formidable catering company. The Board's composition insulated Pearce against criticism. In 1898, the company opened seven new depots (six of them BTT), and earned impressive dividends of 11% and profits of £20,408. Presiding at the new company's second General Meeting, J.P. Hurst partly credited Pearce's "well-thought-out management" with this successful performance.[13]

For Pearce, the turning point in his relationship with the Board of Directors came when Sullivan died, Oldham (another ally) retired and Hurst succeeded Sullivan as chairman. Only later would Pearce encounter Sir Edward's lawyer, who underlined how prophetic was the baronet. "He believed in you, Pearce," he said, and then added: "He always said that there would be trouble after he had gone." Recalling these events, another friend of Pearce's, newspaper editor Joseph Bentley, pointed to the Hurst faction's failure to possess "a thorough grasp of every detail" as mainly responsible for the BTT's collapse.[14]

[11] Williams, *Pearce*, p. 147.

[12] *Daily Mail*, 16 June 1897.

[13] *Financial Times*, 25 May 1899.

[14] Ellis, *Pluck*, pp. 197, 205; Williams, *Pearce*, pp. 147, 153–54; *Temperance Caterer*, 15 Aug. 1908.

Perhaps anticipating a shift in power against which he had little recourse save to place an ally on the Board, Pearce recommended his eldest son, Arthur, who had worked with the firm for some ten years, be appointed assistant general manager with a seat on the Board. Directors unanimously agreed.[15]

When J.P. Hurst became chairman in 1899, the Board's political dynamic altered, dramatically disrupting the previous harmony. After interviewing Pearce years later, journalist Harold Bolce came away with much insight: "Powerful interests grew jealous of the man who had come up pushing a wheel barrow, and forced him out." Those closest to Pearce, notably the Rev. James Ellis, his first biographer, portrayed him in the critical years 1904–1906 as "a man under orders" who, along with his son, was beholden to "those who intended to keep them down."[16] Another Pearce confidant, friend and sympathiser, Joseph Bentley, assessed the power struggle from a unique vantage point. As editor of a leading catering journal, the *Temperance Caterer*, he fully grasped the dynamic forces shaping this sector of the economy. He saw the demise of the BTT as the product of the power struggle between oligarchs who dominated the Board of Directors, on the one hand, and Pearce, representing small shareholders, on the other. Once Pearce resigned, "the descent has been rapid" and predictable: "The strong hand and the personality of the founder of the business had gone." The gentlemen, possessors of vast wealth and commensurate stock and voting power, had triumphed over the player. There was, however, an irony. In the graphic language of one prominent gentleman, "The wrong horse was backed."[17]

Both Pearce and Hurst understood the impossibility of rapprochement, a realisation that fostered much of the distrust and most of the acrimony between them. Hence, the struggle was rooted in achieving absolute control over one's opponent and the company's policies. This explains why directors wanted a general manager whose lack of a seat on the Board underlined his subordinate status.[18]

[15] John Pearce to Editor, 3 Jan. 1899, *Financial Times*, 4 Jan. 1899.

[16] Williams, *Pearce*, p. 157; Ellis, *Pluck*, pp. 195–97; Harold Bolce, "Foreseeing What the People Want: How Initiative, Imagination and a Sense of Value Created an Industry from an Idea," *System* 26 (1914): 160; *Report by the Comptroller of the Companies Department for the Year Ending 31 Dec. 1909*, Board of Trade, p. 16.

[17] *Temperance Caterer*, 15 March 1908.

[18] See pp. 149–52.

To hire another managing director meant that the Board "had not the slightest chance of carrying out reforms which they had set themselves," warned Sir Edwin Galsworthy.[19] Over a managing director, the Board would exercise minimal authority, preventing it from dictating policy.[20] Though unmentioned at least publicly, the direct parallel with the Lockharts Board of Directors' fight with its managing director in these same years must have emboldened Hurst and his allies to govern alone.[21]

Financial woes in these years at the BTT were not initially radically worse than its competitors. The strident debate on its performance must be thus interpreted within this deteriorating wider economic context.

Per capita income slumped almost 10% below its 1903 level, and recovered completely only in 1913.[22] In response, workers economised on meals, leading to the BTT's falling profits and dividends in 1904–1906, the years in which the Hurst faction moved aggressively against Pearce. Net profits declined by a third, while ordinary dividends plummeted still more with a reduction of almost two-thirds (Charts 7.1 and 7.2). Having forced Pearce's resignation from the Board of Directors on 31 March 1905, the outset of this critical period, the Board was deprived of a convenient scapegoat to blame as responsible for the precipitating plunge of profits and dividends.[23] Pearce had to be removed as a prelude to the Board implementing new, more effective policies. To curb the Pearce influence, directors aggressively asserted their authority. Over Pearce's strenuous objections, they created a new position, Inspector of Shops, who reported directly to the Board, altogether bypassing Pearce as the managing director and foreshadowing precisely the subordinate role the Board cast for him.[24] The Hurst faction further instituted a provocative strategy in which it appointed a separate committee to investigate Pearce's handling of the company and recommend changes. Sensing a calculated scheme aimed at undermining his authority, Pearce angrily denounced the "continual pin-pricking and badgering of the Board of Directors." No one, he asserted, needed to instruct him in how to run the company.[25]

[19] *Financial Times*, 14 Nov. 1905.

[20] *Times*, 13 May 1905.

[21] See pp. 133–34.

[22] David Butler and Anna Sloman, *British Political Facts, 1900–79*, 5th ed. (New York: St. Martin's Press, 1980), p. 348.

[23] The Board formally ratified his resignation (*Times*, 13 May 1905).

[24] Ellis, *Pluck*, p. 195; *Financial Times*, 12 May 1906; *Times*, 13 May 1906.

[25] *Times*, 13 and 20 May 1905.

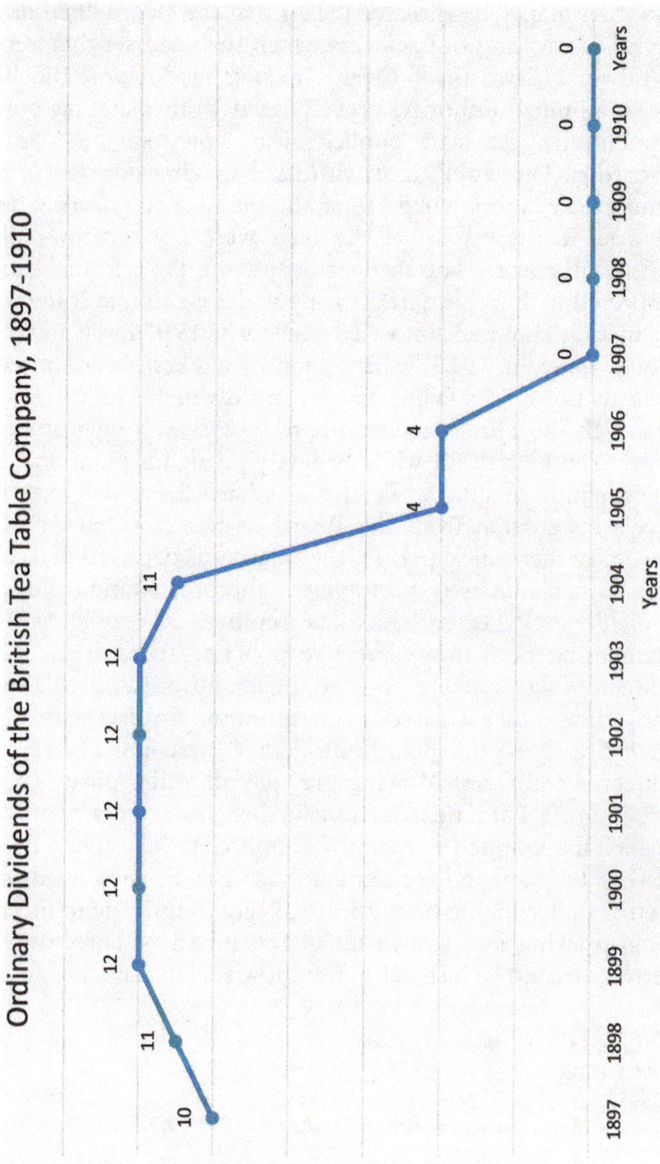

Chart 7.1 Ordinary dividends of the BTT, 1897–1910. Sources: For the years 1896–1910, see the following: *Economist*, *Financial Times*, *Temperance Chronicle* and *Times*

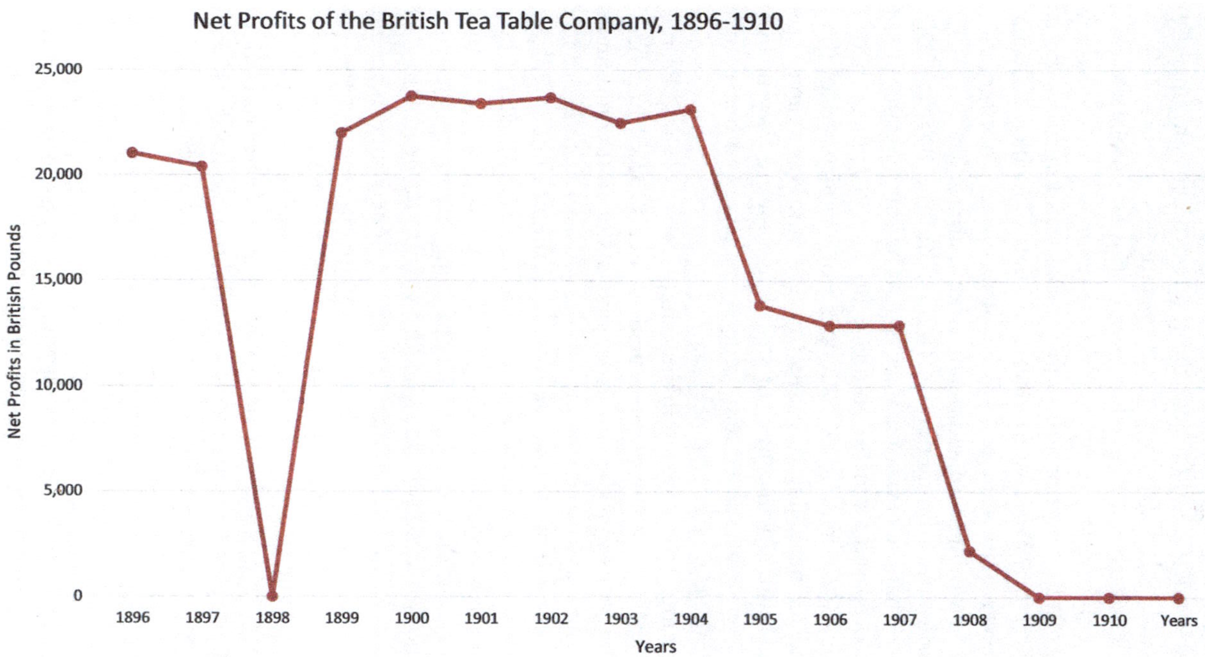

Chart 7.2 Net profits of the BTT, 1896–1910. Sources: For the years 1896–1910, see the following: *Economist*, *Financial Times*, *Temperance Chronicle* and *Times*

While recognising Pearce as the pre-eminent caterer to working-class patrons, Hurst questioned the managing director's insight into the more upmarket middle-class depots trading separately as the British Tea Table restaurants. The plebeian Pearce had gotten above his social station, Hurst insinuated, requiring the company find someone, undoubtedly a gentleman, with greater expertise and higher social standing than the current managing director. "We have to meet a competition which … is managed by men who are quite your equal," Hurst insultingly stressed, an assessment which he would share with many large shareholders.[26]

This assertion was disingenuous. If Hurst and the Board of Directors really believed that the two companies should be run separately, the Board should have prepared a scheme to divide up the BTT, or perhaps set up two managing directors, one for each operation—policy was for the Board to devise and for managing directors to carry out. Was Pearce, however, replaced that easily? Would men of such talent—were they to exist—be prepared to serve as subservient general managers rather than quasi-independent managing directors?

At this point, Hurst was thinking simply of replacing Pearce with another professional in the catering field. Pearce's career after his forced resignation suggests that the Board wrongly assumed it could find someone to equal him; at least, it was the normal activity of the Board to tell its managing director that it was time to go and then to find a replacement. A prudent Board would ponder possible replacements; even if everyone worked with the friendliest of feelings, a Board had to face the possibility that the managing director might let the company down by dying suddenly, and the Board must have some idea what to do next. Hurst's Board of Directors would have been happier with a general manager, but they might have pondered whether Pearce had run so much of the business that they would be prudent trying to keep the managing director system going. This was the perspective which Hurst himself accepted.[27]

Proud, hardworking and confident of his abilities, Pearce reacted strongly to an affront designed to undermine his credibility as decisively as his authority. Intuitively, he sensed its purpose: to force his resignation. The Board's

[26] Ibid.

[27] Pearce characterised his role as managing director who made profits for shareholders, but in no way arrogated the functions of the chairman or Board of Directors. Hence, he played no part in deciding allocation of profits, closure of depots or depreciation of premises (*Financial Times*, 30 July 1908 and 16 Apr. 1909).

lackey, the Inspector of Shops, "went about pulling away the stones" which Pearce had "built up, thus neutralising … Pearce's efforts," wrote Ellis, his biographer. There was no effective appeal. Responding to the managing director's protests, the Board had merely one reply: "We say it shall be so, and so it shall be."[28] His friend Ellis further summarised their plight: "Both father and son's opinions were set aside, their plans overruled, and their conduct subjected to criticism." The "systematic badgering to which he was subjected week after week by the chairman [Hurst] and Mr. Thompson rendered him very miserable," Pearce later told shareholders.[29]

Officially at least, the Board deemed Pearce's performance as inadequate for several reasons. His chief adversary on the Board, Chairman Hurst "suggested that he [Pearce] was hardly progressive enough." Why was it, asked Hurst, that "this company did not get some of the customers from the refreshment depots which had a higher tariff than theirs?" This was scarcely fair, given the financial woes of rivals. Rebuking Pearce had to do with something quite different. Privately, the Board in 1904 told him that at 57, "I was too old" for the position as managing director. This denigrating belief reiterated some shareholder comments made privately at earlier meetings: "Oh, yes, Mr. Pearce was a very good man, but played out." The Hurst faction critique also damned Pearce as complacent: the BTT "had stood still and other caterers had got ahead of them." One powerful incentive for deposing Pearce was the Board conviction that the company's declining revenues could be reversed, provided the BTT spent money upgrading its depots, a viable policy—so it was assumed—only if the post of managing director were eliminated or combined with the position of chairman.[30]

Compared with other leading catering companies in these years, the BTT performed satisfactorily until the 1904–1906 crises. In abolishing the position of managing director and substituting instead a general manager, ABC, Slaters and Lockharts followed an identical strategy which the BTT advocated as a solution to similar problems—declining profits, dividends and gross sales, together with unremunerative shops. What distinguished the BTT from its rivals with economic woes, of course, was its

[28] Ellis, *Pluck*, p. 195; *Financial Times*, 12 May 1906; *Times*, 13 May 1906.

[29] Ellis, *Pluck*, p. 205; *Financial Times*, 13 and 20 May 1905.

[30] *Daily Mail*, 13 May 1905; *Financial Times*, 30 May 1904, 13 and 20 May 1905, 16 May 1907, 28 Feb. 1908, and 26 Aug. 1927; *Times*, 13 May 1905; *Temperance Caterer*, 15 March and 15 Aug. 1908 and 15 Aug. 1909; *Pall Mall Gazette*, 6 May 1905.

inability to institute reforms capable of restoring the company to profitability and declaring acceptable dividends.

Pearce resented Hurst's lack of public transparency as strongly as the chairman's treachery, and so recognised that nothing more could be salvaged from the company as long as the Hurst faction predominated.[31] The Board's collection of "independent reports" on the status of the company depots—predictably critical of Pearce's management—finally precipitated Pearce's forthright decision.[32] Angry, humiliated and impotent, Pearce resigned as managing director in September 1904, though he still retained his seat on the Board itself.[33]

Loss of John Pearce as managing director deprived the company of the outstanding catering authority in England responsible for transforming the BTT into the major caterer of the working and lower middle classes. Not surprisingly, the BTT's performance faltered quickly. Despite £8000 of debentures being issued in 1900, turnover slumped the following year, declining 5% over a three-year period. Its headlong slide started in 1903, as takings decreased 13% in the ensuing two years. Overall, takings slumped a startling 18.5% in the years 1900–1905, an unprecedented fall in the company's history. Net profits, however, remained immune to dwindling sales until 1904, when they too plummeted by 40% within twelve months (Chart 7.2).[34] Pearce & Plenty depots had been losing custom for years, confirming what Pearce himself had predicted when he had urged the Board to move upmarket with the BTT early in the 1890s.[35] After Pearce resigned, however, dividends plunged to 4% in 1905–1906, an unprecedented decline in the company's entire history. Given the minuscule profit margins at this end of the market, the loss of not quite 10% in takings catastrophically affected the company's net profits, which halved in the same year. Contracting net profits translated into modest ordinary dividends of 4%, the lowest amount since the two original companies merged in 1897 (Charts 7.1 and 7.2). The company's weaker performance led to plunging BTT stock.[36]

[31] Ellis, *Pluck*, p. 208.

[32] *Financial Times*, 13 May 1905. These reports have not survived.

[33] Ellis, *Pluck*, p. 196. He gave the required six months' notice of his intention to resign as managing director on 31 March 1904 (*Financial Times*, 9 May 1905).

[34] *Financial Times*, 11 May 1901 and 13 May 1905.

[35] Ibid., 16 May 1907.

[36] *Pall Mall Gazette*, 6 May 1905. Soaring sugar prices, costing the company £4000 more, contributed to declining dividends (*Temperance Caterer*, 15 May 1909).

When they took up the business in mid-1904, the Hurst directors had strong prejudice against the Pearce & Plenty chain, which "for years had been declining" as a worthwhile investment. They turned to the BTT depots, which they "improved and tried to flog them into life," Hurst recalled. Unexpectedly, this tactic failed. The depots, he confessed, "had got [sic] into bad odour with the public, and … they could not remove that."[37] Misplaced faith in its own managerial abilities and jealous as well as resentful of Pearce's financial compensation as managing director, the Hurst faction deluded itself into seeing Pearce's removal as a prerequisite for transforming the company. Until the Pearce influence disappeared altogether, so thought Board members, no reforms could be meaningfully instituted.[38]

Several facts belied this explanation. Pearce had not opposed the Board opening new restaurants, which had increased sharply from sixty-nine (1900) to eighty-four (1904), years in which net profits and dividends had both risen.[39] Most had been the more upmarket BTT outlets, the idea for which had originated with Pearce who had pressed the Board to embrace this new marketing concept—over considerable initial Board opposition—early in the 1890s. Nor had he objected to a new policy, radically expanding items on the menus from 40 to 240 as a marketing tactic for luring more custom. This shrewd move enabled the BTT to publicise it offered customers more choices than Lyons, its bigger rival with deeper pockets.[40] Indeed, given Slaters' economic problems, Pearce had exhibited commendable foresight, a recurring feature of his career. In supporting wider menu choices, he had repositioned the company to offer what customers were now demanding as part of the Edwardian restaurant experience.

For his own part, Pearce indicted policies of the Hurst faction controlling the company as responsible for its faltering performance. Our "dire position is due to the ineptitude and want of experience of the catering trade by the directors," Pearce bluntly charged, a view endorsed subsequently by another director.[41] Based on over twenty years' experience as managing director of a profitable catering company, he knew clearly what

[37] *Financial Times*, 16 May 1907.

[38] Ibid., 14 Nov. 1905.

[39] See Charts 7.1 and 7.2.

[40] Ellis, *Pluck*, pp. 138–40; Williams, *Pearce*, pp. 148–49; *Financial Times*, 30 Apr. 1904 and 14 Nov. 1905; Peter Bird, *The First Food Empire: A History of J. Lyons & Co.* (Chichester: Phillimore & Co., 2000), p. 40.

[41] *Times*, 30 July 1908.

he wanted—"a Board who were in touch with all the details of the company's affairs."[42] But he certainly did not want incompetent directors who obstructed depot managers, a circumstance which he had witnessed much earlier in his career as contributing to failure.[43]

One contentious issue dividing them derived from what Pearce regarded as non-negotiable, the retailing of alcohol. As a life-long teetotaller, he wrote into the company's articles an unqualified ban on retailing or possessing any form of alcohol on company premises as long as he remained managing director. Of the other members of the Board, none was an abstainer.[44] Divergent views on the company introducing liquor licences fomented distrust between Pearce, on the one hand, and directors together with leading shareholders, on the other. Taking an early opportunity in April 1905 after resigning as managing director to reassert his hostility to alcohol, Pearce disclosed his personal pride "that our great business has been run without a drop of alcohol—a helping up business, not helping down [one]." On 15 May 1905, Joseph Bentley published a revealing editorial in which he stated that "Rumour had been busy with a report that if Mr. Pearce could be got rid of, there was to be an attempt to introduce intoxicating drink into the business." Hurst of course, denied this. Another of Pearce's closest friends, the Rev. James J. Ellis, saw the former's testimony before the Royal Commission on Liquor Licensing Laws in 1897 criticising publicans for promoting drunkenness as pivotal in antagonising the "trade" against the caterer. "He was to pay dearly for speaking the truth," argued Ellis. In interpreting the crisis of 1904–1905 driving Pearce to resign, Ellis sought its origins in a much earlier date than many other observers. Ellis referred to "the attempts to reverse the principles on which the company had been hitherto worked."[45]

Pearce himself had no qualms about confronting the issue. In a circular to shareholders, he warned that he could not continue holding shares in the company "if the brewers altered the character of the business," allowing alcohol to be sold at depots. Given the behaviour of Iveagh and

[42] *Financial Times*, 16 May 1907.

[43] *Coffee Public-House News*, 1 Nov. 1884.

[44] Williams, *Pearce*, pp. 164–65. Neither a teetotaller nor prohibitionist, Sir Edward Sullivan loathed excessive drinking as "the damning curse and disgrace of the English people" (Sir Edward Sullivan, *Stray Shots: Political, Military, Economical and Social* (London: Longmans, Green & Co., 1884), p. x).

[45] *Temperance Caterer*, 15 Apr. and 15 May 1905; Ellis, *Pluck*, pp. 188–89, 196; *Evidence on Liquor Licensing Laws*, pp. 240, 242, 244; Williams, *Pearce*, p. 165.

two other unnamed large shareholders in distancing themselves from Pearce and privately accepting his resignation as managing director, the circular merely confirmed their belief in the need for new Board leadership. Accordingly, they now backed the Hurst faction. Pearce, they believed, was out of step with other major catering companies, notably Lyons, which served alcohol with meals, though not at its teashops.[46]

Sharply drawn lines divided the two factions: Pearce wanted not just to regain his post as managing director, but more ambitiously to replace Hurst as chairman. Absolute control of the company must be his; much backroom manoeuvring complicated Pearce's position. Having sought to meet personally with two big shareholders—one of them notably Lord Iveagh, the company's pre-eminent shareholder whom Pearce regarded as a friend—he had been rebuffed, forced to confer with their business associates separately. Pearce left the meetings believing he had the two shareholders' support. Whether they behaved disingenuously (as Pearce later thought) or he deceived himself, remains unclear.[47]

Though still a substantial investor with £8000 of shares, Pearce would learn only later that the Board in a subsequent private meeting with principal shareholders—including his erstwhile friend Lord Iveagh—had accepted his resignation tended in September 1904, effectively denying him any role whatsoever in managing his company. This rankled deeply: "I have been treated unfairly." From his mother, who had influenced him profoundly, he had imbibed the belief that "I must go through life straight."[48] For him, this constituted the ultimate betrayal.

On so many levels this action of major shareholders was insulting—denial of representation despite his sizable shareholdings; apparent unwillingness to confront the former managing director and founder of the company with their decision to repudiate him; and finally, banishing him altogether in their wholehearted embrace of the Hurst faction. No wonder ensuing discussions, debates and divisions became increasingly rancorous, with Pearce's advocates dismayed at his shabby treatment, the Hurst faction's haughty demeanour and the clash of starkly dissimilar business strategies.

[46] *Evidence on Liquor Licensing Laws*, p. 240; Ellis, *Pluck*, p. 196; *Financial Times*, 13 May 1905. At the very first ordinary meeting of Pearce's new catering company, JP Restaurants, in August 1906, he reiterated his long-standing commitment to abjuring alcohol: "He wished it to be clearly known that in no circumstances did the company supply or send out for any alcoholic drinks" (*Times*, 10 Aug. 1906).

[47] *Financial Times*, 13 May 1905; Ellis, *Pluck*, p. 197.

[48] Ellis, *Pluck*, p. 197; *Financial Times*, 13 May 1905.

To consolidate its power, the Hurst faction proceeded to stack the Board with like-minded men. Instead of canvassing shareholders for advice on suitable board members, Hurst, turning to the main shareholders, obtained nominees as possible directors. Colonel Addison, as Lord Iveagh's Secretary, nominated W. H. Campbell (owner of 2000 shares) as a director, as well as Nicholas Tapp to replace John Pearce on the Board. This high-handed tactic infuriated Horace Pearce: "Tapp was entirely ignorant of the catering business."[49]

Warfare between the rival factions commenced when Pearce issued a circular to shareholders on 8 May 1905, calling for the summoning of an extraordinary shareholders' meeting. "I have come to the conclusion that if this business is to continue the shareholders must refuse to elect Mr. J.P. Hurst, also the two nominees of Lord Iveagh, Mr. N. Tapp and W.H. Campbell, and I appeal to them to return me to the directorate with independent colleagues." Few shareholders had the requisite 5000 shares to qualify for appointment as directors, underlining the autocratic concentration of power in few hands. Iveagh owned 20,000 shares, and he and three others together controlled 72,000. To achieve the more democratic board of directors that Pearce sought with himself as chairman, shareholders must change the articles of association reducing the amount of shares required for a director from 5000 to 400 or 500 shares.[50]

At the critical shareholders' meeting on 12 May 1905, Horace Pearce, then BTT managing director, distributed a striking, lengthy circular to shareholders: "Don't throw the pilot overboard because there's a squall! Give him the helm! Have a board constituted as follows: Managing Director, John Pearce (40 years' experience), W. Horace Pearce (8 years' experience), and 3 other practical caterers." Assuming the guise of the democrat, his father urged qualifications for a director be radically reduced, and "thus open this post to a much wider range of shareholders, which … for practical purposes is now reserved to approximately ten shareholders." Were shareholders to endorse his return to the Board, John Pearce vowed to reduce the number of shares required for a director. In resigning from the Board and proposing a directorship drawn from wider numbers of shareholders with modest wealth, Pearce was fomenting a palace revolution. As he affirmed boldly to shareholders, this "had been a fight against

[49] *Financial Times*, 8 and 13 May 1905.

[50] *Times*, 8 and 20 May 1905, and 11 Feb. 1910; *Financial Times*, 8 May 1905; Ellis, *Pluck*, pp. 196–97; *Times*, 11 Feb. 1910.

misrepresentation and wealth." Now, as an outsider, he could challenge the Board without appearing disloyal, and appeal to shareholders to oust the existing (incompetent) directors.[51]

At this meeting, shareholders introduced and then passed overwhelmingly a vote of no confidence in the Board (613–276). Defiant shareholders also voted to return Pearce but not Hurst to the Board. When Pearce attempted to address the meeting, Hurst ruled him out of order, and "amid loud hissing and booing and other demonstrations of hostile feeling," the Board left the room. Three tumultuous hours consumed the confrontation. What Pearce wanted, as he told remaining shareholders, was to see a sympathetic and knowledgeable Board elected, giving him as chairman absolute "control [of] the business." He delivered a masterful speech, praised in the *Temperance Caterer*: "It was made abundantly evident during his remarks that Mr. Pearce commanded the sympathy of the large audience before him, his references to many years' past and faithful service evoking loud and frequent cheering."[52] Readiness of most huge shareholders—themselves "gentlemen"—to support Hurst indicated they agreed that a properly educated gentleman could run the business, which only encouraged Hurst.

When these votes at a later shareholder meeting on 19 May 1905 were weighed according to an individual's shareholdings, however, the results were overturned: Hurst, Campbell and Tapp were all elected to the Board, but not Pearce; and the annual report was accepted.[53]

Votes (12 May)	*Poll (19 May)*
For Pearce (613) (69%)	70,626
Against Pearce (276) (31%)	72,011

Clearly, Hurst's policy of ambitious spending could only have been carried out successfully if a quite skilful leader or committee had managed it. It is much harder to offer any judgement on whether a policy of thrift and frugality could have saved the BTT; 1908 was the low point for the economy, so Hurst's period of management was about as difficult as Pearce's three years of strife.[54]

[51] *Morning Post*, 13 May 1905.

[52] *Financial Times*, 13, 17 and 20 May 1905; *Times*, 20 May 1905; *Temperance Caterer*, 15 May 1905.

[53] *Temperance Caterer*, 15 June 1905.

[54] I am grateful to Trevor Lloyd for this point.

At a subsequent shareholders' meeting, the majority agreed, siding with the Pearce faction, rejecting Tapp and Campbell as directors and refusing to reappoint Hurst as chairman. The Hurst faction' grasp for total power, however, remained undiminished. To forestall appointment of Dr Oldham, son of Sir Henry Oldham, one of the leading shareholders and presumed future ally of the Pearces, the Board nominated instead as director C. Thompson, who along with J.P. Hurst had systematically harassed John Pearce and "rendered him very miserable."[55]

The Hurst faction's manoeuvring went still further. At the critical extraordinary general meeting on 12 May 1905, the Hurst faction increased both the reserve fund and depreciation account as a calculated strategy for reducing the dividend to 4%, thereby potentially infuriating shareholders against Pearce, so Pearce's legal advisor charged. There was some substance in this accusation. Shareholders were prepared to put Pearce on the Board of Directors, but baulked at placing £2000 in the reserve fund. At a subsequent general meeting, Pearce, hopeful of gaining enough shareholder support to control the company, expressed his opinion that, had he been (again) managing director, he would have recommended an annual dividend of 7%, not 4%.[56]

As the supremely self-assured Hurst told shareholders in 1906, "it was child's play to earn [dividends of] 12%." Overconfident and arrogant, the Board decided to govern alone, with Hurst as de facto managing director. Hurst, who had been with the company since 1886, boasted of his commitment to this arrangement: he "had been working daily for many hours, really filling the place of a managing director."[57] Combining the posts of chairman and managing director, even on a de facto basis, was nevertheless controversial. The ABC had embraced this managerial approach since the 1870s, but its disastrous slumping dividends had provoked intense opposition, forcing Chairman George Edwards to accept shareholder demands for hiring an outsider as a general manager. Months before Hurst's speech, Bentley in the *Temperance Caterer* pronounced his verdict on the new order at the BTT: "We have seen Company after Company fail because they have fallen into the hands of inexpert Directors."[58]

[55] *Financial Times*, 9 and 20 May 1905; *Daily Telegraph*, 20 Nov. 1900; *Times*, 19 May 1905; *Morning Post*, 13 May 1905.

[56] *Financial Times*, 13 and 20 May 1905.

[57] Ibid., 14 Nov. 1905 and 12 May 1906.

[58] *Temperance Caterer*, 15 Nov. 1905.

Hurst blamed Pearce principally for the BTT's faltering performance, and for resigning as managing director without presenting an ultimatum to the Board of Directors: choose one of us to remain. Later, at the 1906 annual meeting, Hurst attacked Pearce for defective management and unspecified organisational problems. As the company continued to decline and missed dividends altogether in 1907, Hurst sought to deflect attention from his leadership, making Pearce the scapegoat. To bolster his case against Pearce, Hurst, contradicting what he had stated at the 12 May 1905 annual meeting, asserted the novel claim that when finally the Hurst Board completely controlled the company "the business displayed most marked features of decay."[59]

Chairman Hurst pointed to two vital factors—catering experience and intensifying competition—as impeding the company's recovery. Given the company's declining performance, J.P. Hurst had defended his hand-selected Board members who "had to take over the management, with the details of which they were unacquainted" in 1905. In light of his remark about it being child's play to earn 12% dividends, this was a very peculiar defence of the Board's inexperience. More ironic still, rising competition, which he had dismissed earlier as Pearce's unconvincing reason for the company's miseries, now loomed large in his own analysis of the firm's difficulties under his leadership. Emphasising the role of heightened competition as an explanation for the company's misfortune, Hurst related the experiences of one manageress who complained of twenty-one new refreshment places opening in the immediate vicinity of her depot. Amid escalating competition, Hurst belatedly discovered, "it was far more difficult now to earn 4 percent than the 12 percent which the company used to pay." In 1906, as in the previous year, ordinary dividends stayed at 4%, the last year the company declared any such dividends before sliding into bankruptcy.[60]

To rejuvenate the BTT, the Hurst faction pursued several policies contradicting received wisdom among catering companies. Slaters, later confronting dismal economic problems, would adopt the prevailing philosophy of austerity in which retrenchment became the order of the day. No new expenditure—for new depots or decoration—would be incurred, and the company would cut prices.[61] Rejecting this time-tested tradition, the BTT

[59] *London Daily News*, 13 May 1905; *Morning Post*, 12 May 1906 and 16 May 1907.
[60] *Times*, 12 May 1906; also see *Financial Times*, 16 May 1907.
[61] *Financial Times*, 3 Dec. 1908.

embraced an aggressive approach of transforming its depots into British Restaurants (advertised as "BR"), a chain which required the premises be extensively (and expensively) renovated.[62] These more upmarket restaurants specialised in sixpenny dinners, including one penny for a cup of tea. By mid-1907, the Hurst faction had converted three-fourths of the BTT outlets into BRs. Hurst contended this tactic had stabilised profits, the renovated depots being a "most cheerful and encouraging feature" of the company's new policies.[63] Interviewed in February 1908, he enthused about the company's progress in the post-Pearce period since mid-1904. He lauded "British Restaurants," which then accounted for three-fourths of the company's profitable depots.[64] Yet, this strategy failed, too. For the first time in its history, the company sustained an absolute loss of almost £13,000, and also unprecedentedly passed on ordinary dividends (Chart 7.1).[65]

Notwithstanding Hurst's confidence, the BTT in 1908, as in the previous year, paid neither ordinary nor preferential dividends. After the huge deficit in 1907, profits recovered the next year, rising to a modest £2200, the lowest amount declared since the company began. In late 1908, BTT stock had slumped from 40s. to 2s. or less per share, and by then, he and his Board of Directors had been forced to resign.[66]

On the basis of subsequent performance, Pearce, not Hurst, was vindicated. With uncontested control over the company for several years, the Board failed miserably to implement its promised reform agenda. Never again would the company declare a dividend of any kind. Of the seventy company outlets in 1909, a mere twenty-four were turning a profit.[67]

In retrospect, Pearce had correctly interpreted events. The Hurst faction strategy for reclaiming custom lost since 1900, predicated on eliminating John Pearce and his son from the Board, had dismally backfired. Convinced he could run the company single-handedly, Hurst discovered the shortcomings of acting as an ill-informed de facto managing director,

[62] On assuming control, the Hurst faction failed to reinvigorate BTT depots, which joined the declining profitability of the Pearce & Plenty restaurants (*Financial Times*, 16 May 1907).

[63] Interview with Hurst, 28 Feb. 1908; *Temperance Caterer*, 15 Feb. 1906; *Financial Times*, 16 May 1907.

[64] *Financial Times*, 30 Apr. 1904, and 27–28 Feb. 1908; *Times*, 1 June 1907.

[65] *Times*, 30 July 1908; *Financial Times*, 16 May 1907.

[66] *Financial Times*, 30 Apr. 1904 and 27–28 Feb. 1908; *Temperance Caterer*, 15 Nov. 1908.

[67] *Daily Mail*, 29 May 1909; *Financial Times*, 27 Feb. 1908.

with minimal grasp of the diverse skills needed to operate successfully in a competitive market. After listening to Hurst's speech at the crucial 12 May 1905 meeting, Joseph Bentley had expressed his own contemptuous assessment: "to an expert it showed that he did not understand the business."[68]

Pearce condemned not the policies of the Hurst directors controlling the company but their talent as causes of its faltering performance. Our "dire position is due to the ineptitude and want of experience of the catering trade by the directors," Pearce bluntly charged. Based on over twenty years' experience as managing director of a profitable catering company, Pearce knew instinctively what he wanted—"a Board who were in touch with all the details of the company's affairs."[69]

Returning to the attack, shareholders, who had demanded the Hurst faction's resignations in 1905, appointed an Investigative Committee to inquire into the company's problems on which they truculently placed John Pearce. On hearing of this insolent behaviour, not based on the size of shareholders' ownership of stock, Hurst had exploded, castigating it as "preposterous." Its subsequent report gave a damning account of the Hurst faction control. "The depots," the benchmark of a successful company, "were ill-ventilated and uninviting for want of fresh air and fresh paint." Repairs and renewals, moreover, "were neglected to such an extent that the shops were fast losing their attractiveness for the better class of customers." The report pointed to "mismanagement" at some of the restaurants as a key reason for the company's decline.[70]

One critical reason for failure concerned not just Pearce's resignation, but loss of talented subordinate officials, such as Charles Cann, deputy superintendent of all Pearce & Plenty depots, with some twenty years' experience with the company. Like Pearce himself, Cann imposed rigorous discipline in a light-handed way. The two men were, in fact, identical in character, working-class background and work ethic, with each strongly devoted to total abstinence.[71]

One of the strangest developments in this power struggle concerned the behaviour of Nicholas Tapp, though ostensibly a Hurst ally. Without company records, it is impossible to explain why he had been elected to

[68] *Temperance Caterer*, 15 May 1905.
[69] *Times*, 30 July 1908; *Financial Times*, 16 May 1907.
[70] *Times*, 1 June 1907; *Financial Times*, 16 May 1907 and 27 Feb. 1908.
[71] *Temperance Caterer*, 15 Aug. 1907 and 15 March 1909.

the Board but then repudiated his colleagues, offering damning evidence to support Pearce. Late in 1905 big shareholders received a private circular in which Tapp attacked the Hurst faction for "tinkering with the business" that as a result "was going from bad to worse." Having undertaken a survey of BTT depots, Tapp delivered a critical report in which he disclosed unsatisfactory management, the Hurst faction's minimal understanding of practical business matters, and depot managers who "had hardly any experience in London." Each week, his informants confirmed, receipts had progressively declined. He damned directors as derelict in their duty, implicitly criticising Hurst for acting unwisely as de facto managing director. Hurst, Tapp argued, was responsible for appointing competent depot managers. "A general manager," his report concluded, "should be appointed, as it was impossible for directors to attend to so much detail." What emerged was a Board bereft of expertise, unable to oversee a large company effectively, articulate its policies or arrest the headlong slide into unprofitability. He went further, joining Pearce in demanding the Board's resignation: the company needed "new blood" to manage it. What it needed clearly was Pearce, who, while absent for less than a year, proved irreplaceable.[72]

Unpopular with shareholders, Tapp ultimately resigned from the Board after this episode, and possibly fearful of further encouraging negative publicity, no one on either side of the dispute offered any comments.

Hurst and his faction officially resigned on 30 May 1907. The following month, Hurst, formerly one of the firm's largest shareholders, disclosed that he had disposed of virtually all his stock in the company. This withdrawal from the company also applied to other large shareholders, such as Lord Iveagh.[73] The new chairman, the Rev. Robert Venables Greene, told shareholders that he and his new Board had to deal with extensive abuses, one of them arising from the amateurish Hurst directors who had appointed inexperienced workers in the catering department. A retired missionary and a former window inspector for five weeks with the ABC, Greene himself scarcely possessed the requisite experience for his post. In a headline entitled "The British Tea Table Company: Scandalous Conditions of Affairs," *John Bull* castigated the chairman, directors and manager for "gross mismanagement."[74]

[72] *Times*, 1 June 1907; *Financial Times*, 14 Nov. 1905.

[73] *Morning Post*, 12 May 1906; *Times*, 1 June 1907; *Financial Times*, 6 Feb. 1909.

[74] *London Evening Standard*, 30 July 1908; *John Bull*, 4 July 1908.

Incriminatory evidence came from an unnamed former officer in 1906–1907 in sworn testimony in which he identified a litany of serious problems flourishing under Hurst's leadership.[75] Because virtually nobody held experience as a buyer, a role which Pearce as managing director previously undertook, "thousands of pounds are lost through bad buying." In one area alone, vegetables and fruit, the company paid between 33% and 50% more than its rivals. Another example of overpaying for items occurred in purchasing waitresses' aprons, where the company lost £165 in ordering more expensive but of similar quality aprons than cheaper ones. Yet another breakdown in managerial policy came in terminating the long-standing practice of putting items out for competitive bidding. Orders were placed with just one company in Deptford, with a cheque attached.[76]

Serving superb food, a prerequisite for ensuring customer satisfaction, thus became increasingly problematic. In 1906 the Hurst Board had signed contracts worth £30,000 annually with John Gardner, a meat salesman, to supply genuine British beef. Instead, he substituted inferior imported products. According to Miss Stabb, BTT manageress, Gardner instructed his manager to give the BTT chef a free joint of meat every week. So unappetising was the meat that she needed parsley and tomatoes to disguise its appearance in the show window. Kate Margaret Beck, another manageress who had since left her job, said that "lamb had to be used instead of mutton on account of the complaints." At the Strand branch, manageress Lizzie Stewart noted that customers complained of the mutton as "very dark and wet." The BTT did respond, hardly in a reassuring manner. "The superintendent sometimes told her to take the meat out of the window or there would be a crowd." In another instance, a superintendent voiced his criticism of the substandard food dispatched to depots, but Hurst did nothing. These criticisms gained widespread currency owing to their being published in the *Daily Mail*, a popular daily with a working-class readership.[77] The company accordingly launched a lawsuit, claiming £60,000 in damages. Gardner was found guilty, and

[75] This individual held a position with the BTT between Oct. 1906 and Dec. 1907, with the Hurst faction in control for the first eight months. Precisely who disclosed this information is unclear, but he attended Board meetings and received instructions of a confidential nature (*John Bull*, 4 July 1908).

[76] *Morning Post*, 12 May 1906; *John Bull*, 4 July 1908.

[77] *Times*, 21 Oct. 1908; *Daily Telegraph*, 21 Oct. 1908; *Daily Mail*, 23–24 Oct. 1908.

forced to pay £2500 in damages as well as full legal costs. Another meat supplier was likewise sued for supplying meat of deficient quality.[78]

Still more embarrassing, with potentially devastating consequences for the company's public reputation, *John Bull* disclosed that orders had been issued to chefs that uneaten pieces of meat on plates must be collected and form the basis for entrées such as Vienna steaks. Apparently desperate to revive the company's fortunes, Hurst directed that each depot would acquire a mincing machine to facilitate preparing the new dishes. To thwart waitresses disseminating knowledge of this practice, the Board craftily arranged for them to stay out of the kitchens, thereby guaranteeing that "they should not see behind the scenes." Outraged staff members immediately objected to these departures from standard catering practices. For its part, the Board immediately filed a suit against *John Bull*, though the damage was clearly done already.[79]

Yet, economy as an overriding goal still seemed the order of the day for some time to come. In a desperate but questionable move to save money, the Board slashed menu prices. Several factors should have deterred knowledgeable directors from adopting this strategy. Slaters had already embraced price cutting as a panacea for mounting financial difficulties, but this had failed. As editor of the *Temperance Caterer*, Joseph Bentley drew on lengthy years of observing the fate of price cuts for arguing that workers "have been taught by experience what can be honestly done for a price." Selling below this figure, he stressed, "arouses suspicion."[80]

Instituting economies as a priority pervaded the thinking of directors in other directions. The Hurst Board, "anxious to secure results and study economy, cut down contractor's prices to such a low figure that it was almost impossible for him to recoup himself in the ordinary way of trade," encouraging risky, if not illegal, practices that harmed both the company's reputation and honesty, charged the *Temperance Caterer*. Placed in this position, the company found that "corruption was so rife among the employees that it was exceedingly difficult for the old Board to discover what was going on." For Joseph Bentley, the cause of these

[78] *Temperance Caterer*, 15 May 1909; *Morning Post*, 10 March 1909; *Globe*, 10 Feb. 1910; *Times*, 11 Feb. 1910.

[79] *John Bull*, 4 July 1908; *Financial Times*, 30 July 1908.

[80] *Temperance Caterer*, 15 July 1907. See p. 141.

difficulties was patently obvious: directors "were incapable of managing such a Company."[81]

When the Comptroller of the Companies Department, part of the Board of Trade, delivered its report into the causes of the BTT Company's bankruptcy in 1909, it further undermined the credibility of Hurst's business strategy. Just one year after Hurst's interview, its report concurred with Pearce's assessment. "Bad management and want of enterprise" chiefly doomed the BTT, it concluded. Despite Hurst's glowing account of the new depots, the report characterised the reconverted restaurants as shabby with outdated decor. That "very little was done to improve the company's shops" drove customers away, the report concluded. Another informed source agreed with the Comptroller's conclusions. "We have been advised by persons who have expert knowledge of this business that the depots have scarcely been brought up to date," with front display windows cheerless and unattractive, asserted C.E. Hogg as new chairman of the company in 1909.[82] In fact, these independent assessments in 1909, criticising the Hurst faction's misrepresentation of its performance, reiterated the same conclusions reached by Tapp in 1905, Pearce in 1907 and the Investigative Committee in 1908. Overwhelming evidence thus agreed: the Hurst faction was strikingly incompetent. Hurst as much as the rest of his faction was, as Pearce had contended, inept and unskilled in running the company.[83]

At the meeting of creditors and shareholders early in 1910, Chairman H.E. Burgess pointed to the Hurst faction directors' "slackness of management," unappetising food served badly, and failure to supervise closely and personally the depots as key causes of the company's collapse. Completely misjudging the company's customers, Hurst and his Board had sought unwisely to regain them with reduced prices but to no avail.[84]

Three issues—goodwill, reserves and depreciation—contributed significantly to the BTT's crisis, delaying the company's recovery and undermining its financial strength.

Within the company itself, the Hurst Board policies in dealing with goodwill escaped scrutiny. At its formation, goodwill accounted for

[81] *Temperance Caterer*, 15 July 1907 and 15 Nov. 1908.
[82] *Economist*, 17 Apr. 1909.
[83] *Times*, 1 June 1907; *Temperance Caterer*, 15 Dec. 1909.
[84] *Globe*, 10 Feb. 1910.

£130,000, more than one-fourth of the purchase price.[85] In 1904 Hurst asserted that "the Board never had and did not intend to write down the goodwill." Because the company had growing numbers of outlets, the goodwill had risen, he reasoned. Hurst gave shareholders stark alternatives: retain the current policy or accept lower dividends as the price for writing off goodwill. Adopting the first strategy overvalued the company's net worth, and was questionable if the company's earnings seriously faltered. As the company's economic position deteriorated, the Board entertained the notion of decreasing its share capital, offering another way to reduce the level of goodwill. Reluctant to close unprofitable depots and unwilling to update them, the Hurst faction kept them on the books at their undepreciated values. Kept from shareholders at the critical 1905 meetings was that forty-nine of the company's eighty-two depots incurred losses or earned miniscule profits (averaging £45 each). Desperate to shut hopelessly uneconomic outlets but lacking adequate reserves and confronting sizable amounts of goodwill, the company found itself in an insoluble position.[86] By early 1909, predictably two-thirds of the depots—many of them the newly converted "superior" British Restaurants—generated no profits.[87] Essentially, the company had seriously restricted its manoeuvrability and viable options as its financial crisis deepened from 1905.

The BTT was scarcely alone in mishandling goodwill. Slaters had procrastinated in formulating a policy for writing it down with serious consequences—missing dividends for the war years. Its chairman decided to sacrifice all dividends as a way of ridding the company of £124,500 in goodwill, a huge financial albatross.[88] What made the BTT different, of course, was its bankruptcy.

In failing to create an adequate reserve fund, the Hurst faction blundered yet again. It obfuscated the issue, claiming that funds allocated for repairs and updating "really represented reserve." On other occasions, as in 1902, Chairman Hurst deflected queries, asserting the Board was contemplating placing money in such a fund. According to the Investigative Committee's Report in 1908, however, profits were divided "up to the hilt" when prosperity prevailed, making thoughts of a reserve fund seem-

[85] *Temperance Caterer*, 15 Feb. 1910; *Economist*, 28 May 1898.

[86] Shareholders first learned of this information in 1907. Nothing was said about whether such outlets were BTT or Pearce & Plenty in nature (*Financial Times*, 10 May 1907).

[87] *Financial Times*, 30 April 1904; *Daily Mail*, 29 May 1909; *Temperance Caterer*, 15 May 1907.

[88] *Temperance Caterer*, 15 Dec. 1913. See pp. 140, 207.

ingly unnecessary. No more than £3000 was thus in the reserve fund in 1904, the year before the company's financial crisis.[89] Contrast this with the ABC, which would enlarge its reserve fund by £10,000 in these years.[90] Had the BTT emulated this approach, it could have written down goodwill as a sensible business strategy.[91]

The Investigative Committee in 1908 criticised the Hurst faction's financial ineptness in setting aside not just inadequate reserves but insufficient amounts for depreciations. Nothing prompted the Hurst Board to adopt two defensive policies: earmark funds for dilapidation when leases lapsed; and write off adequate amounts for depreciation.[92] Pearce acquitted himself of being responsible for these shortcomings. In 1901, he wrote off £6115 on furniture, plant and fixtures. Before BTT shareholders in 1909, he declared, "there was a substantial sum written off for depreciation each year [1901–1904], while about £4000 per annum was spent on the upkeep of furniture and fittings." To corroborate his assertions, he cited audited accounts which confirmed that "adequate sums had been reserved for depreciation" in the critical years of 1902–1904.[93]

In Hurst's defence, some catering companies had refused to write off decreasing values of leases in which sales had been declining. In the long run, however, this had serious consequences: when depots had to be abandoned, the company had no choice but to write off the entire initial expenditure. As Slaters' chairman knew so well from experience, vast amounts of unaddressed depreciation "absorbed money urgently required for repairs and redecoration of other shops."[94] This explains why the BTT became so cash-strapped to find funds for upgrading depots in the post-Pearce years in an increasingly competitive market.

Shareholders with limited means too deserved some responsibility for the company's woes and eventual demise. To them, higher dividends outweighed a conservative strategy in which lower dividends would have enabled the orderly writing off of goodwill as well as building up an adequate reserve fund. Hurst had proposed at the 1905 Annual General meeting that £2000 be placed in a reserve fund, but shareholders, anxious

[89] *Financial Times*, 15 May 1902, and 23, 25 and 30 April 1904, and 27 Feb. 1908.
[90] *Financial Times*, 6 Nov. 1906.
[91] *Economist*, 28 May 1898.
[92] *Financial Times*, 27 Feb. 1908.
[93] *Times*, 16 Apr. and 15 May 1909; *Financial Times*, 11 May 1901.
[94] *Financial Times*, 16 Dec. 1909.

to maximise dividends, rebuffed him.[95] This enthusiastic zeal for maximising dividends no doubt reflected the resources of many smaller investors, who keenly supported Pearce. Even slight changes for them in the company's net earnings mattered considerably.

For larger shareholders, much depended on the proportion of their total capital involved in a failing business. Iveagh's £20,000 was a small proportion of his total wealth, whereas Hurst, as a big shareholder, might have had enough of his total wealth in the business to mean that a reduction in his income from it would cause him serious inconvenience and this could have led him to behave irrationally. Pearce was in a quite different position. His £8000 of shareholdings represented probably his major investment, but of course, he relied on his continued earning power—he could always get a job as a manager—rather than his invested money.[96]

Editor Joseph Bentley understood the business with the critical eye of a journalist, drawing upon decades of familiarity, knowledge and insight as the framework for his well-considered judgments. "The success or non-success of a catering business is largely a matter of detail," he reflected. Mindful of Hurst's background, he shrewdly noted that skills obtained in other sectors of business were not necessarily transferable to food retailing. "No matter how eminent the Directors may be in the financial world," he asserted, "if they lack practical experience they lack the one thing needful." Hurst had an exaggerated view of his abilities as head of a major London catering company. "Mr. Hurst," observed the sarcastic Bentley, "was not the heaven-born genius in refreshment catering he thought himself to be." Shareholders themselves would soon come to see Hurst in an altogether different light, though not as the messiah of the City's catering industry.[97]

In interpreting Pearce's pivotal role in the BTT's collapse, his attitudes and motivations merit examination. While he indicated willingness again to work with an experienced, sympathetic and knowledgeable Board, these individuals must give him unfettered "control [of] the business."[98] Resuming his position as managing director with the BTT was hence unthinkable. From early in his career, he had witnessed how incompetent directors had obstructed depot managers and powerfully contributed to

[95] Ibid., 13 May 1905.
[96] I want to thank Trevor Lloyd for the insights in this paragraph.
[97] *Temperance Caterer*, 15 Nov 1905 and 15 Aug. 1908.
[98] *Financial Times*, 13, 17 and 20 May 1905; *Times*, 20 May 1905.

failure.[99] Whether he fully grasped his inability to surrender independence to well-meaning or inept superiors is doubtful; he intuitively sensed a potentially disturbing conflict when his firm, Pearce & Plenty, became a private limited liability company in 1886. On that occasion, he recalled his innermost beliefs: "I felt that I was better on my own. But one thing tempted me. I knew that—alone—everything depended on myself, on the push and drive that were part of me." Without the understanding and support of his friend, Sir Edward Sullivan, Pearce would have undoubtedly baulked at surrendering his autonomy. Marguerite Williams, friend and biographer, wholly agreed: "He did not realize that the day of his freedom was past." In the late 1890s, his friends' death and retirement ended the productive, sympathetic relationship that had sustained him, fostering deep anxieties and exacerbating his acute sense of class differences with Hurst and his Board. Without Sullivan, perceived Joseph Bentley, "men who knew practically nothing of the business [were] trying to control those who did."[100]

Pearce's hypersensitivity to criticism—either outright or implicit—became transparent at a company meeting in 1900, where one brash shareholder demanded to know what fee directors received as a basis for evaluating whether the "amount was excessive." Outraged, Pearce regarded this request as an indictment of his salary. Swift and telling was his sharp riposte: "He did not care to take his fees and feel that they were grudged. He was quite willing to stay on for three months without any remuneration, so as to give them time to find another manager if they were not satisfied with him (Cries of 'No')." In the event, Pearce did not resign, and thereafter, directors' fees subsided as a shareholder issue.[101]

By 1905, some months after resigning as manager director, Pearce saw a solution to the BTT's woes. Were he "elected and able to take the chair, and to get around him a Board who understood the business…," he knew that he "could have pulled it back to its old success." Ironically, he shared with the Hurst faction one assumption: the vital importance of having undisputed authority in running the company. As Pearce recalled much later, he "had suffered very materially through not having a strong hold on the … business of the BTT."[102] This, he knew, would never happen again.

[99] *Coffee Public-House News*, 1 Nov. 1884.

[100] *Temperance Caterer*, 15 Aug. 1908; Williams, *Pearce*, p. 121.

[101] *Temperance Caterer*, 15 June 1900.

[102] *Financial Times*, 17 and 20 May 1905, and 15 Aug. 1911; *Times*, 20 May 1905.

Like the proverbial phoenix rising from the ashes, Pearce salvaged some depots, old friends came forward with money and invested in him anew, and surrounded by family, friends as well as former colleagues, he resumed his role under a new guise—JP Restaurants—as one of London's leading caterers. Within four years, "his reputation as a caterer never stood higher," Bentley proudly remarked.[103]

[103] *Temperance Caterer*, 15 March 1908.

CHAPTER 8

Starting Over

This chapter highlights Pearce's strengths as a London caterer who resurrected his career after his forced resignation to form a new company, remedying previous flaws in organisation while advancing a new business philosophy. Returning to the well-established Victorian family business model, he built a new company, its directors made up of family members and friends, with himself as the undisputed chairman, beholden to no one or nothing except his own considerable skills, judgement and work ethic.

Pearce was an entrepreneurial genius, possessing shrewd insight into marketing, advertising and working-class culture; he did not, alas, grasp finances, except in an elementary way. When exiled from the British Tea Table Company, he unwisely postponed sale of his shareholdings, then worth £25,000, hopeful they would recover their former value as he resurrected his former company. He was wrong, and paid dearly for his miscalculation. Eventually, he disposed of his stock, then nearly worthless, for a mere £250. This provides some perspective for appreciating his remarkable economic recovery after he retired when sixty years old.[1]

Pearce's reputation, much maligned by his critics in the acrimonious struggle to oust him from the BTT Board, became rapidly rehabilitated with his new company. Recalling the expressions of condescending regret—"getting too old" and "not sufficiently up-to-date"—that had dismissed Pearce as a spent force in catering and exiled him, Joseph Bentley

[1] Marguerite Williams, *John Pearce: The Man who Played the Game* (London: Religious Tract Society, 1928), p. 154.

D. W. Gutzke, *John Pearce and the Rise of the Mass Food Market in London, 1870–1930*, https://doi.org/10.1007/978-3-030-27095-7_8

pointed to the successful launching of the new company, JP Restaurants, in 1905 as complete vindication. Based on the new company's restaurants, Bentley declared that "There is to-day in London no stronger or more capable man in the catering world than Mr. Pearce."[2]

When he formed JP Restaurants, a successor to the BTT, Pearce became chairman, not managing director, a post safely in the experienced hands of his son, Guy H. Pearce. Written into company articles shunning democracy, moreover, was the unusual—for Pearce unprecedented—provision that he would hold the chairmanship as a lifetime appointment. Another kindred spirit, Charles Cann, angered at the Hurst faction mistreatment of Pearce and his son, resigned his role as BTT deputy superintendent and joined John Pearce. Debilitating conflict between Pearce and Hurst would not be repeated. Pearce now learned his firm, JP Restaurants, could be quoted on the Stock Exchange only if shareholders possessed the power to remove him at a general meeting.[3] Mindful of recent events and possible future shortcomings of this arrangement, he not surprisingly rejected democracy in the Board Room. No one would ever again wield power that could disrupt, perhaps even endanger, Pearce's personal vision of a successful catering company.

His estrangement from his former company endured for years. Former employees' deep affection for him and resentment at how he had been mistreated presented itself in quite overt ways. Typically, annual reports disclosed controversial topics under a heavy cloak of self-imposed censorship, lest the company's reputation be damaged, together with its share value. But in the 1908 annual report, the BTT divulged that "members of their staff had been acting in the interests of other parties, and had abused their positions of trust by disclosing confidential … information to the detriment of the company." Though not named specifically presumably for reasons of libel, John Pearce was the logical recipient of such confidences. Some employees were deemed not only disloyal but dishonest, prompting directors to fire some and prosecute others.[4]

The Hurst faction wholly misunderstood how employees saw Pearce and so misinterpreted their response. Nothing the Board of Directors did could in any way compensate for the void left after he had departed nor prepare them for anyone else to assume Pearce's irreplaceable role because directors "lacked the knowledge of how to control a business requiring a

[2] *Temperance Caterer*, 15 Nov. 1905.
[3] Ibid., 15 Feb. 1907 and 15 Aug. 1911; *Financial Times*, 15 Aug. 1911.
[4] *Financial Times*, 9 May 1905, and 23 and 30 July 1908.

thorough grasp of every detail." According to Bentley, the staff perceived management's shortcomings and became uneasy, refusing to give loyalty to those who so obviously had neither earned nor deserved it. Directors, he said, "lacked the controlling hand, tact and far-reaching experience of the founder of the business" and then added tellingly: "Pearce was in the eyes of the employees the company."[5]

Whether Pearce rehired such individuals as recognition of their loyalty to him is unknown.[6] He felt personally committed to looking after former employees, much like the protective, solicitous patriarch of a large family. This explains why thirty of Pearce's employees in 1911 had been with him "almost from the beginning" of his career. One of Pearce's attractive features as an employer was that "he knew how to control." This inestimable skill commanded respect, sustained loyalty and endeared him to the staff. Those who came to work as waitresses received generous treatment, getting 9s. per week, free food and commissions on food. Bentley estimated that all these perks translated into a weekly wage of 17 or 18s. This increased still more in 1913, when commissions doubled. Managerial staff also got commissions.[7] Slaters, in contrast, prohibited gratuities, and required waitresses not only work eleven-hour days (8:30 a.m.–7:30 p.m.) with just 90 minutes off for meals and rest, but buy three uniforms at their own expense made from company material. Hence, Pearce never had difficulty recruiting adequate numbers of employees.[8]

Whether in the annual bean feast, the company military band, the annual company outing to a seaside resort or in countless other ways, Pearce displayed the solicitude for his staff's well-being and happiness that bespoke genuine respect, appreciation and indeed affection. Throughout his career he had fostered this loyalty with his employees. This was apparent to a reporter as early as the 1880s. In establishing a rapport with them in diverse contexts, Pearce promoted "closer ties than usually holds a firm's workers together." When Pearce was thus forced to resign, they drew on these durable emotional bonds and gladly threw in their lot with his without regret, exhibiting strong loyalty.[9]

[5] Ibid., 15 Aug. 1908.

[6] Joseph Bentley in an editorial implied that Pearce had recruited "manageresses, waitresses and others" from the BTT (*Temperance Caterer*, 15 Aug. 1908).

[7] Rev. James J. Ellis, *Pluck, Patience and Power: The Life Story of John Pearce of "Pearce and Plenty"* (London: H.R. Allenson, [1910]), p. 204; *Temperance Caterer*, 15 Aug. 1908; *Financial Times*, 19 Aug. 1913; "Fifty Years of Catering," *London Daily News*, 18 Oct. 1911.

[8] *Temperance Caterer*, 15 Feb. 1901 and 15 Oct. 1906.

[9] "Mr. John Pearce: The Man and His Work," *British Journal of Catering* 3 (15 July 1889): 9.

Nothing so underlined the affection and love which the staff held for John Pearce more than his retirement party in 1905 organised at the Hoxton Baths, near where he had been born decades earlier, symbolically attesting to his bonds with former employees. Mr Trent, chairman of the ceremony, articulated the sentiments of countless people—friends, employees, relatives and well-wishers—in the hall: "Sometimes he has talked to us pretty straight, but always as a gentleman, and we honour him for it." Overcome with emotion at the wrenching separation, Trent confessed the feelings of so many in the audience, confiding that "we not only respect him, but some of us have learned to love him." Ever modest, unpretentious and self-effacing, Pearce confessed to his own shortcomings: "I always have felt myself to be a poor, failing, sinful man; but I have tried to do my duty to you and my company." In this candid, humble and spontaneous statement, Pearce, the successful businessman publicly acknowledging his defects and imperfections, could have done nothing more to perpetuate his strong affinity with his staff. It was authentic, candid and heartfelt—for these reasons, those who respected and indeed loved him had their emotional ties reaffirmed with this remarkable man.[10]

As the founder and guiding spirit who personified the ideal relationship with staff and customers, Pearce assumed a persona in which his personality merged entirely with the company's character. In an indefinable way, he became figuratively an extension of the company. To the public, as to his patrons, thought Bentley, Pearce "is one of the best known men in London." Unlike the Hurst faction, "they know him personally"—a connection which convinced staff as much as customers that "his personality spells confidence."[11]

As managing director, Pearce had accentuated the vital importance of ongoing involvement with employees, of inculcating respect and devotion, and of dealing impartially with them. "The Gov'nor'" was beloved and known as one who had sprung from the same working-class roots; the Hurst faction had no such personal relationship with employees and displayed all the arrogance, condescending behaviour and class consciousness typical of so many of Victorian England's governing elite.[12]

[10] Ellis, *Pluck*, pp. 200–01.

[11] *Temperance Caterer*, 15 Aug. 1908 and 15 March 1909.

[12] *Financial Times*, 23 and 30 July 1908; Harold Bolce, "Foreseeing What the People Want: How Initiative, Imagination and a Sense of Value Created an Industry from an Idea," *System* 26 (1914): 158.

Strikingly, Pearce gained fame for not just interacting with staff during lunch-hour rushes, but sitting in the dining room with other diners and ordering food on the menu (partly it should be added to draw attention to less popular dishes). It was inconceivable that any of the "gentlemen" on the Board would have emulated Pearce, either when he personally guided the business as managing director or replaced him. Throughout his career, Pearce remained, despite increased wealth and social mobility, rooted in the working class, an identification reinforced by his philanthropic efforts and evident social concern for struggles of the downtrodden.[13]

On his son's resignation from the BTT in July 1905, ending the Pearce influence, loyalty loomed large in workers' affections: numerous staff members followed him into exile, expressing their solidarity.[14] Some were undoubtedly long-standing employees, capable of recalling his silver wedding celebration exactly a decade earlier. Here, Pearce had disclosed his own altruism: "What he had done … had the effect of helping other people up, and that had been to him a cause of great satisfaction." His uncompromising moral code fostered affection as much as profound admiration from his staff. To his son, Harry, his father and mother epitomised the vital importance "to walk uprightly, honestly, and in fear of God."[15]

Staunchly loyal, Charles Cann, depot superintendent, exemplified why "the Governor" inspired such deep loyalty, love and affection in his staff.[16] When John Pearce resigned, Cann, rejecting an attractive job offer from the BTT, expressed his abiding faith: "I follow the old captain, sink or swim, under whom I served for so many years." This fidelity deeply touched Pearce, who soon rewarded Cann, making him a director in the new company, JP Restaurants. "No man ever had a more faithful and conscientious worker," Pearce readily admitted. Just how many others like Cann departed voluntarily from the BTT and joined Pearce in his new company is unknown, but biographer Marguerite Williams offered her own informed judgement: "The Managing Director had taken its best business brains with him."[17]

[13] Ellis, *Pluck*, p. 199; *Financial Times*, 23 and 30 July 1908; Bolce, "Foreseeing What the People Want," p. 158; Williams, *Pearce*, p. 152.

[14] Ellis, *Pluck*, p. 204.

[15] *Temperance Caterer*, 15 Aug. 1895. He was paraphrasing Micah, ch.6, v. 8, in the Bible.

[16] See p. 173.

[17] *Temperance Caterer*, 15 Aug. 1907; Williams, *Pearce*, p. 154.

Forced into unwanted retirement, John Pearce experienced serendipity when returning from the Bankruptcy Court, where he met Sir Edward Sullivan's former lawyer. "Why, Pearce remarked the lawyer, "you have had a lot of knocking about since I saw you last at Sir Edward's funeral," and then confided: "Been treated badly they tell me." Unburdening himself to the lawyer, Pearce described his predicament, having left his own company and yet feeling a strong sense of responsibility to his former employees. "What are you doing now?" enquired the lawyer. Pearce explained his own plans for a new catering venture for which he had already established three restaurants. Reassuringly, the lawyer replied: "Well, all the Sullivans are not dead, and I've other clients who would like to be with you." Pearce agreed to "come round and see" him; this soon came to fruition.[18]

Members of the Oldham family, together with other former clients, joined him as founders in JP Restaurants in 1905. Four individuals, united by friendship or kinship, formed the nucleus of the new firm: John Pearce (chairman), W. Horace Pearce (managing director), Charles Cann (director) and H. Frederic Oldham (director). Through this network of friends the company began with £40,000 of capital, a testament to Pearce's reputation as the pioneer mass caterer. He and his family took up £5400 or 13.5% of the shares.[19] As a company with a private flotation, those who were allowed to invest were tightly controlled. Because either brewer Lord Iveagh himself or other members of the Hurst faction had previously opposed Pearce—disclosing anonymously to newspaper reporters their belief in his being "too old for the job" as managing director, aligning with the Hurst faction during the 1904–1905 leadership struggle and admitting having "backed the wrong horse"—such malcontents played no role whatsoever in the new company's formation, purchase of shareholdings or leadership. Pearce's reputation, much maligned by his critics in the acrimonious struggle to oust him from the BTT Board, became rehabilitated. Recalling the expressions of condescending regret—"getting too old" and "not sufficiently up-to-date"—that had dismissed Pearce as a spent force in catering and exiled him, Joseph Bentley pointed to the successful launching of the new company, JP Restaurants, in 1905 as complete vindication. Based on the new company's restaurants, Bentley declared that "There is to-day in London no stronger or more capable man in the catering world than Mr. Pearce." As the BTT went into receiv-

[18] Ellis, *Pluck*, pp. 204–05; *Temperance Caterer*, 15 Aug. 1909.
[19] *Temperance Caterer*, 15 Aug. 1905.

ership, a saddened but resolute Pearce purchased some of his old depots in October 1909. Reaffirmation soon followed. After refitting, modernising and reopening them, the founder's hand clearly visible once again, receipts within eight months rose dramatically.[20] This meant his new firm, JP Restaurants, offered Lyons much stiffer competition, which explains in part why Lyons in these immediate pre-war years (1911–1914) declared dividends that stabilised rather than continued phenomenal growth. Dismemberment of the old BTT offered scope for Pearce's JP Restaurants to expand aggressively, with restaurants demonstrating an appeal as alluring as their fashionable décor and store fronts.

Well known for honesty and integrity, Pearce's reputation proved of inestimable value when negotiating with landlords to rent new premises. Hefty rents, he feared, might deter property owners from seeing him as a viable tenant. Once he disclosed his identity, however, they went to great lengths to "help the company in every possible way."[21]

Pearce had been gradually moving geographically outside the City since the late 1880s, a trend which became still more pronounced now. Associated with the theatre trade in more exclusive areas, notably Charing Cross Road and St. Martin's Lane, JP Restaurant shops became as easily recognisable outside the square mile as inside. From the company's beginning, it moved south of the river with an establishment in the Waterloo Road. By 1915, Pearce had opened a new shop at 361 New Oxford Street, advertised as "a first-class restaurant."[22]

Whatever the location, Pearce remained aggressively committed to improvements. Always devoted to introducing the newest technology, he built new bakeries in the Viaduct buildings, "replete with the latest, best, most hygienic and economical appliances," costing some £1500. By 1914, JP Restaurants owned model bakeries, a cold storage for meat and a tea warehouse. Sales of packet teas, still a mainstay of the business, persisted, their advertising stressing full weight, unlike competitors.[23]

Pearce's catering philosophy had likewise evolved in response to newer circumstances. "In catering, as in everything else," he noted in 1908, "the public required more and more, so that what suited now would not do next month or next year," shrewd advice which his former directors at the

[20] Ibid., 15 March and 15 Apr. 1908; *Daily Telegraph*, 25 Feb. 1927; *Financial Times*, 6 June 1910.

[21] *Temperance Caterer*, 16 Aug. 1906.

[22] Ellis, *Pluck*, p. 98; *Temperance Caterer*, 15 Aug. 1909; *Financial Times*, 19 Aug. 1915.

[23] *Financial Times*, 3 Aug. 1906 and 16 Aug. 1913; *Daily Telegraph*, 25 Feb. 1924.

British Tea Table would have been wise to heed. In essence, he envisaged a continually evolving, sophisticated business philosophy, sensitive to ongoing changes in consumer taste, preferences and economic circumstances. No longer would he entertain any notion of replicating his first company in which he created a chain of outlets targeting working-class men in the City; now he transcended class lines in the new company with shops much better than anything with which he had been previously involved. At the outset, two distinct chains were formed: JP Restaurants (nicknamed "JPs"), directed at clerks, typists and tradesmen; and John Pearce Dining Rooms, aimed at workers, formerly called the Pearce & Plenty's.[24] In 1910 he added a third chain, Pioneer Cafés, an intermediate category in-between JP Restaurants, on the one hand, and John Pearce Dining Rooms, on the other. Sensitively positioned and carefully observing nuances of dress and class, Pioneer Cafés would offer prices that, as the *Temperance Caterer* remarked:

> will appeal to a large class whose income … may be somewhat restricted in amount, but have to dress fairly well and therefore are on the look-out for a restaurant where … they get the highest respectability, the best appointments, and good food at reasonable prices, daintily served.[25]

Location of his first shop at 266 High Holborn, headquarters of the new company, underscored his more ambitious agenda. So did his expansion to 79 New Oxford Street. "Of its class there is nothing better in the West End," the *Temperance Caterer* enthused. Even the less partisan *Financial Times* praised the "JPs" for providing "almost all that was procurable at a first-class restaurant." Of all types of the company restaurants, this line became the fastest growing, increasing from one establishment (1905) to thirty-two (1914) and accounting for almost two-thirds of the total. To foster the social widening of customers, some of these newer premises enlarged their menus enormously. The company's motto equally seemed more class-encompassing: "Value for Your Money."[26] In an interesting departure, a new depot at 2 Minories East spanned the classes, with the ground floor and basement catering to the working class in a John Pearce depot, while the two floors above reached socially higher in a

[24] *Temperance Caterer*, 15 Aug. 1908.
[25] Ibid., 15 March 1914.
[26] *Financial Times*, 29 July 1908; *Temperance Caterer*, 15 Aug. 1905, 15 Jan. 1906, 15 Aug. 1908, and 15 Aug. 1909.

Fig. 8.1 JP Restaurants, 3 Victoria Buildings, Victoria Rail Station (Reproduced by permission of the Mary Evans Picture Library)

new chain, John Pearce First Class.[27] Its opening in 1911 commemorated Pearce's four decades as a temperance caterer, with Arthur Henderson (Labour MP and Treasurer of the Labour Party) the key figure at the event. Another experiment, a hybrid JP Restaurant, opposite Victoria Station, consciously aimed at catering to different classes throughout the day (Fig. 8.1). Luncheon patrons could eat meals for 1s. 6d., while those who ate after 6 p.m. paid 2s. for dinners. Here, "the floor is covered with a thick carpet," clearly denoting middle-class décor.[28] Here too Pearce now saw an opening for attracting women. For a long time Pearce restaurants had been serving masculine dinners primarily for the working classes; Pearce's restaurants now expanded with females as a major component of the clientele. Overflowing with young women, the new JP Restaurant in St. Paul's Churchyard also numbered some men.[29]

[27] *Temperance Caterer*, 15 Aug. 1911.
[28] *Financial Times*, 19 Oct. 1911; *Temperance Caterer*, 15 Oct. 1906.
[29] *Temperance Caterer*, 15 Feb. 1910.

Table 8.1 Locations of JP Restaurants, 1905–1906

1905	266 High Holborn (JPR) (headquarters)
1905	John Pearce's Workman's Restaurant, 18 Gray's Inn Road (WC)
1905	John Pearce's Workman's Restaurant, 19–20 Fetter Lane (WC) (Fleet Street End)
	18 St. Paul's Churchyard
	New Bridge Street
	Newgate Street
	3 Victoria Buildings(Opposite Victoria Station)
	Waterloo Road
1906	79 New Oxford Street
1906	John Pearce's Workman's Restaurant,145 Whitechapel Road (EC)
	17 Charterhouse Street, E.C.

Westminster Cafés, begun on the eve of the war, represented a major departure, catering to groups hitherto ignored. Merchants and what George Orwell would later categorise as the lower upper-middle class constituted the types of patrons targeted. Traditional Pearce & Plenty depots, once the backbone of the original firm, still contributed to the company's profits, but overall their role shrank in value, their fifteen depots representing not much more than a quarter of the total (Tables 8.1 and 8.2).

Yet, this movement socially upwards by no means eclipsed his roots in the working classes. He had neither forgotten them nor they him. In the display window of the company's renamed depots, John Pearce Workman's Restaurant (formerly Pearce & Plenty), Pearce proudly hung the photograph of his original "Gutter Hotel" (Fig. 1.2). On the opening of a new restaurant in an old familiar location, Jewin Street in the City, "the patrons came in as though they were coming home." For workers, "he is still the same man who did so much to cheapen their food in the long years ago, and give them comforts before unknown," wrote Joseph Bentley in the *Temperance Caterer*. Well-prepared quality food, sensible prices and attentive staff—these argued the paper retained customers. Equally critical was the proprietor, John Pearce, whose "careful buying and careful management" earned profits for shareholders and gratitude from customers.[30]

[30] Ibid., 15 Oct. 1905, 15 Aug. 1906, 15 March 1908 and 15 Aug. 1909.

Sharply contrasting with policies of the old BTT were those of Pearce's new company. From the beginning, he opposed establishing goodwill as part of the value of the firm, giving him greater latitude in managing a reserve fund.[31] "Every sovereign subscribed had been put into the business," assured Pearce In utilising most of the funds otherwise going into reserve, he expected this money to generate higher dividends, thereby reimbursing shareholders faster than otherwise for their original investment. Within ten years of the company's founding, Pearce announced that all but 5% of investors' original capital had been repaid.[32] Reserve funds did exist, but on a smaller basis than before. Depreciation, the related issue that had caused the old BTT so much trouble, was written off 5% of profits annually, enabling the company to extinguish the cost of leases before they terminated.[33]

Initially, Pearce doubted whether his new company could match the hefty profits of the BTT's pinnacle of its popularity in the early 1900s. "Competition was very keen," he informed shareholders at JP Restaurants' first ordinary meeting, In this more competitive market, the company still declared impressive dividends, with the first year's 5% doubling in the second and reaching 12% in ensuing years (Charts 8.1 and 8.2).

Compared to its competitors, JP Restaurants outperformed Slaters, Ye Mecca and the Express Dairy, while Lockharts recovered and reached 15% dividends briefly (1911–1913)—ironically as a result of the inspired managerial skills of Arthur Pearce. Steadily rising dividends enabled the company to more than double its capital to £100,000.[34] Lyons and ABC, two catering companies with much bigger capital investment more widely dispersed as vertical enterprises than JP Restaurants, remained market leaders.[35]

By June, 1909, JP Restaurants was running twenty-two establishments—fifteen JP Restaurants and seven John Pearce eating-houses—and employing 500 people (Table 8.2). The substantially higher cost of outfitting JP Restaurants compared with John Pearce depots—£2200 versus

[31] In neither buying premises nor merging with other firms, Pearce avoided any shareholder pressures for adding these items under goodwill.

[32] See Charts 8.1 and 8.2. *Temperance Caterer*, 15 Sept. 1914.

[33] In 1907, for example, Pearce placed £500 in a reserve fund (*Temperance Caterer*, 15 Aug. 1907). *Temperance Caterer*, 15 Aug. 1908 and 15 Aug. 1911. The ABC also earmarked no money for goodwill (*Financial Times*, 4 Nov. 1913).

[34] Ellis, *Pluck*, p. 98; *Temperance Caterer*, 15 Aug. 1909; *Times*, 10 Aug. 1906.

[35] See pp. 126–28, 144–52.

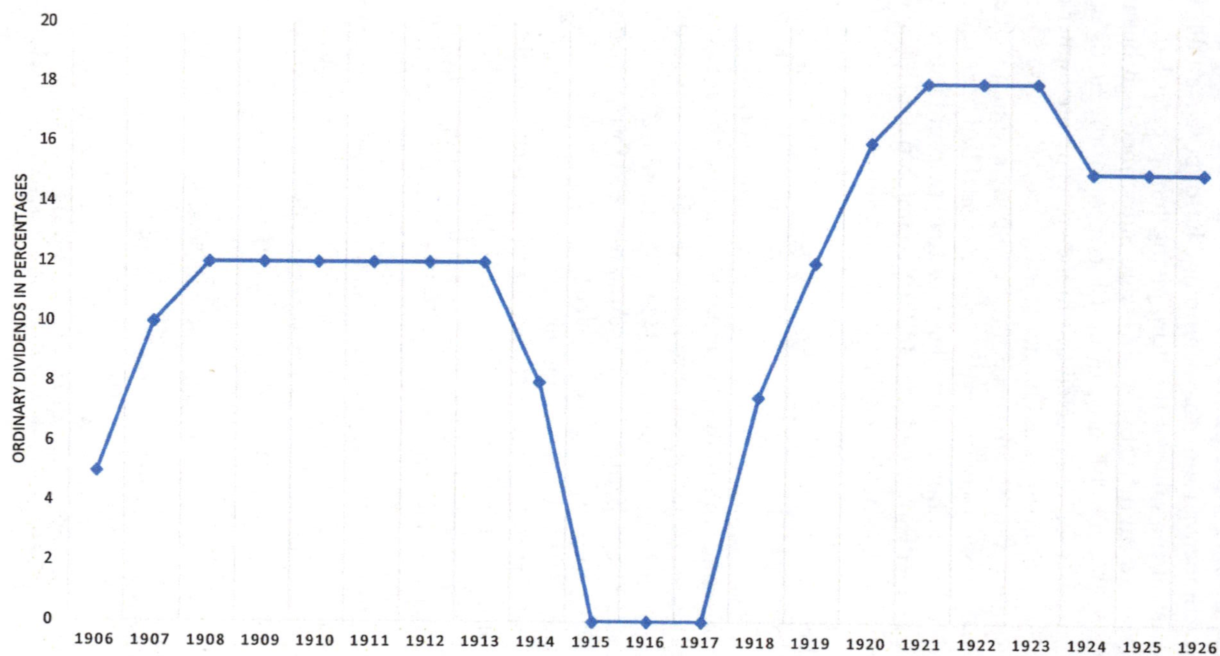

Chart 8.1 Dividends of JP Restaurants, 1906–1926. Sources: For the years 1896–1926, see the following: *Economist*, *Financial Times*, *Temperance Chronicle* and *Times*

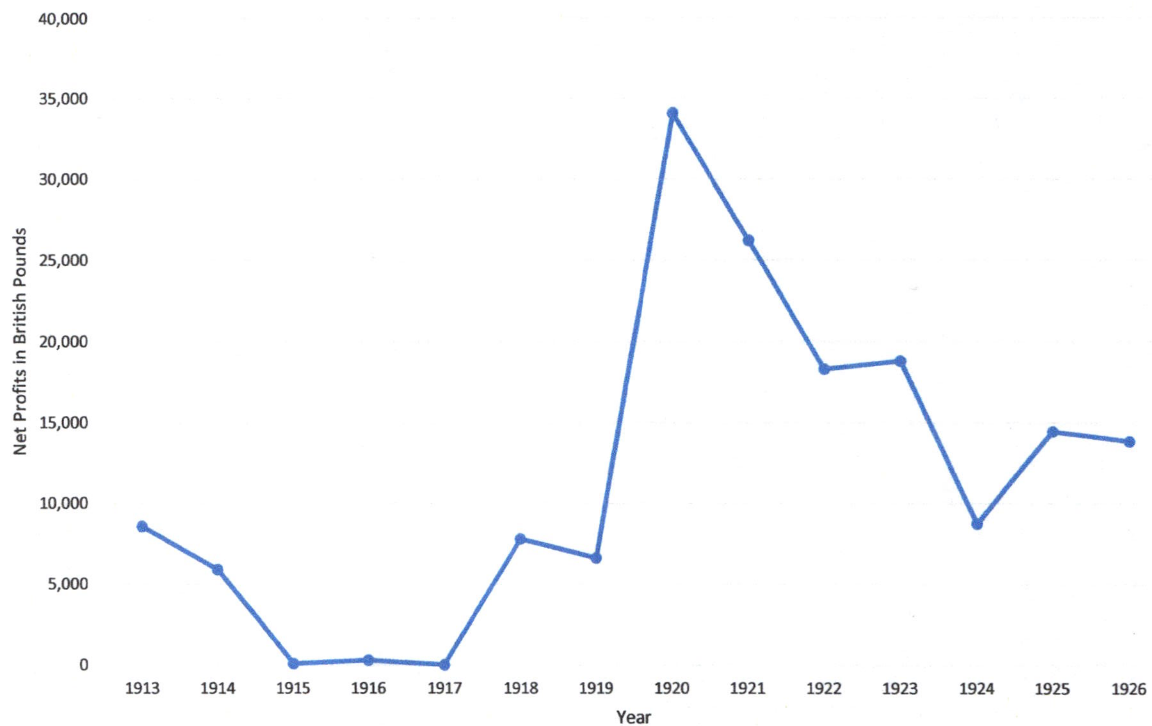

Chart 8.2 Net profits of JP Restaurants, 1913–1926. Sources: For the years 1896–1926, see the following: *Economist*, *Financial Times*, *Temperance Chronicle* and *Times*

Table 8.2 John Pearce's mass catering, 1905–1914

	Westminster Cafés	*JP Restaurants*	*John Pearce First Class*	*Pioneer Cafés*	*John Pearce depots*	*Total depots*	*Employees*	*Capital*
1905		1			2	3		£40,000
1906		8			4		158	
1908		10			7	17	414	£100,000
1909		15			7	22	500	
1909						53[a]		
1910			1					
1911						54	1122	
1913							1304	
1914	6	32		1	15	54	1200	

Sources: *Temperance Caterer*, 15 Oct. 1906, 15 Aug. 1908 and 15 Aug. 1911; *Times*, 10 Aug. 1906 and 20 July 1908; *Financial Times*, 29 July 1908, 24 July 1909, 6 June 1910, 19 Aug. 1913 and 15 Aug. 1914; *Daily Mail*, 21 Feb. 1923 and 28 Jan. 1927; Bolce, "Foreseeing What the People Want," p. 155; *Daily Telegraph*, 25 Feb. 1924; Ellis, *Pearce*, p. 206

[a]The company had purchased 33 depots from the Receiver for the Debenture-holders of the BTT

Table 8.3 Weekly meal sales, 1905–1913

	Workmen's depots	*JP Restaurants*	*Total customers served*
1908	28,000–29,000	28,000–29,000	
1909			100,000
1913			ca. 300,000

Sources: *Temperance Caterer*, 15 Aug. 1908; Williams, *Pearce*, p. 159 (1909); *Financial Times*, 29 July 1908; "The JP Restaurants: The Temperance Catering Movement and One of its Founders," *Financial Times*, 13 Feb. 1913; Ellis, *Pearce*, p. 206

£1500—symbolised the class status of each, as did the terms "restaurants" versus "depots." Such restaurants marked a decided step upwards in quality. As Pearce termed them, they were "more substantial than ordinary tea-rooms gave to their customers." With a big menu advertising the lowest prices in London, his shops generated huge custom, topping 100,000 patrons weekly by 1909 and about 300,000 two years later (Table 8.3).[36]

[36] *Financial Times*, 3 Aug. 1906 and 29 July 1908; Ellis, *Pluck*, p. 206; "Fifty Years of Catering." By 1913, JP Restaurants was selling 50,000 meals daily ("The JP Restaurants: The Temperance Catering Movement and One of its Founders," *Financial Times*, 13 Feb. 1913).

Business became more compressed between the hours of noon and 3 p.m., when fully 90% of the total receipts were earned, reflecting changing eating habits in which working-class men ate just a meal at lunchtime at JPs.[37]

Pearce's more conservative approach delighted frugal shareholders. Within four years of its founding, JP Restaurants was serving about 29,000 customers weekly, justifying expansion of capital from £40,000 to £100,000.[38]

With a brood primarily of boys, Pearce had the foresight to prepare them to enter the business. After brief stints with the BTT and JP Restaurants, Guy Pearce took an informal apprenticeship with Armour & Co., big meat importers in London and Chicago, before re-joining his father. To introduce the most progressive ideas into the business, Guy convinced his father to buy a huge refrigerating plant where some 3000 carcasses could be stored, thereby saving considerable money. With his newly acquired knowledge, he persuaded father John to discontinue the long-standing practice of buying meat with a contract, practised at the BTT and instead get it on the open market. Attaching great significance to this innovation, John observed that "it was only by purchasing in bulk that they were able to serve their customers at reasonable charges and still make a profit." In fact, he regarded this practice as of such importance because with it, patrons could eat more cheaply at "JPs." Guy's older brother, Horace, had gained experience as a confidential clerk with the BTT, and succeeded his father as its managing director for three months. Having resigned, he re-joined his father with the new family firm, assuming the role of managing director of JP Restaurants. John's oldest son, Arthur, had served as general manager of Lockharts in 1905 before joining his father as managing director with the family firm just before the war.[39]

Pearce's subsequent catering success indicated that he still possessed far greater insight into the catering market than the Hurst faction. Ever the astute marketer, he perceived scope for his JP Restaurants given a renewed life in the changed circumstances. The reciprocal relationship with his customers now sustained him. "Thousands of his patrons who had followed him had grown in prosperity and wanted more luxuries," wrote Bolce.[40]

[37] *Financial Times*, 17 Aug. 1912 and 21 Aug. 1922.

[38] *Temperance Caterer*, 15 Aug. 1908.

[39] Ibid., 15 Feb. 1907 and 15 Dec. 1910; *Financial Times*, 16 Aug. 1910 and 16 Aug. 1913. Arthur had served as assistant general manager of the BTT.

[40] Bolce, "Foreseeing What the People Want," pp. 155, 160.

Public support had been apparent from the first JP Restaurant's opening in 1905 on High Holborn, just outside the City's limits. As Joseph Bentley recorded in the *Temperance Caterer*, "the public is showing in an unmistakeable manner in which direction its sympathy goes. At the luncheon hour there is often difficulty in obtaining a seat."[41] The *Caterer & Hotel-Keeper* recognised Pearce's stature as one of the country's pre-eminent caterers.[42] In this same year, the *Temperance Caterer* quoted one observer who remarked that "the people are sure to follow John Pearce wherever he goes."[43]

Though he paid dearly for retaining his shareholdings in the BTT, his involvement in its winding-up stages enabled him to acquire some of the depots at the most promising sites.[44] Soon after procuring former BTT depots and totally redesigning and renovating them in 1910, they became incredibly lucrative outlets for JP Restaurants. Under the proper management, these thirty-three within eight months were performing outstandingly, increasing their receipts by an astonishing 90%. This owed too to a man whom the Hurst faction had dismissed contemptuously as "too old" at 57.[45] These were years, moreover, in which caterers experienced rising demand but reduced earnings and less profitability.[46]

Pearce discovered his peacetime activities had ill-prepared him for wartime disruptions. By 1916, restaurateurs testified that prices across the board had soared by some 75%. Contributing to disorder, experienced staff took better wages in munitions work, leaving him constantly shorthanded with inferior replacements. "Among his temporary staffs he found the biggest thieves he ever knew," remarked biographer Marguerite Williams. German Zeppelin attacks demolished three of his restaurants, and the coachman of the brougham who drove him to inspect them afterwards disappeared. Poison gas factories gave the surroundings a saffron-coloured look. Bombs had not directly hit some civilians, but many nevertheless showed distinct signs of exposure—sickness, deranged behaviour and unattended horses whose boy minders had been killed. Her health giving way under the strain, Pearce's wife was moved to safer quar-

[41] *Temperance Caterer*, 15 Aug. and 15 Oct. 1905.

[42] *Caterer & Hotel Keepers' Gazette*, 16 Jan. 1905.

[43] *Temperance Caterer*, 15 Aug. and 15 Oct. 1905.

[44] Williams, *Pearce*, p. 154.

[45] *Financial Times*, 6 June 1910 and 26 Aug. 1926; *Daily Telegraph*, 25 Feb. 1927; *Temperance Caterer*, 15 Sept. 1910. Pearce's purchase of BTT outlets, moreover, included a half dozen in the less profitable category (*Economist*, 17 Apr. 1909).

[46] *Economist*, 1 Jan. 1910.

ters in Tunbridge Wells. After a visit to bring her some requested items, Pearce returned home to find it empty, his three maids having plundered it and fled. In 1916, Pearce's wife, companion, supporter and helper, died, leaving him more isolated than he had been since he married.[47]

JP Restaurants, though experiencing wartime dislocation, was far from decimated. One source of work and profit involved two nationalised areas, Enfield and Woolwich, where he served 10,000 and more factory workers.[48] Like other catering firms, his declared no dividends for three years (1915–1917), but recovered quickly, posting 7.5% dividends in 1918, 12% the following year and still more impressive results of 16% (1920) and 18% (1921–1922). What had not changed were miniscule profits on each meal served. With over half of the amount going to overhead charges, JP Restaurants earned just 4% of every shilling of receipts.[49] Towards the war's end, the pre-war five separate branches of restaurants had consolidated into three (Table 8.4).

Enormous numbers of women, generally young, began frequenting JP Restaurants from 1915 onwards. To this influx of females, Pearce attributed rising receipts of 21–22% in 1920. Though they initially spent much less on midday meals than men, Pearce thought such women "were much better customers individually than they used to be." Formerly, "well-dressed women came into their restaurants, occupied the best seats, and remained a long time consuming a glass of milk and a bun." Now, however, they ate ample meals instead of such light fare.[50]

Table 8.4 Branches of JP Restaurants, 1917

Branch name	*Total number*	*Located in EC London districts*
JP Restaurants	21	19
Pioneer Cafés	19	14
John Pearce Dining Rooms	16	9

Source: *Temperance Caterer*, 15 Apr. 1917

[47] Williams, *Pearce*, pp. 186–91; *Temperance Caterer*, 15 Sept. 1916 and 15 Sept. 1917.

[48] Williams, *Pearce*, p. 188.

[49] *Times*, 21 Feb. 1923.

[50] *Temperance Caterer*, 15 Dec. 1915, and 15 July and 15 Sept. 1917; *Financial Times*, 15 Aug. 1915 and 24 Aug. 1920; *Daily Mail*, 24 Aug. 1920. Easily outnumbering men, growing numbers of respectable women likewise began frequenting public houses from early

Soaring rents, rates and taxation, together with intensifying competition in the City combined to obstruct the company's expansion. As Pearce despairingly informed shareholders in 1922, "the time has now arrived when it is almost impossible to carry on successfully a working-class trade." Rents especially soared.[51] In one outrageous case, a property owner demanded a £20,000 premium for a 21-year lease for a ground floor and basement in Kensington. Rents, Pearce stressed, were "simply abominable, so it has become impossible to run a cheap trade." In the mid-1920s, Pearce portrayed JP's bleak prospects: "the only reason why the firm had not opened more premises last year was that there was no chance of anyone making money except the landlord."[52]

To these new commercial pressures, Pearce responded in different ways. Doomed were his traditional working-class depots, the Pearce & Plenty chain with which he began so many decades ago. Low-cost meals became unattainable owing to new economic constraints. As he noted, "It is impossible to sell goods cheaply, because high wages, heavy cost of building, heavy rents, all have to be passed on to the consumer." Pearce & Plenty houses either closed down or were converted into more upmarket premises. The quintessential example of the latter transformation came at St Martin's Court, Ludgate, long a popular workers' depot, which Pearce closed and renovated for a wealthier clientele. Another such depot, 26 High Street in Whitechapel, in East London, became a "JP." Other caterers of the working class had similar experiences with catering for plebeian patrons.[53]

JP Restaurants not only survived serious wartime dislocations, but recovered faster than any other catering company in the post-war era, even outperforming huge competitors such as Lyons and ABC. Of the five major catering companies,[54] JP Restaurants—the second smallest with £100,000 of share capital—had achieved a yield of £10 in the years 1921–1924, the closest competitor and smallest company, Ye Mecca,

1916 (David W. Gutzke, *Pubs and Progressives: Reinventing the Public House in England, 1896–1960* (DeKalb, Illinois: Northern Illinois University Press, 2006), p. 53).

[51] *Daily Mail*, 4 Oct. 1920. See below, p. 203 for rising coffee prices.

[52] *Financial Times*, 21 Aug. 1922 and 26 Aug. 1925; *Daily Mail*, 26 Aug. 1924 and 26 Aug. 1926; *Portsmouth Evening News*, 26 Aug. 1925.

[53] *Financial Times*, 21 Aug. 1922, and 26 Aug. 1925.

[54] By 1923 W. Hill & Sons, bakers and confectioners took over Lockharts, while the Express Dairy Co. was excluded from the calculation owing to much of its trade being dominated by milk delivery.

recording a yield of £7 11s. 3d. To accomplish this feat, JP Restaurants had posted impressive dividends of 18% (1921–1923) before declining slightly to 15% (1924). Commenting on this astonishing performance, the *Economist* reflected:

> Apparently profits depend entirely on efficiency of management, and in seeking investments in this direction the cautious person will look more to the man behind the organisation than to historic names and undertakings who are living upon their past.

Such a thoughtful investor, too, would dismiss Pearce's age of 77 as worthy of any consideration. Were further evidence needed of his sagacious assessment of the catering trade, the same periodical reported that JP Restaurants remained unchallenged two years later, its yield remaining at £10.[55] In achieving this outstanding performance, JP Restaurants defied intensifying competition in the City. Refreshment houses proliferated here to a greater extent than other businesses along London's main arteries, notably Oxford Street, Holborn and the Strand.[56]

To the end of his career, Pearce embraced new ideas, especially in regard to the welfare of his staff. Tried on an experimental basis, he introduced profit sharing at some thirty or forty restaurants in the City and West End as a way of guaranteeing staff families ate recently cooked meals. Employees paid nine shillings for booklets of ten tickets, each of which was accepted at a full shilling when buying meals, providing staff with a 10% discount.[57]

To what did Pearce owe this sustained level of astonishing success? The *Financial Times* pointed to JP Restaurants' shrewd strategy in crossing class lines with both middle- and working-class shops as responsible for its popularity. Food distribution ensuring the freshest cooked food likewise distinguished the company from rivals. Competitors centralised food preparation at one site, where they cooked food and then distributed it to branches, which reheated it for customers the following day. JP Restaurants, in contrast, cooked food at one site in the early morning before dispatching vans with it to branches.[58] This was what his firm had done before the war, and now continued it.

[55] *Economist*, 13 Dec. 1924 and 13 Feb. 1926.
[56] *Financial Times*, 21 Aug. 1923.
[57] *Daily Telegraph*, 25 Feb. 1927.
[58] *Financial Times*, 11 Aug. 1922 and 26 Aug. 1926.

CHAPTER 9

Into the War and Beyond

For catering companies, the years between 1914 and the depressed 1920s fundamentally transformed assumptions governing their business in the late Victorian and Edwardian years. Lower-middle-class workers benefited from reduced hours, and had less reason to frequent nearby caterers when employers arranged for tea trolleys to take food and refreshments to their staff desks. Between 1895 and 1920, passengers on railways doubled, so workers could return home faster without stopping for dinners. For even market leaders such as Lyons, fewer customers and their lower expenditure hit particularly hard, given that profit on typical meals consisted of a farthing. High turnover had amplified miniscule profits, but this relationship no longer existed. In the case of Lyons, for example, some teashops incurred losses for the very first time.[1] Further squeezing profits were inflationary pressures, driving up rents, wages and menu charges. Coffee prices reflected this new dynamic. For long, a cup of coffee had cost 2d., but this pre-war figure began increasing incrementally by ½d. during the war, reaching 3½d. in 1920.[2] Customers complained most about putting an extra ½d. on buns.[3]

[1] Peter Bird, *The First Food Empire: A History of J. Lyons & Co.* (Chichester: Phillimore & Co., 2000), pp. 108, 111–13.

[2] *Daily Mail*, 4 Oct. 1920. To resist such pressures, leading catering companies had agreed to a price-fixing arrangement with 2½d. established as the going rate in 1915. Slaters withdrew from the understanding late in 1916, but other big companies upheld it (Minute Book, ABC, Board of Directors, University of Exeter, MS 326, 26 Oct. 1916, f. 50).

[3] Minute Book, ABC, Board of Directors, MS 326, 31 July 1919, f. 35.

D. W. Gutzke, *John Pearce and the Rise of the Mass Food Market in London, 1870–1930*, https://doi.org/10.1007/978-3-030-27095-7_9

During World War I and into the 1920s market changes forced caterers to adopt different retailing strategies. Throughout these years, Lyons, its size and diversified businesses making the firm an anomaly, remained profitable, though not to the same extent as formerly. For the other major catering companies—Slaters, Lockharts, Ye Mecca and the ABC—this same period resulted in dismal economic performances, delaying repairs and decorations of premises. Profits and dividends plummeted, prompting some firms to seek security against persisting financial woes with enlarged reserved funds. What created the most challenging context was the faltering patronage of pre-war working-class customers, which had devastating impact especially on Lockharts where Arthur Pearce inspired leadership ended before the war. That talented leadership was vital became apparent when Edward Hart directed Ye Mecca's remarkable recovery. This small company also underlined how merging with other firms in part enabled transition to new market conditions. The quintessential example was the ABC, which acquired control of Lockharts and JP Restaurants. Another survival strategy involved moving upmarket, establishing upscale subsidiary lines such as Picard's Cafè's (Ye Mecca) and Beta Tea Rooms (Slaters) or doing so informally as in ABC's case. Firms also began experimenting with hybrid diners/restaurants in which customers had diverse choices—alcohol, dancing, better food and wider offerings.

Largest of the country's catering companies, Lyons occupied a category quite separate from its competitors, owing to its unique position as a multifaceted caterer. Central to its leadership was its 250 teashops, a chain following standardised practices which Cadby Hall supplied with food as well as other items. Three traits distinguished the chain, and contributed most to its success. Committed to giving the public dependably good value at competitive rates, Lyons teashops served exceptional tea, combining the best blends with outstandingly reasonable meals, even challenging working-class caterers. Roast beef and two vegetables, priced at 10d. and easily the top choice of diners, was as popular as the table d'hôtel lunch at a Corner House obtainable for 1s. 6d. Second, considerable thought—and expense—went into acquiring the best sites. Finally, exploiting the twin economic advantages of labour surplus and abundant clerical staff, Lyons implemented sophisticated systems of portion control and checking designed to eradicate waste and theft. No transaction however small escaped scrupulous inspection. One revealing facet of this system involved the waitress check which Major Salmon, a company director, instituted. After consuming a meal at a Lyons restaurant or teashop and armed with the waitress check,

> the customer gives [it] up at the paybox … [where it] goes through something like eight pairs of hands at Cadby Hall and stage by stage it is classified, checked, analysed, credited to the waitresses and recorded in its proper place as a unit of the business done that day by that depot. If anywhere a leakage has occurred it is detected within a few hours and the individual responsible among all the twenty-two thousand employees of the company is known.[4]

Easily overlooked is that from its beginnings in London, Lyons developed a subsidiary component of teashops, food processing. Placed in front of teashops (and later the Corner Houses), stood a shop retailing tea, but burgeoning business compelled Lyons to create a special agency for sale and distribution by 1904. In the 1920s, ice cream, bread and cakes were likewise distributed wholesale through a separate agency. During the 1920s and into the early 1930s, Lyons transitioned from teashops and Corner Houses to food processing and distribution as the chief basis of business. On the eve of World War II, what the firm retailed was staggering. As historian D. J. Richardson observes, Lyons "sold its tea through two hundred thousand agents, produced three and a half million gallons of ice cream, and baked sixty-three thousand tons of bread and cake each year." Mass production and innovative factory techniques and processes—the product of Lyons' engineers solving the challenges of manufacturing on a scale previously unimagined—together with scientific recipes devised by Lyons' laboratories, all contributed to Lyons spearheading food processing and distribution in Britain's second industrial revolution. Centre of this transformation, Cadby Hall (Hammersmith) itself was a marvel. Consider the daily production of Swiss rolls, which when placed one after the other would have stretched several miles.[5]

Of all the catering companies, Lyons survived the war with least dislocation. It continued making substantial profits and declared smaller but still respectable dividends of 25% (1915–1918), easily surpassing ABC, the next biggest company.[6]

With more capital (£3.5 million) at its disposal, Lyons earned on average 28% dividends before the depression, though the declining profitability of teashops and the corner houses started emerging already in the

[4] *Hotel Review*, Oct. 1922; D.J. Richardson, "J. Lyons & Co. Ltd.: Caterers and Food Manufacturers, 1894 to 1939," in Derek Oddy and Derek Miller (eds.), *The Making of the Modern British Diet* (London: Croom Helm, 1973), pp. 167–69.

[5] Richardson, "Lyons," pp. 169–70.

[6] Bird, *Lyons*, Appendix B.

second half of the 1920s. “The popular image of Lyons as a company based predominantly on catering became increasingly misleading,” remarks Richardson.[7]

The Edwardian crisis in catering came later to Slaters than other competitors in the City, but was nevertheless quite devastating. Late in 1915 the previous year’s dividends of 6% vanished altogether. Enraged shareholders appointed an Investigative Committee, which ousted the chairman and the four directors. Shareholders elected two new board members who possessed considerable experience: J. Salter Cox, a butcher by trade, had worked with former chairman Crowle fifty years earlier, while Mrs Louisa Sampson had been a vocal critic of Ye Mecca’s Board members.[8]

The Investigative Committee reserved its harshest criticism for overall oversight and supervision of restaurants. “Inadequate, inefficient, and antiquated”—these adjectives in the eyes of the Committee characterised the company’s “system of accounting.” Of utmost importance was the need for a modern bookkeeping system. The many far-flung branches of the company—fish, meat, grocery, provision, florists, green groceries and restaurants—desperately needed centralised control. Detailed shortcomings were enumerated about the branches, indicating systematic problems of long standing. “They express surprise, not that the business has deteriorated, but that it has for so long survived,” confessed the Investigative Committee.[9]

Three neglected areas required urgent attention: the central office must scrutinise purchases; directors must assert direct control over restaurant managers; and restaurants must be closely supervised. However well-intentioned these reforms, they yielded nothing substantive in the war’s last three years (1916–1918) to alter fundamentally the company’s financial standing: its cumulative net losses in profits stood at almost £15,000 and no dividends were declared, so outstanding repairs totalling £16,000 remained unaddressed. Depreciation on investments at least had been substantially written down from £76,000 to £42,000. Apart from realising this long-sought change, the war had proven utterly disastrous for Slaters.[10]

[7] Richardson, “Lyons,” p. 169; Bird, *Lyons*, Appendix B.
[8] *Financial Times*, 11 Dec. 1915, and 11 March and 30 Dec. 1916.
[9] *Financial Times*, 28 Feb. 1916.
[10] *Economist*, 14 Dec. 1918; *Financial Times*, 28 Feb. and 30 Dec. 1916.

One insuperable problem concerned the number of restaurants unprofitable now for a dozen years. Although the Committee's Report prompted closing one of them, further contraction posed difficulties. Many uneconomic restaurants "are mostly held on long leases, some with a covenant to maintain the business, and could not therefore be closed, even if desirable," related one Board member.[11]

Long leases became more problematic because of how the company had historically dealt with goodwill. Predictably, shareholders' views shaped Slaters' policy. There was a historic struggle between the short-term thinking of shareholders, wanting optimal dividends, on the one hand, and sound long-term company financial strategy, which meant diverting some of the profits to writing down goodwill, on the other. These antithetical goals, in fact, were understood but never considered as anything more than theoretical considerations, except by the Board. Since the firm's formation, nothing had been written off goodwill, which stood at over £124,000 pounds in 1913, one-third of the capital. In that same year continued modest dividends of 7% prompted Sir David Burnett (chairman) to candidly inform shareholders that "until this item was extinguished no very large dividends could be expected." Had goodwill disappeared from the balance sheet, "it would be possible on the present trading results to pay dividends of 12 percent to 13 percent." With vast sums invested in premises with long leases, the company rather belatedly earmarked a special fund called "leases reserve" to recoup the unprotected capital. This sound but long overdue policy explains in part why the company passed dividends for the war years and into 1919.[12]

One shareholder pointed to the company's gratuity policy as an important factor decreasing profits from afternoon teas. Slaters' restaurants in the City primarily derived profits from the lunch trade, for which patrons had no objections to tipping table staff. People stopping for afternoon tea, with several slices of bread and some butter, however, baulked at paying gratuities. Had Slaters banned them, so thought this shareholder, afternoon business would have increased sharply.[13]

Outside the company some critics emphasised other factors as responsible for Slaters' protracted financial woes. Shrewd and informed, newspa-

[11] *Financial Times*, 28 Feb. and 11 March 1916.

[12] *Temperance Caterer*, 15 Dec. 1913; *Financial Times*, 3 Dec. 1913, and 28 Feb. and 11 March 1916; *Economist*, 14 Dec. 1918.

[13] *Financial Times*, 7 Dec. 1911.

per editor Joseph Bentley focused on three problems with one paramount. "The real cause for the set-back in Slaters may … be found in the subsidiary enterprises with which the Company is connected." This view contradicted the chairman's own belief that regarded the company's diversified trading as insurance against disaster. "Should bad times overtake us in any department, we may hope to compensate ourselves in one or other of the other departments."[14] Related to shortcomings of this strategy was investment in overseas "speculative businesses." To Bentley this constituted having "too many irons in the fire," evoking the decline of Spiers & Ponds. Finally, he noted the role of John Crowle, an earlier chairman, whose death had deprived Slaters of shrewd, gifted skills.[15]

For Slaters, as for most other catering companies in the City, the war years had meant not just negative profits and passing of dividends, but shabby premises, with repairs and other important structural changes deferred as a result partly of scarcity of both skilled tradesmen and materials. "The very appearance of a Slaters restaurant, proclaimed aloud that it was a concern struggling to keep its head above water," admitted Chairman W.E. Catesby. Once free of the war, Slaters spent some £33,000 on redecorations and updating its restaurants, including installing new stoves replacing those dating from when shops had opened.[16]

Impressed with Lyons' diverse customer appeal, Slaters departed from long-established custom, and pioneered licensed restaurants. By the mid-1920s, the firm had established seven of them. Complementing adoption of this new business strategy, Slaters merged with Bodega Co., a long-established concern with business as caterers, hotel proprietors and licensed victuallers running a chain of wine shops. With the addition of £400,000 of Bodega stock, the enlarged Slaters traded with a capital of £1,000,000.[17]

Emerging in the 1920s, Slaters implemented a novel policy aimed at new types of customers. Continuing pre-existing practices of preparing and cooking food at each restaurant rather than emulating other catering firms which centralised kitchens at one site for subsequent distribution, Slaters opened an entirely new line, "Beta" Tea Rooms, targeting "the

[14] See *Temperance Caterer*, 15 March 1896; *Financial Times*, 14 June 1897, 15 Nov. 1902, and 11 Sept. and 1 Dec. 1905.

[15] *Temperance Caterer*, 15 Dec. 1906; Bryan Morgan, "A Short History of Spiers and Pond," in *Express Journal, 1864–1964: A Centenary History of the Express Dairy Company Limited* (London: Newman Neame, 1964), pp. 134–35.

[16] *Financial Times*, 1 Jan. 1920.

[17] Ibid., 5 Dec. 1925 and 21 Nov. 1928.

rank and file of City workers" with light, fresh, recently cooked food. Appropriately, Aldersgate Street, the site of Pearce's first venture in the City, was designated as home of the first Beta in 1925. With the opening of the third Beta on Oxford Street, Slaters moved well beyond mere catering into a broader area in which it offered space for dances, dinners and other social functions, a hybrid between the traditional eating facility and a modern restaurant emulating what Lyons pursued so successfully.[18]

Faced with the most serious financial crisis in its history before 1914, Slaters thus creatively instituted changes in the 1920s, enabling a complete turnaround in its trading. Making sizable profits from 1919, the firm declared modest dividends of 4–5% for several years and then incrementally increased them each year until the amount reached 10% (1928), a level last achieved two decades earlier. Two interrelated issues, the reserve fund and goodwill, became part of the recovery plan. Long-standing practice of distributing profits reasonably to shareholders rather than "up to the hilt" had permitted growth of a sizable reserve fund, somewhat depleted by wartime austerity. Nevertheless, the Board decided to apply the existing £55,000 reserves to goodwill, then standing at £124,000, with the ultimate goal of eliminating them both.[19] Slaters recovered and performed well in the 1920s, making it an exception among London's catering companies; others experienced greater difficulty.

For Ye Mecca, a decade of flat dividends of 3% (1904–1913) meant especially difficult war years. Profits were tiny, leaving the company no choice but to continue the practice started at the war's outset of passing dividends.

Underground locations of most of its depots deterred Ye Mecca from attracting more patrons. Board member Percy Pickard recalled that such basement facilities had "horrible tiles arranged in a kind of mosaic which for some reason, always reminded me of the Albert Memorial," typifying how so many other people reacted. Unattractive depots alone, however, scarcely explained why Ye Mecca failed to draw greater numbers of customers. Since depots were designed neither to cook food nor to serve lunches, reconstruction seemed inevitable as a solution. To alter fundamentally the depots and what they served would require sizable investments from shareholders, an unlikely strategy, given the company's unsatisfactory financial performance. The company's dismal record of earnings equally precluded the idea of selling out to a larger rival.[20]

[18] Ibid., 30 Dec. 1920, 5 Dec. 1925, 4 Dec. 1926, 26 Nov. 1927, and 30 Nov. 1928.
[19] Ibid., 24 Nov. 1923, 19 Nov. 1926 and 11 Aug. 1928.
[20] http://meccadancehalls.kett.ch.; *Financial Times*, 28 Feb. and 4 March 1914.

Edward Hart's appointment as chairman marked Ye Mecca's turning point. Charles Rees, who knew him well, paid Hart the ultimate accolade as a catering expert: "What he does not know about it is not worth knowing." In the company's recovery, provincial depots played a vital role. Accounting for one-fourth of the total depots, they spearheaded the company's rebranding as a restaurant business. On taking over Picard's Cafés, Ye Mecca displayed new initiative and energy. The change was staggering: with 670,000 more cups of tea and coffee consumed in 1919 than in 1915, takings dramatically increased by 58%. Ye Mecca earned £6500 in net profits, allowing payment of 2.5% dividends, the first time since 1913 the company paid shareholders anything. Greater turnover enabled Ye Mecca to offset rising costs of commodities and wages, while addressing the backlog of outdated premises. Eight new depots were transformed into restaurants, and existing depots were run as coffee/tea cafés. Throughout the chain, Hart had cash registers installed and redecorated older depots. Adopting a conservative strategy, Ye Mecca, like Slaters, opted to declare modest dividends and enlarge its reserve fund.[21]

In the 1920s the company adopted several new policies. Dancing, the rage of the interwar years, was introduced into large branches such as at Ludgate Hill, where it became "an enormous attraction." Here, too, this branch acquired a wine and spirit licence, broadening both its clientele and appeal. Dividends remained consistently respectable, with 4–5% as the benchmark. Symptomatic of the more optimistic Board, Ye Mecca doubled its capital to £250,000. These additional funds sustained an expansionist programme in which the company purchased new restaurants, and either reconditioned or redecorated many more.[22]

Lockharts' late Edwardian recovery demonstrated, as in Ye Mecca's case later, the vital component of talented leadership. Arthur C. Pearce's remarkable recovery strategy was in retrospect an aberration in which Lockharts posted high dividends for three years. Once Pearce resigned to join his father in 1913, the absence of his acumen immediately became apparent when the company faltered, the war itself exacerbating longstanding unsolved problems.

[21] *Economist*, 13 Dec. 1924; *Financial Times*, 23 Feb. 1911, 1 Apr. 1920.

[22] David W. Gutzke, *Pubs and Progressives: Reinventing the Public House in England, 1896–1960* (DeKalb, Illinois: Northern Illinois University Press, 2006), pp. 166–68; *Financial Times*, 3 May 1928 and 6 May 1929.

Catering to workmen, especially in the building trades, for three meals, beginning with a hearty breakfast, Lockharts encountered two problems—shorter work days and extension of the tube—enabling patrons to cut their meals outside home to just lunch. A related problem concerned new government legislation imposing rationing. Under the Public Meals Order (1916), restaurants could only serve two courses in the daytime and three courses in the evening. Another equally devastating factor arose indirectly from the war. "Their customers," lamented Chairman C.B. Thring, "were the working men who went on active service, and Lockharts' shops were thus empty." Rising prices, impossible to pass on to patrons entirely, resulted in closure of four uneconomic depots. Should Lockharts want to increase prices as a strategy for offsetting inflationary pressures, Thring confessed, "within a week … they would have emptied their shops, and might close their doors." Food shortages compounded the firm's woes. True to well-established working-class custom, Lockharts regulars sought a tantalising cut from a joint of meat, not unappetising, despised wartime substitutes such as curries, hashes and stews. Desperate to regain patrons, the firm went so far as to introduce "vegetarian, egg and cheese substitutes." Regulars responded with silent but unmistakable contempt: "Many of them disappeared." These circumstances together explain why the company incurred losses during the war, precluding ordinary dividends. One vital decision occurred in 1919 when the company, apparently at the behest of anxious shareholders, offered modest dividends of 5.5%, the first such payments since 1914. An outstanding issue, most notably the writing off of depreciation, not done since 1915, was ignored entirely, because it would have reduced, if not eliminated entirely, dividends.[23]

Lockharts' problems, however, had a systemic dimension, chronic under-capitalisation. For decades, the Board had made the case for issuing debentures of £30,000, but almost two-thirds of this had been unmet in 1904. Again in 1915, the Board appealed to shareholders to increase Lockharts' capital, though this too went unanswered, perhaps because the troubled firm had written off substantial amounts of goodwill and share capital of nearly 60% in 1909. Quite simply, the catering market had changed substantially, rendering a firm such as Lockharts, based solely on working-class custom, inviable. For this reason, the company had closed

[23] *Financial Times*, 11 June 1914, 20 June 1916, 17 June 1917, 11 July 1918, 10 July 1919, and 14 Nov. 1922; *Times of India*, 25 Oct. 1922; *Temperance Caterer*, 15 Nov. 1913 and 15 July 1916.

twenty depots—about one-third of the total—opening one new one and renovating two others aimed at a new, different class of clientele branded as Ideal Restaurants.[24]

Lockharts' demise came quickly after an embarrassing loss of £3085 in profits in 1922. No ordinary dividends had been posted since 1919, while preference shares of £42,000 were seven years in arrears.[25] ABC directors proposed a merger with Lockharts because of interest in acquiring not its customers, but its "well-sited shops." Class prejudice loomed large in this thinking. ABC directors viewed Lockharts' working-class clientele as incompatible with their socially upmarket image. According to the *Financial Times*, the ABC Board "would probably be frightened of the old Lockharts customers if they turned up in any strength" after the merger. Any talk of the war as having a socially levelling impact had not reached the Board rooms of leading companies. In taking over the business, the ABC contemplated choosing only the most desirable restaurants to run, which possessed pre-war leases with terms unattainable in the inflationary post-war era. Ultimately, the merger talks collapsed. Early the following year, W. Hill & Son, bakers and confectioners, bought Lockharts. Ironically, Arthur C. Pearce, former general manager of Lockharts just before the war, held this same position now with W. Hill & Son.[26] Publicly, Lockharts' name disappeared altogether, being replaced with Goodfare Dining Rooms.

Another troubled company had been the ABC. Unofficial Board policy in Edwardian England had been "directed along the lines of least resistance," Chairman George Harvey admitted. This lacklustre approach had provoked a shareholder revolt against the unimaginative chairman and managing director George Edwards, who had reluctantly yielded to demands for appointing an outside expert. The ultimate choice, Horace Pearce, second son of John, had confirmed the worst fears of the shareholder committee, but its combined criticism produced no lasting fundamental alterations.[27] Hence, when the war disrupted trade, the ABC had little choice but to address serious, long-standing difficulties.

[24] *Financial Times*, 29 June, 11 Oct. and 14 Nov. 1922. For the origins of Ideal Restaurants, see pp. 135–36, 211–12, 225.

[25] *Sheffield Daily Telegraph*, 21 Oct. 1922.

[26] *Daily Mail*, 19 Feb. 1923; *Financial Times*, 2 and 11 Oct. 1922; *Economist*, 10 and 12 July 1919, 17 Jan. 1920, and 1 July and 2 Oct. 1922.

[27] See pp. 146–48.

For the ABC, the war years resulted in steadily declining profits, with the company actually incurring huge losses approaching £15,000 and declaring no dividends in 1917, the first time this occurred apparently since the firm's formation in 1861.[28] When the war ended, new chairman George Harvey disclosed to shareholders that "the company had felt the steady pressure of competition for some years, and their shops and general service conditions were allowed to remain in a very backward state." Such were the ABC's financial weaknesses that a prominent firm had launched a takeover bid.[29] Whether this factor proved crucial in the ABC's gradual withdrawal from the City is unclear, but other catering companies such as Lyons and JP Restaurants—much better off financially—retained their outlets there.[30]

New blood for the ABC was perceived as an overriding need, so the Board policy embraced an aggressive expansionist campaign meant to "raise its tone and give it more life and elasticity than could be obtained by adhering to the tea-shop business pure and simple on ABC lines." Acting on this belief in 1918, the ABC purchased Buszard, a smaller company and manufacturers of chocolate and confectionery, as a strategy for transforming the staid ABC menus with Buszard products. From this new relationship the ABC Board expected to "reconstruct the service arrangements of many of their shops."[31]

Expansion with complementary businesses was fruitful in other ways. That same year, the ABC also purchased Bertram & Co. and signed a catering contract with Oval. Recovery soon resulted in soaring profits, dividends reminiscent of the prosperous Edwardian years just before the war and ABC's growth with new share capital. Its ordinary capital now reached £1.5 million. Widening its base of operations, the ABC invested heavily in W. Hill & Son, bakeries and confectioners, purchasers of Lockharts in 1923.[32]

[28] *Financial Times*, 18 July and 11 Oct. 1922. Historical records of the ABC's performance have not survived, save for a few volumes of minute books (Gareth Shaw, Louise Curth and Andrew Alexander, "A New Archive for the History of Retailing: The Somerfield Collection," *Business History Archives* 84 (2002): 29–34).

[29] *Financial Times*, 24 Sept. 1918. What company made the bid was never mentioned in the press.

[30] Robert Leon, "Rise and Fall of the Aerated Bread Company," *Camden History Review* 25 (2001): 49. This reversed company policy of consolidating its outlets in the City, inaugurated in the 1890s (Ibid., p. 48).

[31] *Financial Times*, 24 Sept. 1918.

[32] ABC, Minute Book, Board of Directors, 8 Dec. 1927, and 17 Jan. and 6 March 1928, MS 326, ff. 216–17, 240, 272; *Daily Mail*, 20 Dec. 1927.

In 1927 the ABC, nearly ten times larger than JP Restaurants, bought its rival for £176,000, with JP directors given £10,000 to split among themselves.[33] For the preceding three years, Pearce's company had outperformed the ABC, earning dividends of 15% annually compared with the ABC's 10%. To reflect this disparity, each JP share was exchanged for 1¼ shares of ABC.[34] What ultimately ended Pearce's remarkable career owed nothing to market changes, intensified competition or outmoded ideas, but rather to his octogenarian status. Rapid consolidation, too, in the catering sector would have posed problems greater than he had ever confronted in his entire career. Pearce, now 80, meanwhile accepted a role as a consultant, while working as a director of JP Restaurants (Fig. 9.1). Of all the company's mergers and investments, the most important was the

Fig. 9.1 John Pearce photographed in 1930 (Reproduced by permission of Daryl Pearce)

[33] JP Restaurants had increased its capital to £100,000 in 1908 (See Table 8.2).

[34] *Daily Mail*, 6 May 1927; Minute Book, ABC, Board of Directors, 21 Apr. 1927, MS 326, ff. 107–08.

takeover of JP Restaurants in 1927. It was rumoured in the press that Arthur Pearce's joining the ABC the preceding year had "paved the way for the acquisition." As part of the strategy to introduce more dynamic ideas and policies, Pearce was appointed as general manager. Widely experienced in the catering trade and serving as JP's managing director, Arthur came to the ABC as a remarkably talented executive, having rescued Lockharts from financial ruin in the depths of the Edwardian catering crisis.[35] The ABC had embarked on a new policy, the establishment of fully licensed, upscale restaurants. On the most expensive of these, located on Wilton Road, near Victoria Station, the ABC spent the unprecedented sum of £12,798. ABC named the Empire Restaurant, its immense expense reflected its premier status, as the company's flagship restaurant.[36]

Arthur Pearce identified wages of waitresses as causing the ABC considerable problems. He saw the wage scale as a chief reason in "many leaving the Company's service." A case in point was at the recently reconstructed branch at 233 Oxford Street, where inability to hire qualified staff had delayed its reopening. In presenting a convincing case, Pearce was instrumental in persuading the chairman to raise wages from 17s./week to 20s./week at reconstructed premises. Showing his father's humanitarianism, he also proposed that ageing manageresses, whose infirmities prevented their continuing in their job, be employed as cashiers with good pay (25s./week) and food allowances. To this too, the Board acceded.[37]

Poorly light and ventilated, ABC teashops also desperately needed modernising. Within eighteen months, Pearce had reconditioned twenty-seven of the defective teashops; the investments fully justified the expenditure, as patronage expanded considerably.[38]

Acquiring new companies and an experienced general manager had one immediate consequence: the ABC decentralised cooking from preparing food dishes at a central site in Camden Town the night before their delivery and reheating the following day at depots to instituting food preparation at each restaurant. Spiralling takings reinforced this devolution of control. Unlike other catering companies, the ABC rejected creating a separate line of depots as a move targeting more refined customers;

[35] See pp. 135–36, 211–12, 225. *Sheffield Daily Telegraph*, 27 Apr. 1927.

[36] Minute Book, ABC, Board of Directors, MS. 326, 2 June 1927, 28 Feb. 1929, ff. 103, 129; *Daily Mail*, 9 Dec. 1926; Leon, "Aerated Bread Company," p. 48.

[37] Minute Book, ABC, Board of Directors, MS. 326, 29 March, 3 and 19 Apr., and 1 May 1928, ff. 285, 287, 295, 303–04.

[38] *Financial Times*, 14 Jan. 1932.

instead, the ABC distinguished between different kinds of clientele with a distinct nomenclature—depot for the working classes and restaurant for the middle classes. In shifting from dependent depots to autonomous restaurants, the company consciously sought to lure patrons more socially upmarket than what it currently drew. Another distinctive group was the teashop, a term now employed to designate an outlet offering a menu of snacks with coffee or tea without any preheated food available.[39] In pre-war terms caterers would have called these light refreshments.

Eighteen months after he was appointed, the ABC Board reaffirmed faith in Arthur Pearce with a new, generous contract. In recognition for enlarging the company's business primarily through the reconstructed depots and teashops, the Board offered him a seven-year contract in which he received a salary of £3000 and 2% of the company's annual profits, a quite generous proposition. That ABC was already experiencing a decided slump in both sales and dividends in 1928, yet still expressed confidence in his continued successful performance, attested to its strong faith in his managerial abilities.[40]

Pearce's modernisation programme coincided with the 1929 depression in which ABC net profits fell by two-thirds and dividends plummeted to zero. Not surprisingly, a disturbed Board of Directors became less inclined to spend sizable sums on refurbishments, particularly when the expenditure on nineteen projects had reached £48,000, more than twice as much as the firm's then annual net profits. Seeking a scapegoat for its financial crisis, the Board attacked the company architect for failing to obtain its approval for estimates. Under ordinary circumstances, the long overdue updating and modernising of premises was wholly defensible, since the average cost of £2536—taking into account post-war inflation—compared closely with the average £2200 that JP Restaurants had laid out in updating premises in the Edwardian era.[41]

ABC's conservative pre-war culture, which had thwarted Horace Pearce's attempts to modernise the company, now resurfaced in yet another financial crisis, with a second son of John Pearce blamed for long-standing deficiencies. Charged with rashly instituting improvements that

[39] Minute Book, ABC, Board of Directors, MS. 326, 30 June, 15 Sept. and 8 Dec. 1927, 17 Jan. and 6 March 1928, ff. 137, 163, 216–17, 240, 272.

[40] *Economist*, 13 Dec. 1930; Minute Book, ABC, Board of Directors, MS. 326, 25 Oct. 1928, ff. 15–16.

[41] Minute Book, ABC, Board of Directors, MS. 326, 28 Feb. and 21 Nov. 1929, ff. 103. 316; *Economist*, 13 Dec. 1930. See pp. 193 and 196 for JP's pre-war expenditure.

had not repaid investments, Arthur Pearce was summarily ordered to submit his resignation as the general manager and the company manager was fired. Within a fortnight's of his dismissal, the Board received a "list of depots in a bad state of decorative repair."[42]

Despite the Board having offered Pearce a seven-year contract in appreciation for commendable performance one year earlier, he now became fall guy for the ABC's faltering performance. Summarily dismissed, he was shabbily treated, given one week's wages in lieu of notice. Eager to make Pearce the culprit of the ABC's financial miseries, the company besmirched his reputation, recording its views in the private minutes: "Pearce was looked upon generally in the market as an incompetent buyer." Why had this not been raised earlier as a factor when renewing and extending his contract? Pearce was allowed to confront neither his accusers nor given the chance to defend himself.[43]

Antagonism between the Pearce family and Lord Greenwood originated in the nature of the merger between the firms.[44] In an interview published in the *Birmingham Daily Gazette*, Guy Pearce asserted that Greenwood wanted his brother Arthur not just fired as general manager, but removed entirely as a director from JP Restaurants and the ABC, along with two other family members, John and Guy, also serving in a similar capacity. Should John Pearce accept this proposal, Greenwood promised to resell JP Restaurants to him. Relations between the main participants remained strained and contentious. "My father accused Lord Greenwood of carrying on a vendetta against him and his sons," Guy Pearce claimed to the paper's reporter.[45]

Averse to being unfairly censured for the ABC's financial debacle, Arthur Pearce hired a solicitor and confronted the ABC, eventually being entirely vindicated. Rather than a week's pay in lieu of notice, the court, mindful of his contract worth £3000 annually, awarded him £15,000 of damages plus court costs. Thus, he cleared his reputation from charges of incompetence, and exposed the ABC's dishonesty in refusing to accept some responsibility for the company's uninspired performance.[46]

[42] Minute Book, ABC, Board of Directors, MS. 326, 10 Oct., 19 and 29 Nov. and 6 Dec. 1929, ff. 268, 310, 324, 332.

[43] Ibid., 12 Dec. 1929, f. 338.

[44] As Sir Hamar Greenwood, he served as a cabinet minister in Lloyd George's post-war government.

[45] *Birmingham Daily Gazette*, 28 March 1930.

[46] *Financial Times*, 14 Jan. 1932.

By the end of the 1920s, the late Victorian catering world had disappeared. Three stalwart companies—the BTT, JP Restaurants and Lockharts—had liquidated or been taken over. Lyons, in a distinct category, was flourishing, but soon would be moving into food processing as the main basis of business. Ye Mecca, smallest of catering companies, survived the decade, though the 1930s would force its departure from catering altogether.

On the verge of Lockharts' takeover in 1922, the *Financial Times* remarked that John Pearce as chairman of JP Restaurants "saw how things were going and developed the business in those directions whose profit and prosperity were to be secured." Again, Pearce grasped how market conditions changed in the 1920s; Lockharts had not.[47] Of all the leading caterers, he alone understood how the present bore little resemblance to the past. But then it underlined his acumen and intuitive grasp of catering, a clear-sightedness that had guided him unfailingly for more than sixty years.

[47] Ibid., 11 Oct. 1922.

CHAPTER 10

Conclusion

John Pearce launched his career as the quintessential penny capitalist with £1 in 1867, saved £1200 in the following thirteen years and, reinvesting these profits in his business, went on to cater to millions, riding the crest of this economic transformation and the social mobility it entailed. His was literally the rags-to-riches story in which he left a gross estate of £51,073, an apt testament to his entrepreneurial flair and devotion to hard, unrelenting but joyous work.[1] Had he held government bonds, he would have earned a 3½% interest rate amounting to £1785, almost enough to put him in the very limited category of rich people who paid supertax, the threshold starting at £2000.[2]

John Pearce's career possessed a curious symmetry: he devoted nineteen years (1867–1886) in business for himself moving from the Gutter Hotel to working with Sir Edward Sullivan, another nineteen years (1886–1905) labouring in the private and then public company called British Tea Table and finally spent twenty-two years (1905–1927) running JP Restaurants, possibly doing less day-to-day work as he approached his eightieth birthday. In fact, he celebrated this milestone on 29 January 1927, not quite three months before he sold his company to the ABC.

To what extent did temperance influence the business attitudes and profitability of the City's caterers? Most leading late Victorian catering compa-

[1] *Daily Mail*, 26 June 1930.
[2] I want to thank Trevor Lloyd for this point.

D. W. Gutzke, *John Pearce and the Rise of the Mass Food Market in London, 1870–1930*, https://doi.org/10.1007/978-3-030-27095-7_10

nies embraced temperance, except Slaters and the smaller companies, Ye Mecca and the Express Dairy Company. Hence, to serve alcohol constituted a deviation from the norm. The Aerated Bread Company (ABC) assumed one stance in which it banned the sale of alcohol. Less exacting was Lyons, which later in the early 1890s followed a similar posture in prohibiting alcohol but just in its teashops. Ronald McDougall's temperance sentiments were displayed boldly on restaurant windows and walls: "No intoxicants sold." One of his cafés advertised itself as the "People's Temperance Café." More confrontational, Lockharts deliberately sited its cocoa rooms literally next door to pubs. On opening his first Glasgow cocoa room in 1875, Robert Lockhart hired total abstainers exclusively and encouraged customers to sign teetotal pledges in a book available at each restaurant, something which became a standard feature at all his houses. Taking his opposition to alcohol consumption one step further, he sought to dissuade friendly societies from meeting on licensed premises. Lockharts also distinguished itself from temperance-minded competitors in placing customer abstinence pledges on walls of the company outlets.[3]

How did Pearce fit into this anti-alcohol environment? Fiercely opposed to alcohol, he permitted temperance organisations to meet at his depots, provided some commercial advantage resulted. Lacking this compelling evidence, he discontinued the practice. Further than this, he was unprepared to go. Had an unfamiliar patron encountered his depots, in half of the instances, he (or infrequently she) would have seen above the ground floor the signage proclaiming "Pearce's Temperance Hotel." In public, he certainly made no effort to conceal his beliefs: he referred proudly to himself as a "temperance victualler," assumed offices in leading temperance catering organisations and attended their conferences and finally spoke candidly about how he thought alcohol blighted the lives of so many Londoners.[4]

As Pearce's business ventures expanded from the mid-1880s, promoting temperance never receded far from his view. Of his forty-six restaurants in the 1890s, fourteen had temperance hotels connected with them, where customers—however poor and humble—had their own bed. Here he endeavoured to uplift his working-class clientele with what Victorians

[3] *Temperance Caterer*, 15 Sept. 1900.

[4] *Evidence of the Royal Commission on Liquor Licensing Laws*, 1898, 36 (Cmnd. 8694), pp. 242, 244. From 1889 he participated in the National Temperance Caterers' Association. He likewise served as director of the Temperance Caterers' Journal Co. Not surprisingly, he categorised himself unequivocally as a "temperance caterer," who regarded alcohol consumption as anathema.

called rational recreation, outfitting the hotels with libraries, pianos and rooms designated for smoking, reading and writing, all part of the night's charges. When a new trust was established for the Old Vic Theatre in 1891, Pearce secured pride of place in the front with the understanding that he would operate (another) temperance restaurant. No one anticipated that Pearce would indulge drinkers with alcohol on his menu. Not only did he refuse to sell intoxicants, but he forbade their being brought into his restaurants.

Publicly, Pearce refused to allow his hostility to alcohol abuse to consume his entire business life. For him, alcohol he knew was a problem for many, not an evil substance worthy of demonisation. He raised no objections to accepting investment in the British Tea Table from Irish millionaire brewer Lord Iveagh (Arthur Guinness, Son & Co.), so long as Pearce could write his uncompromising hostility into its company articles: whatever the beverage, Pearce vowed no alcohol would ever be served on the firm's premises. Throughout his life, he never compromised on this belief.[5]

He had a clear view of his purpose, which had nothing to do with philanthropy. Pearce conducted business as a matter of making a profit by activity that respected his own moral principles, while giving customers what they wanted at a price they could pay. An avowed teetotaller, he sought to offer workingmen an alternative to rum and milk for breakfast and beer at the pub for lunch. Pearce regarded men's excessive consumption of alcohol as the product of dirty coffee houses, pubs and beerhouses seldom closed, and nothing to consume on licensed premise save booze. In giving workers an attractive substitute, he viewed himself as contributing to their temperate habits, something in which he took immense pride. Victorian temperance advocates labelled such activities as "counter-attractions." "Catering," Pearce reflected, "helps people to be temperate." Strikingly different from coffee public-house philanthropists, he assessed the market as a businessman who saw an unfilled need for good, inexpensive and nutritious food. To succeed, he knew he had to make profits, so nothing in his approach involved the common philosophy, "philanthropy plus five percent."[6] Customers went to Pearce & Plenty for

[5] How he reconciled his uncompromising hostility to alcohol, on one hand, with ABC's new post-war policy of serving liquor is unclear.

[6] Marguerite Williams, *John Pearce: The Man Who Played the Game* (London: Religious Tract Society, 1928), pp. 90, 163–64; John Nelson Tarn, *Five Per Cent Philanthropy: An Account of Housing in Urban Areas between 1840 and 1914* (Cambridge: Cambridge University Press, 1973), pp. 43, 46.

its prices, substance and quality, not for its commitment to teetotalism. On the firm's premises, nothing reminded patrons of the virtues of temperance—no placards, no prominently displayed books in which patrons pledged their adherence to temperance, no outspoken temperance-minded staff and no signage on windows proclaiming bans on alcohol.

Recalling his forty years in catering in 1906, Pearce claimed that "he and those associated with him were the pioneers of this temperance refreshment business." They had been, he believed, the "forerunners in the business." To bolster this assertion, Pearce cited the fact that "they were often looked up to by other caterers for hints in connection with their business." Soon after arriving and establishing a depot, he became the City's dominant working-class caterer. A former licensed victualler thought Pearce & Plenty had earned the immense gratitude of workers, filling a niche with huge potential in the catering market. By the end of the 1880s, he was being characterised as the Spiers & Pond for London's working-class men.[7]

Pearce's antipathy to serving alcohol on company premises led to his opposing Lord Iveagh, Dublin brewer and large shareholder, in the managerial crisis of 1904–1905. Envious of Lyons & Company's selling of alcohol at its more upmarket restaurants, Pearce's critics regarded him as an unnecessary and outmoded obstacle to increasing the BTT's profitability. With Pearce exiled from the Board, the pro-alcohol Hurst faction, supported by Iveagh and other big shareholders, could conceivably revise the company articles prohibiting the sale of alcohol.

Attitudes of the pro-Hurst faction must be inferred from what several key individuals stated publicly about their chief motivation. Joseph Bentley reported a rumour that pointed to the dismissal of Pearce as a necessary prelude to rewriting the BTT's articles prohibiting alcohol. His future biographer, the Rev. James J. Ellis, attributed hostility to Pearce as the result of the latter's public testimony before a royal commission in which he blamed publicans for encouraging drunkenness. A less conspiratorial view would be that Iveagh was simply concerned with getting beer into the hands of sellers, whether publicans or caterers. Like other brewers, Iveagh sought retribution in the 1905 crisis, Ellis contended. Finally, Pearce as

[7] *Financial Times*, 10 Aug. 1906; *Temperance Caterer*, 9 Nov. 1889 and 25 Jan. 1890. Spiers & Pond specialised in providing refreshment at rail stations and on trains (Bryan Morgan, "A Short History of Spiers and Pond," in *Express Journey, 1864–1964: A Centenary History of the Express Dairy Company Limited* (London: Newman Neame, 1964). pp.132–33).

managing director circularised shareholders' warning that if brewer shareholders repealed the ban against alcohol, he would sever ties with the BTT. In response to Pearce's forthright challenge, Iveagh, together with other huge shareholders, backed the Hurst faction, and proceeded to accept Pearce's resignation at a private meeting from which he had been excluded.[8]

Pearce & Plenty's growth, however, had less to do with Pearce's attitudes to alcohol than with shrewd positioning as a caterer. His uncanny ability to anticipate evolution of the catering market remained a persisting trait in his long business life, never deserting him or distorting his judgement. Throughout the 1880s, Pearce astutely differentiated Pearce & Plenty from rivals, offering customers food more substantial than Lockharts and more savoury than the ABC. Into the early 1900s, the firm continued to work on small profit margins, selling in bulk while generating a smaller return per unit sold than ABC or Slaters' shops. This applied as well to the more upmarket BTT shops, which sold cups of tea or coffee at half the price charged at ABC teashops. Nothing better explains the enormous sales of 80,000 meals daily at the BTT and Pearce & Plenty shops.[9] As the dominant force in the company's success, Pearce was ambitious, never greedy.

His business strategy also differed markedly from his two chief rivals, Lockharts and the ABC. Lockharts' North Country Coffee Taverns in northern England, founded in 1879 with a capital of £220,000, specialised in retailing cakes and pastries, not hearty meals to the working-classes. With this same formula, the company spread to London in the mid-1880s.[10] The ABC had concentrated in the bakery business, selling bread and cakes. Not until the late 1880s in response to customer demands did the ABC introduce tea and milk, initially at one shop near London Bridge. Expanding custom resulted in the shop devoting a separate room for teas, a development with which the company would become most closely identified.[11] Customers could patronise Pearce & Plenty restaurants, in contrast, for more substantial (high protein) fare and all three meals. For breakfast or

[8] See pp. 166–68. This same issue re-emerged in the 1920s, when Slaters and the ABC breaking with tradition began serving alcohol at restaurants which had obtained liquor licences. By this time, Pearce had sold his company and so the question for him became moot.

[9] *Temperance Caterer*, 9 Nov. 1889, and 15 June 1903.

[10] *Refreshment News*, 18 Aug. 1888; *Financial Times*, 30 July 1895; *Temperance Caterer*, 15 June 1901; *Coffee Tavern Gazette*, 22 Jan. 1887.

[11] *Temperance Caterer*, 15 Nov. 1912; *Times*, 19 Oct. 1912.

luncheon, his establishments offered haddocks, eggs and bacon; at dinner, customers typically ate cuts from the joint and vegetables.[12]

Displaying considerable business acumen, Pearce decided to go upmarket with a new chain of restaurants early in the 1890s, though directors opposed what they saw as a potentially disastrous repositioning of the company. Such a move might antagonise the firm's base of plebeian patrons, and provoke criticism of Pearce as getting above himself socially, views which even his friends on the Board forcefully argued. For his part, an undeterred Pearce stressed that he was not so much personally ambitious as eager to follow his old customers whose social standing had risen over time. Central to this debate on clientele was the unshakeable belief that social mixing of classes on the same premises was inadvisable, even untenable: patronising establishments which blurred class lines portended serious loss of status for transgressors. Pearce's view was vindicated, paving the way for creation of a new firm, the British Tea Table Company.

This perspicacity remained a hallmark of Pearce's business outlook and integral to his strategy for sustaining profitability. Of the leading catering companies in the City, his was the first to form a new subsidiary firm, the British Tea Table Company, aimed explicitly at the petit bourgeois. Again, after being forced out of the BTT, he founded as part of JP Restaurants what the public dubbed the "JPs," catering to clerks, typists and tradesmen, though on a more attractive basis than the old BTT depots. Targeting more sophisticated customers was the next line, Pioneer Cafés, billed as better than the plebeian John Pearce Dining Rooms but one step below the "JPs."[13] On the eve of the war, Pearce went further upmarket with another subsidiary line, Westminster Tea Cafés, pursuing a group of patrons previously well beyond what the public associated with him. Thus, in pre-war London, Pearce more than anyone else focusing on the lower end of the catering industry came to personify the visionary entrepreneur, a characteristic wholly unappreciated by scholars. Predictably, his eldest son, Arthur Pearce, implemented a similar subsidiary, Ideal Restaurants, at Lockharts. After the war, two other companies, Ye Mecca and Slaters, embraced the same strategy of going upmarket with their own subsidiaries, respectively Picard's Cafés and Beta Tea Rooms (Table 10.1).

[12] Rev. James J. Ellis, *Pluck, Patience and Power: The Life Story of John Pearce of "Pearce and Plenty"* (London: H.R. Allenson, [1910]), p. 163.

[13] Ultimately, just one such restaurant, the Railway (Approach, London Bridge), opened (*Temperance Caterer*, 15 Jan. and 15 March 1914).

Table 10.1 Establishment of subsidiary catering cafés and restaurants

Company	*Outlet*	*Began*
BTTC	BTT	1892
J. Lyons	Lyons Tea Rooms	1894
JP Restaurants	"JPs"	1905
J. Lyons	Corner Houses	1909
Lockharts	Ideal Restaurants	1909
JP Restaurants	Pioneer Cafés	1910
JP Restaurants	Westminster Tea Cafés	1914
Ye Mecca	Picard's Cafés	1919
Slaters	Beta Tea Rooms	1925

In this, as in so many other senses, Lyons occupied a category alone. Given its considerable financial clout, contacts and prior experience, Lyons established multiples with its famous tearooms. While continuing this strategy, it spent prodigious sums on dining establishments, promoted as "Corner Houses." Between 1909 and 1928, Lyons built three such restaurants in London: Coventry House (1909), the Strand (1915) and New Oxford Street (1928). One reason why Lyons never emulated its rivals in establishing subsidiary catering cafés and restaurants derived from these "super restaurants," which its official historian describes as a "multi-storeyed structure of carefully segregated catering rooms—each with its own menu and price range." Combining food, drink (including alcohol) and music at one site, the Corner House projected a truly revolutionary concept. Essentially, Lyons created a miniature city or what today would be called a shopping mall within the confines of an extended roof encompassing diverse attractions—food shops, hairdressing salons, shoe-shine parlours, a theatre-ticket booking office and a telephone bureau. With this broad array of options, customers had little reason to leave the premises. Corner houses carried forward the concept of targeting specific social classes spanning the entire class spectrum from the working to the upper classes. This was an immense breakthrough in conceptualisation, class appeal and retailing.[14]

To what factors then did Pearce owe his remarkable business career and social mobility? First-hand knowledge of his clientele's lives afforded him enormous insight into late Victorian social mobility, retailing and beverage taste. Much impetus for his pioneering mass catering derived from this

[14] Peter Bird, *The First Food Empire: A History of J. Lyons & Co.* (Chichester: Phillimore & Co., 2000), pp. 98–101.

symbiotic relationship with working-class people, awareness of their struggles and innate sense of their needs. Initially, his own suffering daily as a penniless orphan confronting hunger and unremitting struggle to survive gave him the indispensable experience as well as remarkable acuity to provide others with what he had been unable easily to find for himself—inexpensive, nourishing food prepared to his high standards and rapidly dispensed to literally thousands (and later tens of thousands) of customers daily.[15]

No one, save perhaps the Rev. Carter, assumed a role in his life greater than his mother, who inculcated her uncompromising moral values that left an indelible mark on his character. As he oft-recalled: "I must go through life straight." Evangelical religion, astute marketing skills, selflessness, advertising, business acumen, innovation, showmanship and capacity for remaking himself—all these also formed components of his multifaceted character. Tenacity tempered by altruism, ambition combined with humility, shrewd assessment of catering market changes, enduring class consciousness and empathy with the working class help explain his remarkable social mobility. He rigorously followed his own homely motto: "Get things right, and keep on keeping them right." With sales of coffee and other beverages from an itinerant stall, innumerable penny capitalists had sought profit, the more ambitious even social mobility. Few of them, however, unflinchingly and unfailingly confronted the arduous demands vital to ensuring loyalty of his customers. Making painstaking efforts to procure fresh bread and brew fresh coffee meant rising at 2 a.m., so that he could be at his pitch two hours later, comprised a daily feat unequalled by any rivals. To these sacrifices, even endured in inclement weather, Pearce would later in part attribute his success.[16]

Difficult to assess but still vital as a factor in his social mobility was Pearce's symbiotic relationship with Cockneys. Despite his rise from the residuum, into the working and then the middle class, Pearce never forgot his plebeian origins. Mindful of his early career as an unassuming coffee bar keeper, he later placed, in easy sight, a photograph of the "Gutter Hotel" in his office at Aldersgate and then Farringdon Street (Fig. 10.1). In glancing

[15] Harold Bolce, "Foreseeing What the People Want: How Initiative, Imagination and a Sense of Value Created an Industry from an Idea," *System* 26 (1914): 156.

[16] "A Fortune Made from a Coffee Stall: The Romance of 'Pearce and Plenty,'" *Fortunes Made in Business: Life Struggles of Successful People* (1901), p. 42; Bolce, "Foreseeing What the People Want," p. 158.

Fig. 10.1 Christmas card commemorating Pearce's beginnings at the Gutter Hotel. This photograph was misdated, as his hotel would not presumably have been doing quite so well in 1866, when he started the business (Heritage Image Partnership Ltd/Alamy Stock Photo)

at it regularly, it served as a continual reminder of "the pit from whence I was digged [sic]."[17] Lacking formal education, much less attendance at an elite public school, he spoke with the untutored language and accent of his youth, not entirely grammatical as the quotation above reveals, an easy cultural identifier for customers seeking to place and then embrace him as one of their own. No other managing or general director of a big City of London catering firm could assert such credentials, or perhaps cared to do so. In this, as in so many other ways, Pearce stood out as an anomaly, a fact which his customers readily saw, appreciated and reciprocated by loyally dining at his depots or restaurants for years, if not decades.

Pearce's pronounced social conscience, product of his deprived upbringing, empathy with the downtrodden and influence of evangelicals such as Carter and Moody, likewise motivated him into becoming a public

[17] "Caterers for the Common People," *Review of Reviews* 14 (1896): 524; *Temperance Caterer*, 30 July 1887.

figure whose reputation became deeply embedded in London's poverty-stricken districts through his altruism. Unintentionally, Pearce regularly facilitated this personal rapport with customers in visiting one of his own houses daily while customers ate lunch or dinner, when many addressed him affectionately as "Sir John" or "Old John." His widespread participation in London's philanthropic world magnified his public image among his working-class customers, underlining that he had not forgotten his East End origins. Few who knew Pearce well would have been surprised to learn of his having donated about £250,000 to diverse philanthropic enterprises over the course of his long life.[18] As one friend observed, Pearce, ever diffident, modest and self-effacing, liked keeping his good deeds quiet. Viewed in a wider context, Pearce gave away about five times his final estate, an astonishing figure itself and still more so, given his plebeian origins.[19] His truly was the rags-to-riches story so beloved of so many Victorians.

Pearce also owed his success to business colleagues, who sometimes shared his temperance sentiments or kindred spirits wanting for philanthropic or class reasons to assist the impoverished. He was thus an extraordinary individual whose complex personality originated in diverse influences.

Of all the circumstances contributing to Pearce's achievement in surmounting poverty, a single-parent upbringing, and meagre personal funds, mere luck (or possibly intuitive timing), often ignored as a factor, favoured him.

Coffee public houses in the 1860s–1870s, combining philanthropy with commitment to 5% profits or more for investors, spearheaded a new approach to reforming working-class eating habits. Parliamentary legislation introducing the concept of limited liability companies enabled the commercialising of catering. Late in the 1870s, some 150 coffee and cocoa companies became incorporated, flourishing in Liverpool and Manchester and also later in London. From the North would come Ronald McDougall and Robert Lockhart, two men who had participated in the first stage of mixing philanthropy with profit; both would establish commercial catering depots in London. McDougall's career underlined

[18] Williams, *Pearce*, p. 226; Frederick Willis, *A Book of London Yesterdays* (London: Phoenix House, 1960), p. 176. Pearce's son obtained this figure from his father's executors.

[19] Had Pearce sold his BTT stock before its value plummeted after 1905, he would have augmented his gross estate by £25,000 (Williams, *Pearce*, p. 154).

the critical importance of entering catering as a recruited, tested proprietor of the Liverpool British Workman's Public House Co. These traits under normal circumstances should have produced success, but the unanticipated arrival of sweeping changes—advent of the mass market—upended him.

McDougall's reputation as London's pioneering mass caterer in late Victorian England rested on quite slim evidence, an interview published in London's *Star* in 1912 some three decades after he had been a London caterer with the People's Café Co. On becoming its manager in 1876, he claimed that it became "a remarkable success." McDougall pointed to profit sharing, uniformed waitresses, payment at the desk system, removal of standard partitions between seats, gender segregated rooms, prohibition of tips, and sale of Scotch scones (genuinely made in Scotland) as persuasive proof of his revolutionary impact.[20] Though unaware of this interview, historian Kathleen Heasman supported McDougall decades later, arguing that the People's Café Co. "made it general for the teashops of the 1890s to accommodate both men and women and so began the modern custom of catering for both sexes."[21] Unfortunately, we have only McDougall's own account as the basis for establishing his claims to having introduced radically new developments in London's catering.

In retrospect, McDougall assumed a pivotal role in the advent of mass catering in London. Although coffee public houses had encountered recession from the late 1870s, the slump was worst and deepest in London than elsewhere. By 1883, the *Coffee Public-House News* depicted the pessimism in which some coffee-house companies fired employees as a preliminary to shutting premises, while others seemed willing to accept any price as acceptable for selling out.[22]

To understand McDougall, one must see that nothing in his past prepared him for London's suddenly deteriorating conditions. Over-confident about and over-committed to the expansion of the People's Café Co., he encountered declining profits, and arrival of the mass market upended McDougall's quest to launch himself as a formidable force in feeding

[20] [Interview with Ronald McDougall], "Originator of London Tea Shops," published in the *Star* and reproduced in the *Temperance Caterer*, 15 Nov. 1912.

[21] Kathleen Heasman, *Evangelicals in Action: An Appraisal of their Social Work in the Victorian Era* (London: Geoffrey Bles, 1962), p. 143.

[22] *Coffee Public-House News*, 1 July 1882, 1 Feb. 1883, 1 May 1884, and 22 Feb. 1887; E.T. Bellhouse, "The Coffee-House Movement," *Transactions of the Manchester Statistical Society* (1880): 119.

London diners dispersed well beyond the City. The swiftness of his demise appeared late in 1882 when he declared bankruptcy. Clearly, advent of the mass market ranked as one leading factor in his demise, but so did his boom/bust career as a businessman. Capitalisation, timing, depot concentration, class and gender, all were factors in his collapse as an entrepreneur. But so was his personality in which he cleverly presented himself as a remarkable entrepreneur whose skills would literally transport Liverpool's thriving teashops to the capital. Key to understanding McDougall was his chameleon ability to assume different personas: the successful Liverpudlian who established teashops, on the one hand, and the genius who revolutionised catering for London diners, on the other. What ultimately overwhelmed him, denying McDougall any chance of being seen as the pioneer of mass catering in London, were the ill-timed arrival of the mass market, together with his extraordinary ability to market himself as a catering genius.

For Pearce, luck—call it intuition perhaps—favoured him. His entry into the City of London's catering market came in the mid-1870s, when he switched from a peripatetic stall to a fixed shopkeeper on Type Street. Two years later on Aldersgate Street, he opened bigger premises, coinciding with the advent of the retailing revolution. Pearce & Plenty, the chain that would be most closely associated with Pearce, established its first depot in the City in 1883, where he "revolutionized the catering trade in London."[23] From the very beginning, Pearce unlike McDougall, had another source of revenue, the profitable temperance hotels located above many of his depots which to a large extent insulated him against economic downturns. Rejecting McDougall's dispersed depot strategy, Pearce concentrated on the City, facilitating both distribution of food and supervision of restaurants. Sensitive to erratic market conditions, Pearce delayed expanding the number of depots until after 1886, by which point London's catering trade had recovered. Absence of ready capital likewise instilled a cautious attitude.

In yet another sense timing proved decisive. Soon after Pearce opened his Farringdon Street shop, Mr Morrison (Secretary of the Aerated Bread Co.), informed Pearce that his company would soon enter the refreshment business: "Well, don't come anywhere near me!" Pearce warned, exhibiting a strong territorial business mentality.[24]

[23] Williams, *Pearce*, p. 90; "Pearce's Coffee Bar, Farringdon Street, London," *Coffee Public-House News*, 1 Feb. 1883.

[24] [Interview with John Pearce], "ABC Jubilee," published in the *Star* and reproduced in the *Temperance Chronicle*, 15 Nov. 1912.

Rapidly expanding multiple branches, one of the mass market's key features, chiefly distinguished his early years. By the end of the 1880s, Pearce & Plenty had opened fifteen branches selling some 30,000 meals daily. As useful adjuncts, twelve of the fifteen branches had temperance hotels over the depots on the first and second floors. A decade later combined total daily meal sales at Pearce & Plenty and the BTT, the new chain, had more than doubled, and the newly-floated company held shareholdings of £1½ million, the fourth largest catering company in the City.

For a man given little to introspection, Pearce fully grasped some of the reasons for his survival. Over decades in a volatile market, his "careful buying and careful management" had produced profits, stability and expansion, ensuring his company's success. It had nothing to do with what the self-confident J.D. Hurst had boasted to shareholders in 1906 after Pearce had resigned: "It was child's play to earn [dividends of] 12%."[25]

The Edwardian catering crisis underlined how Pearce's managerial skills had sustained the BTT's years of financial success. All catering companies with middle- and working-class customers in the City confronted serious problems—declining profits, dividends and gross sales, together with unremunerative shops—from 1903 to 1906 (and some beyond as well). In this respect, the BTT conformed to the overall trend. Once he left it and started anew with JP Restaurants in 1905, however, the new company performed outstandingly well. His rivals struggled for years thereafter, in some cases up to or into World War I. Of these firms, just Lockharts recovered first in 1910, ironically under the guidance of Arthur Pearce, John's eldest son, as general manager. In less propitious circumstances, Horace Pearce had a rancorous battle to introduce new ideas into the ABC catering culture. For him, inspired leadership meant acumen, vision, perseverance and, most significantly, lengthy first-hand experience. In depriving the BTT of a man of John Pearce's calibre and permitting John Hurst to act as de facto managing director, the Board of Directors representing huge shareholders committed the same error as did Chairman Hurst, assuming that running the company was straightforward and earning 12% dividends a matter of mere "child's play." This brazenness, typifying the cultured but amateur "gentleman" asserting control over the talented but plebeian "player," led to the company's steady decline, culminating in humiliating disgrace and ignominious bankruptcy.[26]

[25] *Financial Times*, 12 May 1906; *Temperance Caterer*, 15 Aug. 1906.

[26] D.C. Coleman, "Gentlemen and Players," *Economic History Review* 26 (1973): 108–09; John F. Wilson, *British Business History, 1720–1994* (Manchester: Manchester University Press, 1995), p. 116.

Table 10.2 Social hierarchy of outlets of JP Restaurants

Name	*Clientele*	*Began*
Westminster Tea Cafés	Merchants; high-class trade	1914
JP Restaurants	Clerks, Typists and Tradesmen	1905
Pioneer Cafés[a]	Car men & mechanics	1910
John Pearce Dining Rooms[b]	Workers	1905

Sources: Williams, *Pearce*, pp. 159–60; *Financial Times*, 6 June 1910; *Temperance Caterer*, 15 Jan. and 15 March 1914, and 15 Feb. and 15 Apr. 1917

[a]Formerly John Pearce First Class Restaurants, and renamed in 1914
[b]Formerly Pearce& Plenty

Nothing demonstrated Pearce's resiliency better than his capacity for remaking himself as a principal caterer at the age of 58. While other leading catering companies in the City endured crises of management, lost substantial share value and declared lower or, worse, no dividends whatsoever in the decade from 1905, Pearce had by far the most productive, creative and in many ways most satisfying period in his entire career, an apt testament to his superb skills as a masterful caterer.

Within a decade of founding JP Restaurants, Pearce had fashioned a company with a reconceptualised business philosophy, and wider clientele transcending both class as well as gender boundaries, together with a new hierarchy of four tiers catering to distinct social classes (Table 10.2). Symbolically, he detached himself from his former City working-class base and all for which it stood, and established his company in Holborn, centre of his catering firm, more geographically dispersed and more representative of a cross-section of London's class and gender composition. Core of his clientele and mainspring of his prosperity for so many years, working-class patrons shrank in importance, as he grafted other groups of patrons onto the base. Whether he was responding to the new freedom of being chairman of his own company or fundamental changes in the catering market remains uncertain. Without company records, nothing definite can be stated. Precisely where he derived insight into evolving a vibrant business culture is unclear, for as an unintrospective individual he could reveal nothing about the process in interviews, personal testimony to a royal commission or even conversations with future biographers. We must judge then by what he did, not by what he said. In this regard Pearce's relationship with his sons is extremely suggestive.

As the pre-eminent caterer of the working class, Pearce acquired and sustained his business prowess in part through three sons, a theme wholly ignored by contemporaries (including his biographers) and scholars alike. All three had gained experience under John's watchful tutelage. Starting as a mere employee, Arthur, the eldest, had spent a decade acquiring skills before his father promoted him to general manager of the BTT in 1894, a post he held for three years. Horace, his younger brother, worked as a confidential clerk, a superintendent with the BTT and then assistant general manager before replacing father as managing director in 1905. Having trained two sons in his catering business, John Pearce must have derived considerable parental satisfaction on their assuming managerial roles with his competitors, Arthur with Lockharts and Horace with the ABC. How such capable men came to "direct the huge catering concerns of London" in Edwardian England was worth pondering, thought the *Morning Leader*. Of these three men, the *Leader* wrote in 1910, "We should imagine that they will feed the majority of those who take their meals in London restaurants." Arthur and Horace, however, were still more vital in another broader sense: they personally oversaw two enormous catering companies through the most serious, potentially even fatal, economic crisis of the preceding thirty years.[27]

Horace Pearce's tumultuous tenure as general manager of the ABC in 1910 provides much understanding into the character of John, who had struggled with John Hurst at the BTT in 1904–1908. Like his father, Horace sought a chairman of "more progressive ideas" who knew the overriding importance, not of economising on décor but of spending money on keeping depots attractively decorated and filled with customers. To Horace it was imperative that the chairman "spend money to improve shops" for the company to generate business. Epitomising the reactionary old guard, ABC chairman George Edwards, like John Hurst at the BTT, baulked, unwilling to surrender authority to someone whom he regarded as subordinate, and whose ideas he resented as strongly as he reviled rebellious shareholders who clearly knew not their place. Here again was the classic but uneven power struggle between the gentleman and player, between Edwards (stand in for Hurst), on the one hand, and Horace Pearce (stand in for his father), on the other; education, wealth and class of the gentleman pitted against the plebeian player whose

[27] *Daily Telegraph*, 13 May 1905; *Temperance Caterer*, 15 Feb. 1907 and 15 Apr. 1913; *Morning Leader*, 3 Sept. 1910.

lengthy training, experience and perception had produced success but not equal standing between them. In both cases, the outsider lost against powerful wealthy shareholders but with dire consequences: one company ultimately driven into bankruptcy while the other (avoiding such an ignominious fate owing to its diversified retailing and manufacturing businesses) forced to yield significant concessions in the company's management.[28] Throughout the struggle on the fate of these two companies, Horace, convinced of his father's sagacity, embraced the same goal: replacement of the chairman with a managing director more astutely attuned to a changing catering market.

Trained under John's supervision, experienced in widely ranging jobs and promoted to positions of leadership with London's major catering companies, his three sons—Arthur, Horace and Guy—assumed key positions with JP Restaurants in the immediate years before World War I.

Here was the nucleus of talent, knowledge and Pearce acumen that, with father John at the helm, guided JP Restaurants into becoming the most dynamic catering company from the eve of World War I until well into the 1920s. This influx of Pearce's sons displayed itself quickly in the new company's dynamic approach to wooing new customers. Women now became integral to the clientele, clerks, typists and tradesmen forming the backbone of the JPs, the sector of the company which underwent its most explosive growth in Edwardian England. With just one restaurant in 1905, the firm reached thirty-two by the war. This chain's spanning of classes and catering to dissimilar clienteles throughout the day—these became two critical factors in its remarkable development. That these outlets were designated restaurants, not depots, likewise underlined their departure from the pre-1905 model.

To learn from the past and respond with creative changes for the future became John Pearce's defining trait as London's premier caterer. Towards the end of his association with the BTT, Pearce grasped that its woes were rooted in three issues—goodwill, reserves and depreciation—that would bedevil the firm's financial strength and eventual survival. Of the three, goodwill, assessed in 1897 on the formation of a new, larger company, was, by whatever objective standard, derided as excessive. No other factor loomed larger in the firm's ultimate demise. Too much emphasis was placed on the firm's goodwill, representing fully half of the total purchase price; too little on managerial skills. Critics would be more blunt: the shares were overvalued. Given these circumstances, the Board had two

[28] ABC meeting, *Financial Times*, 30 Oct. 1891.

other interrelated decisions: determining the amounts either placed in the reserve fund or written off as depreciation. Had other paths been followed, catastrophe might have been averted. Adopting one viable strategy, the company might have declared lower dividends as a way of writing off goodwill and lease expirations, on one hand, or providing sums for paying anticipated premiums, thereby establishing an adequate reserve fund, on the other. Alternatively, the company might have created a sizable reserve fund as a tactic for writing down goodwill and lease expirations, while preparing for premiums. Solicitor Martin Gilbert expressed the persisting received wisdom in business in a 1950 novel:

> Every well-run business which operates on leasehold premises puts aside a fund against the day when the lease expires—for repairs and dilapidations, to say nothing of the premium that they may have to pay to get the lease renewed.[29]

Having gained insight as a result of the BTT's debacle, Pearce as chairman of JP Restaurants evolved his own distinctive managerial philosophy answerable to no one else. Breaking with received wisdom in the industry, Pearce placed small amounts in the reserve fund, but protecting the company, claimed nothing whatsoever as goodwill. The money thus saved was invested in the business as a way of generating higher dividends. Accordingly, this strategy reimbursed investors at a faster rate, so that the total paid out in dividends over the next decade covered 95% of the original cost of the shares made by investors. Inadequate funds had been earmarked for depreciation in the BTT, preventing money from being allocated for updating premises and extinguishing leases, whereas in JP Restaurants Pearce systematically wrote off 5% of profits annually, enabling the company to terminate leases on a timely basis and keep premises in tiptop condition. Learning from BTT's past mistakes, he addressed old problems in entirely new ways, displaying his ongoing mastery of London's restaurants in an ever-changing commercial environment.

For a man allegedly past his prime, Pearce defying pessimistic predictions again, not just survived his banishment but recovered from it with astonishing speed. No other catering firm outperformed JP Restaurants in its yield earned on investment in the 1920s, an extraordinary achievement indeed for "a very good man, but played out," a phrase uttered in 1905.

[29] Michael Gilbert, *Smallbone Deceased* (London: Hodder and Stoughton, 1950), p. 140.

To the very end, Pearce fought for influence but also his reputation. Having sold virtually all of the company stock to the ABC chain, he opposed bitterly efforts to remove his sons and himself from JP's Board of Directors in 1930.[30] Vowing to fight this development, he returned home, only to die later that day of a heart attack, eighty-four years old.

During his long life, he had an enormous impact on those with limited funds who wanted nutritious, tasty fast food. Writing in 1905, Canon Barker believed that Pearce "might almost be called the Father of the Great Cheap Catering Trade." In a review of Ellis' biography of Pearce some years later, the Dean of Carlisle endorsed this verdict.[31] "One of the earliest pioneers of the temperance catering movement," Pearce had "done more than can be readily recognised to render London a sober city," commended the *Financial Times.* Of all the pre-war testimonials, the best by far came from his old friend, Joseph Bentley, editor of the *Temperance Caterer*, who thought that both Pearce & Plenty and the BTT "were practically the pioneers in London of the movement for feeding the mass of people on moderate terms, and in this way helped forward Temperance Reform."[32]

Of these assessments, what did Pearce himself think? He predictably recorded nothing in print, except on one special occasion, his jubilee celebrating fifty years' catering when he became uncharacteristically reflective and forthcoming about his life. Noting that his company restaurants then dispensed some 40,000 meals daily, Pearce affirmed modestly: "I think I may claim to have started the [mass catering] movement."[33] Nothing would have pleased him more than the accolade which Lord Greenwood, chairman of the ABC, his old rival, offered on Pearce's death. Much contested by McDougall in 1912, Pearce's contribution to London catering was now fully upheld by Greenwood: Pearce, he stated simply, had been "the founder of the tea shops of London."[34]

[30] No surviving records reveal why Pearce sold his flourishing business rather than turn it over to his capable sons. Marguerite Williams finished her biography in 1928, two years before Pearce died.

[31] Williams, *Pearce*, p. 90; *Daily Mail*, BTTC prospectus, 16 June 1897; Ellis, *Pluck*, p. 58; Dean of Carlisle's review, *British Journal of Inebriety* 8 (1911): 42.

[32] *Financial Times*, 13 Feb. 1913; *Temperance Caterer*, 15 Aug. 1908.

[33] "Fifty Years of Catering," *London Daily News*, 18 Oct. 1911.

[34] John Pearce's obituary, *Lancashire Evening Post*, 26 March 1930.

Bibliography

Primary Sources

Archives

Bishopsgate Institute Library (London)
Restaurant Files
London Metropolitan Archives
Aerated Bread Co. Minute Book
J. Lyons & C., Annual Report and in-house magazine
Museum of English Rural Life
Express Dairy Company, Annual Reports
History of the Express Dairy Co.
Pure Food: The Record of a Great Public Service (n.p., [1929])
University of Exeter
Aerated Bread Co., Minutes of Board Meetings, MS 326, 1919–31

Newspapers

Birmingham Daily Gazette
Caterer & Hotel-Keepers' Gazette
Church of England Temperance Chronicle
Coffee Public-House News
Coffee Tavern Gazette
Daily Mail
Daily Telegraph
Derby Daily Telegraph

D. W. Gutzke, *John Pearce and the Rise of the Mass Food Market in London, 1870–1930*, https://doi.org/10.1007/978-3-030-27095-7

Economist
Edinburgh Evening News
Figaro
Financial Times
Glasgow Herald
Globe
Hampshire Telegraph
Hartlepool Northern Daily Mail
Hearth & Home
Hotel Review
Illustrated London News
John Bull
Lancashire Evening Post
Leicester Chronicle
Liverpool Mercury
London Daily News
London Evening Standard
Morning Leader
Morning Post
Norwood News
Pall Mall Gazette
Pearson's Weekly
Portsmouth Evening News
Refreshment News
Reynolds's Newspaper
Salisbury Times
Sheffield Daily Telegraph
Shields Daily News
South London Chronicle
Star
Straits Times
Sunderland Daily Echo
Temperance Caterer
Temperance Chronicle
Times
Times of India
Weekly Dispatch
Western Morning News
Western Times
York Herald

Parliamentary Papers and Official Publications

Evidence of the Royal Commission on Licensing (England and Wales), 1929–32.
Evidence of the Royal Commission on Liquor Licensing Laws, 1898, 36 (Cmnd. 8694).
Report by the Comptroller of the Companies Department, Board of Trade, for the Year Ending, 31 Dec. 1909.

Interviews/Personal Portraits

Bolce, Harold. "Foreseeing What the People Want: How Initiative, Imagination and a Sense of Value Created an Industry from an Idea." *System* 26 (1914): 154–60.
"Caterers for the Common People." *Review of Reviews* 14 (1896): 523–24.
Fitz-Gerald, S.J. Adair. "Chats with Caterers: Mr. John Pearce." *Caterer & Hotel Keepers' Gazette*, 16 Jan. 1905.
Fitz-Gerald, S.J. Adair. "Chats with Caterers: Joseph Lyons." *Caterer & Hotel Keepers' Gazette*, 15 June 1904.
"A Fortune Made from a Coffee Stall: The Romance of Pearce and Plenty." *Fortunes Made in Business: Life Struggles of Successful People* (1901), pp. 42–3.
[Interview with Horace Pearce]. *Financial Times*, 14 Oct. 1911.
[Interview with Horace Pearce]. *Morning Leader*, 3 Sept. 1910.
[Interview with John Pearce]. "Fifty Years of Catering," *London Daily News*, 18 Oct. 1911.
[Interview with John Pearce]. "The JP Restaurants: The Temperance Catering Movement and One of its Founders." *Financial Times*, 13 Feb. 1913.
[Interview with John Pearce]. *Financial Times*, 10 Aug. 1906.
[Interview with John Pearce]. *Daily Mail*, 23 Jan. 1926.
[Interview with John Pearce]. *Sun*, 15 Aug. 1898.
[Interview with John Pearce]. "ABC Jubilee." *Temperance Chronicle*, 15 Nov. 1912.
[Interview with Ronald McDougall]. "Originator of London Tea Shops." *Star*, 15 Nov. 1912.
"Interview with W. Horace Pearce." *Temperance Caterer*, 14 Oct. and 15 Nov. 1911.
"Mr. John Pearce: The Man and His Work." *British Journal of Catering* 3 (15 July 1889): 9.
"Our Portrait Gallery: Mr. and Mrs. John Pearce." *Temperance Caterer*, 15 June 1912.
Pearce, John. "'I Started Gutter Hotels': Founder of the Famous Poor Man's Restaurants." *Pearson's Weekly*, 5 Sept. 1914.
"A People's Caterer." *Caterer*, 15 Jan. 1897.

"Representative Temperance Caterers: John Pearce." *Temperance Caterer*, 30 July 1887 and 15 June 1897.

"Representative Temperance Caterers: Mr. W.H. Peskett." *Temperance Caterer*, 3 Sept. 1887.

"Ronald McDougall." *Biograph and Review* 5 (1881): 118–19.

Wintle, W.J. "Round the London Restaurants." *Windsor Magazine* 4 (1896): 447–48.

BOOKS AND ARTICLES

Babcock, B.F. "The Liverpool Cocoa Rooms." *Methodist Temperance Magazine* 9 (1876): 221–23.

Bellhouse, E.T. "The Coffee-House Movement." *Transactions of the Manchester Statistical Society* (1880): 115–27.

Bentley, Joseph. "Temperance Restaurants and Coffee Houses in Britain." In John Newton Stearns, ed., *Temperance in All Nations: History of the Cause in All Countries of the Globe*. New York: National Temperance Society and Publication House, 1893, 2: 378–83.

Birch, H. "About Coffee Houses--How to Manage Them." *Coffee Public-House News*, 2 Jan. 1882.

Booth, Charles. *Life and Labour of the People of London*. London: Williams and Norgate, 1889, vol. 1: *Industry*, "Pubs and Cocoa Rooms."

Bosanquet, Helen D. *The Standard of Life and Other Studies*, 2nd ed. London: Macmillan & Co., 1899.

Bourne, Stephen. "The Social Influence of the Coffee-House Movement." *Coffee Public-House News*, 1 Sept. 1881.

British Tea Table Depots, 1908. London: BTTC, 1908.

"British Workman Public-Houses and Other Aids to Temperance, 1868–73." In P.T. Winskill, ed., *The Temperance Movement and Its Workers: A Record of Social, Moral Religious and Political*. London: Blackie & Son, 1891, 3: 213.

Calkins, Raymond. *Substitutes for the Saloon: An Investigation Made for the Committee of Fifty Under the Direction of Francis G. Peabody, Elgin R.L. Gould and William M. Sloane*. Boston: Houghton Mifflin Company, 1901.

Callow, Edward. "City Taverns, Chop and Coffee Houses, & Co." *City Press*, 15 Jan. 1898.

Caulfield, Sophia F.A. "Women's Clubs in London." *Independent Living* 11 (1890): 146–47.

Clarke, Benjamin. "Temptations to Temperance." In Rev. Benjamin Waugh, ed., *Sunday Magazine* (1887), pp. 42–3.

Clarke, James Freeman. *Coffee Houses and Coffee Palaces*. Boston: George H. Ellis, 1882.

"The Coffee-Shop." *Punch* 82 (1882): 84.

"Coffee-Houses in Great Britain." In Charles E. Bolton, *A Model Village of Homes, and Other Papers*. Boston: L.C. Page & Co., 1901, pp. 63–6.

"The Coffee Public-House Movement." *Chambers's Journal* 56 (1879): 144.
"The Coffee-Shop." *Punch* 82 (1882): 84.
Coffee Tavern Guide. n.p., 1884.
Coffee Tavern & Temperance Hotel Guide. n.p., 1885.
Cotton, Elizabeth R. [Lady Hope]. *Lines on a Dark Ground*. n.p., 1879.
Cotton, Elizabeth R. [Lady Hope]. *More about Our Coffee-Room*. London: J. Nisbet & Co., 1878a.
Cotton, Elizabeth R. [Lady Hope]. *Our Coffee-Room*. London: James Nisbet & Co., 1878b.
Dendy, H. "The Position of Women in Industry." *National Review* 1616 (1894): 807–14.
Ellis, Rev. James J. *Pluck, Patience and Power: The Life Story of John Pearce of "Pearce and Plenty."* London: H.R. Allenson, [1910].
"Female Poaching on Male Preserves." *Westminster Review* 129 (1888): 293.
Garrett, Rev. Charles. "The History of the British Workman Public-House Company in Liverpool." *The National Temperance Conference, Chester, 1895*. n.p., n.d.
"Gold in the Tea-Cup." *Daily Mail*, 9 Nov. 1904.
Gore, Frederick. "The Causes of Success and Failure in the Coffee House Movement." *Coffee Public-House News*, 16 July 1885.
Hall, E. Hepple. *Coffee Taverns, Cocoa Houses and Coffee Places: Their Rise, Progress, and Prospects*. London: S.W. Partridge, [1878].
[Hilliard, S.H.]. "Coffee-Houses." *Cyclopaedia of Temperance and Prohibition*. n.p., 1891, pp. 83–4.
Hogben, Thomas. "Causes of Failure in London." *Coffee and Public-House News*, 1 Aug. 1882, 1 Feb. 1883 and 1 May 1884.
Hogben, Thomas, "The Coffee Public-House Movement." In Robert Rae, ed., *The National Temperance League's Annual for 1881*. London: National Temperance Publications Depot, 1881, pp. 123–24.
Hobgen, Thomas. "The Coffee Public-House Movement." In *A Hand-Book of Temperance History*. London: National Temperance Publications Depot, 1882, pp. 119–23.
Jepson, J. "The Coffee Tavern Movement in London." *Supplement to the Temperance Caterer*, 10 Sept. 1887a.
Jepson, J. "The Coffee House Movement in London." *Coffee Public-House News*, 1 May 1884.
Jepson, J. "Coffee House Movement in London." In P.T. Winskill and Joseph Thomas, eds., *History of the Temperance Movement in Liverpool and District, from its Introduction in 1829 Down to the Year 1887*. Liverpool: Joseph Thomas, 1887b, 3: 175.
Langley, Andrew. *The Selected Soyer: The Writings of the Legendary Victorian Chef, Alexis Soyer*. Bath: Absolute Press, 1987.

Lockington, Eve and Win Trickey. "The Coffee House Movement." *Loughton & District Historical Society* 154 (Oct. 2002a).

London Correspondent. "Bar and Dining Room to Editor." *Western Morning News*, 24 Sept. 1883.

Machray, Robert. *The Night Side of London*. London: John Macqueen, 1902.

[Manley, J.J.] "The Temperance Refreshment House Movement." *British Almanac Companion* 53 (1880): 47.

Mayhew, Henry. *London Labour and the London Poor*. London: Griffin, Bohn & Co., 1861. vol. 1: *The London Street-Folk*. London: Griffin, Bohn & Co., 1861, pp. 160–207.

McChesney, Dora Greenwell. "The World of the ABC." *Daily Mail*, 15 Apr. 1903.

National Temperance Congress: Liverpool, June, 1884. Liverpool: National Temperance Publication Depot, 1884.

"No Intoxicants Sold." *Leisure Hour* 31 (1882): 116–17.

Orczy, Baroness [Emmuska]. "The Fenchurch Street Mystery." *Royal Magazine* 6 (May, 1901).

Page, H.A. "Coffee Palaces." *Good Words* 18 (1877): 680.

Paul, Mrs. C.S. "Lunch for Ladies in London." *Hearth & Home* No. 578 (12 June 1902): 274–75.

"Pearce's Coffee Bar, Farringdon Street, London." *Coffee Public-House News*, 1 Feb. 1883.

Peskett, W. "Work in Liverpool." *Coffee Public-House News*, 1 Aug. 1884.

A Pictorial and Descriptive Guide to London: Its Public Buildings, Leading Thoroughfares, and Practical Hints for the Management of Coffee Taverns. London: Coffee Tavern Company, [1878].

Principal Objects of Interest. London: Ward, Lock & Co., 1902.

Scott, Clement. *How They Dined us in 1860 and How They Dined us Now.* [London: Trocadero Restaurant, 1900].

Sims, George R. "Looking Back." *Daily Mail*, 5 Oct. 1921.

Smith, C.C. "The Coffee House Movement in Provincial Towns." *Coffee Public-House News*, 1 May 1884.

Smith, Mrs. Hind. "British Workman Public-Houses; or, Public-houses without the Drink." *Transactions of the National Association for the Promotion of Social Science*. London: Longmans, Green, Reader & Dyer, 1872.

Sullivan, Sir Edward. *Stray Shots: Political, Military, Economical and Social.* London: Longmans, Green & Co., 1884.

Williams, Marguerite. *John Pearce: The Man Who Played the Game*. London: Religious Tract Society, 1928.

Winskill, P.T. (ed.), *The Temperance Movement and its Workers: A Record of Social, Moral, Religious, Political Progress* (London: Blackie & Son, 1891).

Winskill, P.T. and Joseph Thomas. *History of the Temperance Movement in Liverpool and District, from its Introduction in 1829 Down to the Year 1887.* Liverpool: Joseph Thomas, 1887.

Secondary Sources

Assael, Brenda. *The London Restaurant, 1840–1914.* Oxford: Oxford University Press, 2018.

Bailey, Peter. *Leisure and Class in Victorian England: Rational Recreation and the Contest for Control, 1830–85.* 1978, reprint ed.: New York: Methuen & Co., 1987.

Ball, Michael and David Sunderland. *An Economic History of London, 1800–1914.* London: Routledge, 2001.

Benson, John. *The Penny Capitalists: A Study of Nineteenth-Century Working-Class Entrepreneurs.* New Brunswick, New Jersey: Rutgers University Press, 1983.

Benson, John. *The Rise of Consumer Society in Britain, 1880–1980.* London: Longman, 1994.

Benson, John and Laura Ugolini. *Cultures of Selling: Perspective on Consumption and Society since 1700.* Aldershot: Ashgate, 2006.

Bevan, Brad. *Leisure, Citizenship and Working-Class Men in Britain, 1850–1945.* Manchester: Manchester University Press, 2005.

Bird, Peter, *The First Food Empire: A History of J. Lyons & Co.* Chichester: Phillimore & Co., 2000.

Bowley, A.L. "Changes in Average Wages (Nominal and Real) in the United Kingdom between 1860 and 1891." *Journal of the Statistical Society* 58 (1895): 223–78.

Broomfield, Andrea. *Food and Cooking in Victorian England: A History.* Westport, CT: Praeger, 2007.

Brown, J.B. "The Pig or the Stye: Drink and Poverty in Late Victorian England." *International Review of Social History* 18 (1973): 380–95.

Burnett, John. ed. *Destiny Obscure: Autobiographies of Childhood, Education and Family from the 1820s to the 1920s.* Harmondsworth: Penguin, 1984.

Burnett, John. *England Eats Out: A Social History of Eating Out in England from 1830 to the Present.* London: Pearson Longman, 2004.

Burnett, John. *Liquid Pleasures: A Social History of Drinks in Modern Britain.* London: Routledge, 1999.

Burnett, John. *Plenty and Want: A Social History of Diet in England from 1815 to the Present Day.* 1966; rev. ed.: London: Methuen & Co., 1983.

Carnaffan, Gladys. "Commercial Education and the Female Office Worker." In Gregory Anderson, ed., *The White-Blouse Revolution: Female Office Workers since 1870.* Manchester: Manchester University Press, 1988, pp. 67–87.

Chinn, Carl. *They Worked all their Lives: Women of the Urban Poor in England, 1880–1939.* Manchester: Manchester University Press, 1988.

Clayton, Anthony. *London's Coffee Houses: A Stimulating Story.* London: Historical Publications, 2003.

Coleman, D.C. "Gentlemen and Players." *Economic History Review* 26 (1973): 92–116.

Davin, Anna. "City Girls: Young Women, New Employment, and the City, London, 1880–1910." In Mary Jo Maynes, Birgitte Sland, and Christina Benninghaus, eds., *Secret Gardens, Satanic Mills: Placing Girls in European History, 1750–1960.* Bloomington: Indiana University Press, 2005, pp. 209–23.

Davison, Andrew. "'Try the Alternative': The Built Heritage of the Temperance Movement." *Journal of the Brewery History Society* 123 (summer, 2006): 103–04.

Dingle, A.E. "Drink and the Working-Class Living Standards in Britain, 1870–1914." In Derek J. Oddy and Derek S. Miller, eds., *The Making of the Modern British Diet.* London: Croom Helm, 1976, pp. 117–34.

Dingle, A.E. "Drink and Working-Class Living Standards in Britain, 1870–1914." *Economic History Review* 25 (1972): 608–22.

"Dr. Barnardo Turned a Gin Palace into a Coffee House." *Look & Learn* 666 (9 Nov. 1974).

Dyos, H.J. "Workmen's Fares in South London, 1860–1914." *Journal of Transport History* 1 (1953): 3–19.

Elliott, Malcolm. "The Leicester Coffee-House and Cocoa-House Movement." *Transactions of the Leicestershire Archaeological and Historical Society* 47 (1971–72): 55–61.

Flynn, Michael, Caroline Ritchie and Andrew Roberts. *Public House and Beverage Management: Key Principles and Issues.* Oxford: Butterworth-Heinemann, 2000.

Fraser, W. Hamish. *The Coming of the Mass Market, 1850–1914.* London: Macmillan Press, 1981.

Fry, Terry. "The Pleasures of Tea and Coffee: An Account of Tea Gardens and Coffee Houses in and around Nottingham in the 18th and 19th Centuries." *Nottinghamshire Historian* 57 (autumn/winter, 1996): 7–10.

Gainer, Bernard. *The Alien Invasion: The Origins of the Aliens Act of 1905.* London: Heinemann Educational Books, 1972.

Geddes Poole, Andrea. *Philanthropy and the Construction of Victorian Women's Citizenship: Lady Frederick Cavendish and Miss Emma Cons.* Toronto: University of Toronto, 2014.

Gibson, Paul. *A Toast to the Town: A History of Beverley's Public Houses.* Kingston upon Hull: n.p., 2001.

Gilbert, Michael. *Smallbone Deceased.* London: Hodder and Stoughton, 1950.

Girouard, Mark. "Pubs with No Beer: The Victorian Coffee Public House." *Country Life* 158 (1975): 926, 928.

Golby, J.M. and A.W. Purdue. *The Civilisation of the Crowd: Popular Culture in England, 1750–1900.* New York: Schocken Books, 1985.

Gutzke, David. "Gender, Class and Public Drinking in Britain During the First World War." *Histoire sociale/Social History* 27 (1994a): 367–91.

Gutzke, David W. "Gentrifying the British Public House, 1896–1914." *International Labor and Working-Class History* 45 (1994b): 29–43.

Gutzke, David W. *Pubs and Progressives: Reinventing the Public House in England, 1896–1960*. DeKalb: Northern Illinois University Press, 2006.

Gutzke, David W. "Rhetoric and Reality: The Political Influence of British Brewers, 1832–1914." *Parliamentary History* 9 (1990): 78–115.

Gutzke, David W. "Sydney Nevile: Squire in the Slums or Progressive Brewer?" *Business History* 53 (2011): 960–69.

Gutzke, David W. *Women Drinking Out in Britain since the Early 20th Century*. Manchester: Manchester University Press, 2014.

Harrison, Brian. *Drink and the Victorians: The Temperance Question in England, 1815–72*. 1971, 2nd ed. Keele University: Keele University Press, 1994.

Haydon, Peter. *The English Pub: A History*. London: Robert Hale, 1994.

Heasman, Kathleen. *Evangelicals in Action: An Appraisal of their Social Work in the Victorian Era*. London: Geoffrey Bles, 1962.

Heasman, Kathleen Joan. "The Influence of the Evangelicals upon the Origin and Development of Voluntary Charitable Institutions in the Second Half of the Nineteenth Century." Ph.D. thesis, Univ. of London, 1959.

Holcombe, Lee. *Victorian Ladies at Work: Middle-Class Working Women in England and Wales, 1850–1914*. Newton Abbot: David & Charles, 1973.

Holt, Richard. *Sport and the British: A Modern History*. Oxford: Oxford University Press, 1989.

Jakle, John A. and Keith A. Sculle. *The Gas Station in America*. Baltimore: Johns Hopkins University Press, 1994.

Lambert, W.R. *Drink and Sobriety in Victorian Wales, c. 1820–c. 1895*. Cardiff: University of Wales Press, 1983.

Langdon, Philip. *Orange Roofs, Golden Arches: The Architecture of American Chain Restaurants*. New York: Alfred A. Knopf, 1986.

Leon, Robert. "Rise and Fall of the Aerated Bread Company." *Camden History Review* 25 (2001): 47–50.

Lockington, Eve and Win Trickey. "The Coffee House Movement." *Loughton & District Historical Society* 154 (Oct. 2002b): 3.

Longmate, Norman. *The Waterdrinkers: A History of Temperance*. London: Hamish Hamilton, 1968.

McCracken, Scott. "Embodying the New Woman: Dorothy Richardson, Work and the London Café." In Avril Horner and Angela Keane, eds., *Body Matters: Feminism, Textuality Corporeality*. Manchester: Manchester University Press, 2000.

McIntosh, James R. "Alcoholism." In Jack S. Blocker, Jr., David M. Fahey, and Ian R. Tyrrell, eds., *Alcohol and Temperance in Modern History: An International Encyclopedia*, 2 vols. Santa Barbara: ABC-Clio, 2003, 1: 32.

Macqueen-Pope, Walter. *Goodbye Piccadilly*. London: Michael Joseph, 1960.

Mathias, Peter. "The British Tea Trade in the Nineteenth Century" In Derek J. Oddy and Derek S. Miller, eds., *The Making* of the *Modern British Diet*. London: Croom Helm, 1976, pp. 91–100.

Morgan, Bryan. *Express Journey, 1864–1964: A Centenary History of the Express Dairy Company Limited*. London: Newman Neame, 1964a.

Morgan, Bryan. "A Short History of Spiers and Pond." In *Express Journal, 1864–1964: A Centenary History of the Express Dairy Company Limited*. London: Newman Neame, 1964b, pp. 134–35.

Mountjoy, Peter Roger. "Thomas Bywater Smithies, Editor of the *British Workman*." *Victorian Periodicals Review* 18 (1985): 46–56.

Obelkevich, James. "Consumption." In James Obelkevich and Peter Catterall, eds., *Understanding Post-War British Society*. London: Routledge, 1994, pp. 141–54.

Oddy, Derek J. *From Plain Fare to Fusion Food: British Diet from the 1890s to the 1990s*. Woodbridge, Suffolk: Boydell Press, 2003.

Oldcorn Reid, Caroline. "Middle Class Values and Working Class Culture in Nineteenth Century Sheffield." Unpublished Ph.D. thesis, University of Sheffield, 1976.

Osborn, Bob. *The History of Yeovil's Pubs*. n.p., n.d.

Othick, John. "The Cocoa and Chocolate Industry in the Nineteenth Century." In Derek Oddy and Derek Miller, eds., *The Making of the Modern British Diet*. London: Croom Helm, 1976, pp. 77–90.

Parratt, Catriona M. "Making Leisure Work: Women's Rational Recreation in Late Victorian and Edwardian England." *Journal of Sport History* 26 (1999): 471–87.

Pettigrew, Jane. *A Social History of Tea*. London: National Trust, 2001.

Richardson, D.J. "J. Lyons & Co. Ltd.: Caterers and Food Manufacturers, 1894 to 1939." In Derek Oddy and Derek Miller, eds., *The Making of the Modern British Diet*. London: Croom Helm, 1973, pp. 161–72.

Shaw, Gareth. "The Evolution and Impact of Large-Scale Retailing in Britain." In *The Retailing Industry*, vol. 2: *The Coming of the Mass Market, 1800–1945*, eds., John Benson and Gareth Shaw. London: I.B. Tauris, 1999, pp. 233–63.

Shaw, Gareth, Louise Hill Curth and Andrew Alexander. "Creating New Spaces of Food Consumption: The Rise of Mass Catering and the Activities of the Aerated Bread Company." In John Benson and Laura Ugolini, eds., *Cultures of Selling: Perspectives on Consumption and Society since 1700*. Aldershot: Ashgate, 2006, pp. 81–100.

Roberts, Robert. *The Classic Slum: Salford Life in the First Quarter of the Century.* Manchester: University of Manchester Press, 1971.

Rowell, George. *The Old Vic Theatre: A History.* Cambridge: Cambridge University Press, 1992.

Shannon, H.A. "The Limited Companies of 1866–83." *Economic History Review* 4 (1933): 290–316.

Tarn, John Nelson. *Five Per Cent Philanthropy: An Account of Housing in Urban Areas between 1840 and 1914.* Cambridge: Cambridge University Press, 1973.

Thompson, E.P. *The Making of the English Working Class.* London: Victor Gollancz, 1963.

Thorne, Robert. "Places of Refreshment in the Nineteenth-Century City." In Anthony D. King, ed., *Buildings and Society: Essays on the Social Development of the Built Environment.* London: Routledge & Kegan Paul, 1980, pp. 228–53.

Trentmann, Frank. "Beyond Consumerism: New Historical Perspectives on Consumption." *Journal of Contemporary History* 39 (2004): 373–401.

Vamplew, Wray. "The Sport of Kings and Commoners: The Commercialization of British Horse-Racing in the Nineteenth Century." In Richard Cashman and Michael McKernan, eds., *Sport in History: The Making of Modern Sporting History.* St. Lucia, Australia: University of Queensland Press, 1979, pp. 307–25.

Walker, Lynne. "Vistas of Pleasure: Women Consumers of Urban Space in the West End of London, 1850–1900." In Clarissa Campbell Orr, ed., *Women in the Victorian Art World.* Manchester: Manchester University Press, 1995, pp. 70–85.

Willis, Frederick. *A Book of London Yesterdays.* London: Phoenix House, 1960.

Wilson, John F. *British Business History, 1720–1994.* Manchester: Manchester University Press, 1995.

Index[1]

[1] Note: Page numbers followed by 'n' refer to notes.

D. W. Gutzke, *John Pearce and the Rise of the Mass Food Market in London, 1870–1930*, https://doi.org/10.1007/978-3-030-27095-7

FSC
www.fsc.org
MIX
Papier | Fördert
gute Waldnutzung
FSC® C083411

Kolibri 360 GmbH
Ferdinand-Jühlke-Straße 7
99095 Erfurt, Deutschland
produktsicherheit@kolibri360.de